MAN *and* VALUES

A PERSONALIST ANTHROPOLOGY

MAN
and
VALUES

A PERSONALIST ANTHROPOLOGY

CORMAC BURKE

 Scepter

© 2007 Cormac Burke

Published by Scepter Publishers, Inc.
www.scepterpublishers.org
All rights reserved

ISBN: 978-1-59417-064-5

Printed in the United States of America

Cover Design: Eric Sawyer/Rose Design

Text Design: Carol Sawyer/Rose Design

CONTENTS

Preface   ix
Introductory Note   xi

PART 1. FREEDOM AND VALUES

1. THINKING ABOUT HUMAN LIFE Who Am I? What Will I Become?   2
   Controlled or Free?   3
   Free and Autonomous?   5
   Happiness, Evolution, Progress   8
   The Importance of Meaning   10
   Free, but Not Autonomous   11

2. HUMAN FREEDOM   15
   Freedom and Commitment   17
   Fear of Commitment   18
   Freedom Not To Act   19
   Freedom and Motivation   19
   Freedom and Responsibility   21
   Love   22
   Love and Freedom: "Free Love"   24
   Doing Someone Else's Will   26
   Freedom and Authority   27

3. VALUES   29
   Freedom and Preferences   29
   Appreciation   31
   Scale of Values; Criterion   33
   Relativity of Values   34
   Response to Values   35

4. CONDITIONS FOR FULFILLMENT   40
   Openness to Values   41
   Acceptance and Assimilation of Values   42
   Ambition and Human Stature   46

5. INTELLECT, WILL, AND FEELINGS IN THE PROCESS
   OF FULFILLMENT   50
   Formation of the Mind; Recognizing the Truth in a Value   52
   Formation of the Will; Choosing the Goodness of a Value   53
   Interrelation between Mind and Will   54
   "Easy" and "Difficult" Truths   55
   Affectivity in the Process of Personal Growth   57

6. CONSCIENCE   60

     Faculty, Feeling, Judgment?   60
     In What Way Is "My" Conscience Mine?   62
     Rights of Conscience   64
     Duties toward Conscience   65
     Freedom of Conscience   66
     Self-awareness, Self-acceptance, Self-esteem, Self-fulfillment   67

PART 2. PERSONAL FULFILLMENT AND OTHERS

7. PERSONAL AND INTERPERSONAL FULFILLMENT   72

     Responding to Values in Other People   73
     Envy or Admiration   74
     Appreciating Others   76
     Learning from Imperfect Persons   79

8. SOCIAL LIFE   83

     The Structure of the Human Community   84
         Freedom and Responsibility   84
         Education   84
         Work   86
         Politics   88
         Justice and Law   90
         The Common Good   91
         Human Rights   91

9. THE HUMANIZING ROLE OF SEXUALITY   94

     The Two Modalities of the Human Person   95
     The Response to Sexual Values   97
     Traditional Conception of the Masculine and Feminine Characters   98
     The Sexual Identity of Man   101
     The Sexual Identity of Woman   104
     Femininity   106
     Unisexism   109
     Fashion   109
     Complementarity and Integration   111

10. MARRIAGE Fulfillment through Sexual Gift and Union   113

     Sexual Giving and Conjugal Giving   115
     Giving—or Just Lending—One's Self?   117
     The Three Essential Properties of Marriage   119
     United, but Distinct   121
     The Conjugal Act   123
     Complementary Differences   126

11. **THE FAMILY** Personal Growth in the Context of Sexually
   Structured Love   128
     Interpersonal Relations in the Family: Education for Social Life   130
     Families with "Personality"   133
     Interpersonal Family Relations and Sexual Education   135

PART 3. **TRANSCENDENCE**

12. **BEYOND ANTHROPOLOGY?**   138
     Is Death the End?   139
     Self-actualization or Self-transcendence?   142
     God as an Anthropological Hypothesis   143
     Halfway Born?   145
     Wanting to Meet the Artist   146
     The Problem of Evil   148
     Salvation   149
     How High Can We Rise?   151

13. **TRANSCENDING** From What, To What?   154
     The Issue of Human Nature   156
     Nature and Freedom   157
     Values   160
     Which Can Go Farther, Imagination or Reality?   163
     Conscience: Whose Voice?   166
     God: On Stage or Off Stage?   171

14. **APPENDIX I** Science, Reason, and God   174
     Atheism: Freedom and Joy, or Deadend and Nausea?   179
     Not Coping with the Riddle . . .   181
     The Hollow People   183

15. **APPENDIX II** Individualism and Collectivism;
   Personalism and Community   186
     Personalism   187
     Individualism   188

16. **BIBLIOGRAPHICAL REFERENCES**   194

"Till we can become divine we must be content to be human, lest in our hurry for a change we sink to something lower."

—*ANTHONY TROLLOPE*

✲✲✲

PREFACE

There are two ways in which we can be taught by others. On the one hand, a person who knows something we do not seeks to bring us into possession of that knowledge. On the other hand, a far more difficult task, the teacher enables us to recognize what we already know. The second method can be called the Socratic, and it characterizes the book you are about to read.

From the very opening pages, the reader senses that he is being addressed by a wise man. Nonetheless, he is being addressed as an equal. Cormac Burke has developed what he calls an anthropology of freedom, a personalist anthropology. The great accomplishment of his book is that the reader ends by realizing that he already holds that anthropology. In a subtle mix of uncovering the obvious and displaying the untenability of alternatives, Burke enables the reader to see that, whatever he might have said on the level of chatter, deep down he has convictions about what it is to be a human being.

One is of course already a human being, but to be a person is to have a task. Every act is an effort to gain something we do not have, something that we consider it would be good to have. That we might not do what we do, that we might have acted otherwise, these are truths everyone knows. And in knowing them, we know that we are free. The most delicate achievement is to see our freedom in context. We are not so free as to be a law unto ourselves, as if whatever we did were a good thing for us to do. How establish that? Burke employs historical and literary figures to bring home the point that claims to absolute autonomy, total freedom, lead to enslavement and despair.

What kind of an argument is that? It is more a reminder than a revelation, and any reader will have sufficient personal experience to ground his agreement with the author. In doing so, he will not feel that he is adopting a new position. Rather, all along it has been implicit in his acts and his thoughts about those acts. In the Socratic metaphor, Burke is the midwife, but the reader comes forth with the ideas. The development is from the implicit to the explicit.

The historical Socrates made unabashed appeal to his belief in God, assuming that his interlocutor shared that belief. Cormac Burke is writing in what has been called the post-Christian era, an age characterized by skepticism and doubt, often outright atheism. In his socratic task, he cannot make the appeal the original Socrates did. And yet here is an extraordinary thing about this book: after the calm and self-effacing treatments of personal and social values, seen as embedded in our implicit knowledge of what we are, Burke ends with the suggestion that what we have now made explicit suggests something more. And he leaves it to the reader to see whether that something more is avoidable.

In short, this is a wise book, and one that has the delightful effect of enabling the reader to see that he himself is not devoid of wisdom. It is a pleasure to recommend *Man and Values*.

Ralph McInerny
University of Notre Dame

INTRODUCTORY NOTE

Personal identity; personal fulfillment. Two issues that obsessively occupy the modern mind.

Who am I? Whatever other answer may be given, it is indisputable that I am not myself, not yet. The me of today is inevitably giving way to the me of tomorrow which is slightly different, and sometimes (after particular choices or experiences) notably or even radically different.

How am I? What do I want to be? What am I in fact becoming? Some people prefer to turn aside from these questions, and yet few can avoid them. We can do something with time, but we cannot stop it. Either we shape it or it will shape us. The past is behind us; we cannot change it, though we can try to learn from it. The future is yet to come; in that sense it still lies in our hands. The "tomorrows" of each one are coming quickly, but they still have to come. What will they bring? What will I make of them, or what will they make of me? Is the future actually in my hands, or am I in its hands? Does it shape me inevitably, or am I free to give it shape? Is my sense of freedom real, or am I in fact controlled and determined by some more powerful force or destiny?

"Will I be happy?, will I be successful?, will I be free?" There is little satisfaction in the fatalistic answer, "que será, será—what will be, will be," for it is not really an answer at all. Not only when one is young (although especially then), it is logical to react and say, "No, No! My life, and especially my future, is still in my hands. It can be what I want. I can still make what I like of my life."

My life will undoubtedly be what I make of it; of that I can be sure. But will what I make of it be to my liking? Will I really be happy and free? Of this I cannot be sure at all. It depends on so much, on so many imponderables and ponderables. The purpose of this book is to consider some of the ponderables; in other words, to examine main elements or factors of human existence and development which, if properly put together, can give shape to a fulfilled life, and so at least in part help resolve the question—the crisis—of human identity.

This, then, is a book about the life of each of us, as it can be, i.e. as we can make it. It traces a program for human fulfillment, examining major aspects of our personal and social life, asking fundamental questions, proposing some more obvious (though not necessarily politically correct) answers, along with a few that may not be so obvious. The chief purpose however is not to offer answers, but to expand horizons, to prompt interest in looking higher and reaching farther. As a consequence, most of the issues considered are left open so that the reader, helped perhaps by the analyses given, can provide his own answers and examine where they may lead.

In the main body of the book (Parts I and II) I examine the unfolding of human possibilities. I try to show that these possibilities are real and great, but not unlimited; nor inevitably realized.

The dominant anthropological theme is that one has to *open* oneself to "values" and, by responding to them, to happiness and fulfillment. The aim is to show what this means and—since happiness is not an automatic or guaranteed result of any sort of life—why it can be difficult and how it can be achieved.

The book is meant for those of this new millennium who, being immersed in the problems being posed to personal life, are not fully satisfied with answers being given; or are finding no answers. A glance at the bibliography will show that many contemporary authors are quoted, and many more of preceding generations. While this latter point may put some people off, the reason for it should be clear. It is hard to understand the present if you do not know the past. I cannot know myself if I do not know my roots. Without perspective I will never properly grasp the mindset of the age in which I live, or be able to judge the way it tends to shape my own mind and my choices.

◊ ◊ ◊

Chapters 1–11 derive from a course in anthropology that the author taught during the 1990s in Rome at the *Studium Rotale* (the specialized postgraduate school for would-be advocates of the Roman Rota), and subsequently at Strathmore University, Nairobi. It might be described as an experiment in analyzing "man" and his possibilities at a purely human level, without any reference to religion, transcendence, or God. It is left to each one to conclude whether and to what extent an "anthropology of values" leads to a transcendent view of life.

Chapters 12 and 13 (Part Three), along with Appendix I, have been added in order to give some idea of the horizons which the christian transcendental view opens. They may be considered superfluous by the reader who feels little urge toward transcendence.

PART I

FREEDOM AND
VALUES

1

THINKING ABOUT
HUMAN LIFE
Who Am I? What Will I Become?

Anthropology—the study or science of "man"[1]—is a relatively modern term. Certain scientific usages restrict it to the study of primitive man and/or contemporary societies that live in a primitive state. The anthropology presented in these pages centers on "man" in himself, and focuses not on distant or early and elementary expressions of humanity, but on the human life that is present and seeks to develop in each one of us. It is less interested in man's external behavior, or even certain aspects of his inner life (which may be the more particular concern of law, sociology, psychology or ethics), than in his "structure" and growth as a living, thinking and willing being.[2]

But, is this a possible *scientific* enterprise? It is evident that men exist, and that each one can be an object of study: individual after individual. But does a "science of man" exist? In other words, do men have something *in common*,

---

1. "Man" is understood here in a genderless sense; i.e. it covers both sexes indiscriminately. It is used in the same general sense throughout the present work, except in cases that will be obvious from the context.

2. "No period like the present has had so many and such varied notions on man. None has succeeded like ours in presenting its knowledge about man so effectively and fascinatingly, and in communicating it so rapidly and easily. It is also true however that no period has known less than ours what man is. Man has never assumed such a problematic aspect as in our days": M. Heidegger, *Kant e il problema della metafisica*, Genoa, 1962, pp. 275–276.

from the study of which valid norms can be drawn for the positive development of both individual and social human life? Rather than proposing the point for debate (which one certainly can do), we take it here as a necessary presupposition of anthropology. If there is nothing in common among men, then no logical discourse is possible on the subject of "man."

What is "man?" We can state a few obvious things that help pin down his identity. In the first place, he is not an inert object or a piece of dead matter, but a living and changing being. Moreover, he is a living-changing being who *thinks*: this is evident. Otherwise neither would I have written these lines nor would you be following them. It is likewise evident that man is a being who *wills*. It is by an act of the will that I have written and that you are reading—and can stop reading at any moment.

We are used to assessing change in economic or social affairs in terms of "development," whether positive or negative. If man's life is a sequence of changes, it seems we ought to be able to measure positive human or personal development, in which possibilities of improvement or growth are achieved; and equally to distinguish lack of human development (underdevelopment), implying that certain possibilities have not been realized or have been poorly realized. All education, after all, is based on the supposition that the human being can develop towards a more complete or fulfilled form; and moreover that the absence of education places him at a disadvantage for his development.

What does human development consist in? What peculiarities does it show, as distinct from the development of other living beings? Which principles govern this development? Does it arrive at its culminating moment? Is it possible to speak of human "completion" or fulfillment? Does man, after perhaps reaching a peak in his development, go into decline? Is such decline inevitable? What does it mean to say "Life ends?" What meaning is to be attributed to death? Is it absolutely the final point of the history of each individual? Anthropology can and should ask these questions, including the last one—although going beyond it may not be within its competence.

In any case, it is clear that human development, fulfillment, or "realization" is a main issue that any study or science of man must examine.

Controlled or Free?

We have said that man thinks and wills. That will be readily admitted. The issue most debated here is not whether man thinks or wills, but whether he is free in doing so. Is man free? One cannot present any rational anthropology without taking a clear position on this question. Two answers can be offered, and they involve two fundamentally opposed ideas of man: on the one hand, man conceived as a being dominated by forces beyond his control; on the other, man conceived as a free being able to shape his own destiny and fulfillment.

According to the first view, man does not have his own proper and personal fulfillment, but is just one more element inserted into a cosmic or historical or economic order—or perhaps disorder. Anthropology, so conceived, becomes practically absorbed in economy, sociology, historical cosmology, etc.

In this perspective, either man is not free or his freedom is an element of little importance, almost an illusion, since he remains controlled by more powerful and more important processes and realities than he can ever establish himself. Each individual exists for these greater realities—the world, history, society—but his life has no further purpose, he has no destiny in or for himself. To accept such a philosophy radically diminishes man in his own estimation and self-awareness, because it tells him that he has no personal dignity, that he is not free, or that whatever freedom he appears to possess is without real purpose as far as he is concerned.

Within this deterministic approach we could make these distinctions:

1) Biological, psychological, or environmental determinism:

    a) *Determinism "ab intra":* we do not govern ourselves, but are governed or controlled by internal forces—inheritance, genetic elements, sexual impulses, phobias . . . —which mold and form our "psyche";

    b) *Determinism "ab extra":* our lot and destiny are imposed on us by environment, circumstances, education, society (other people), government . . .

2) Economic or political semi-determinism:

    a) *Market determinism (consumerism):* the individual as a pawn in a huge game of economic forces. He can believe he is free, it is even good that he does believe it. Advertising can encourage him to think that freedom is a purchasable commodity: "Buy this Land Cruiser and you will have acquired freedom." In fact, however, his "freedom" can do nothing against the real powers that manage his life.[3] Further, his value consists almost exclusively in his power of acquisition. Whoever possesses nothing is worth nothing: he is reduced to a valueless being.

        The first standard by which a society should be tested is whether it answers real human needs. It is only when people can achieve what they need, not just what they want, that their lives can progressively become humanly fulfilled. The advertising/consumer society, where people are

---

3. The more you control people's freedom, the more you guarantee your market. Nothing is so profitable and reassuring as a captive consumer public.

programatically conditioned to want what the Controllers of society think *they should want*, creates "an illusion of meaning" for their lives,[4] but no sense of deeper achievement or genuine and ultimate purpose. The lives of those who let themselves be uncritically integrated into such a society are likely not just to remain humanly underdeveloped but to be subjected to a process of gradual dehumanization.

b) *Collectivism:* the individual as a "piece" of an immense social reality which surpasses him, or of a huge historical or cosmic movement where the personal history of each one is totally subordinated to collective history, having practically no importance or value in itself. The individual does not have his history—a life-story endowed with meaning; history is something which belongs only to the cosmos or to the collectivity.

It is not possible to build any real anthropology on a deterministic basis.

In the other view, man is conceived as a free being, in some way in control of his personal existence: open to possibilities, able to choose, capable of fulfillment. It is not enough to be. In order to be truly a man or a woman, one has to *become* one. There is a potential to be realized. Each individual can and should regard his humanity as a job to be completed by means of his own free efforts. Here also two fundamental and very different formulations are to be noticed: (1) man is a free *and* autonomous subject; (2) man is a free subject, but is not *autonomous*.

These formulations are of more interest to us, and call for an examination in greater depth.

Free and Autonomous?[5]

According to this view, man is self-sufficient, in the sense that he can make or fulfill himself from within. Life and the world are his to mold. He has no need to come out of self, but can simply reach out from within himself and pick whatever he chooses, using it as he likes as raw material for building his own life.

In this hypothesis, then, man is a subject capable of self-fulfillment[6] without the need to follow given norms or laws, simply expressing himself from within.

---

4. Cf. C. S. Lewis: *The Abolition of Man*, p. 79.

5. Here we use the term "autonomous" in its literal sense, as implying that man, at least in his spiritual faculties, is subject to no law outside himself.

6. "The idea of self-realization is peculiar to modern philosophy": Leonardo Polo, *Presente y Futuro del Hombre*, Madrid, 1993, p. 193. If the idea is taken in an immanent sense, if man is "causa sui," it would follow that he has his own fulfillment within himself.

Here man identifies himself in complete freedom; he is a subject of "self-identification" or "self-definition." This is a dominant principle underlying much of modern popular psychology. It tends to permeate education, and is reflected at the highest level of contemporary civil jurisprudence, being set forth as a basic principle of the majority judgment in the 1992 U.S. Supreme Court case, *Planned Parenthood v. Casey*: "At the heart of liberty is the right to define one's own concept of existence, of meaning, of the universe, and of the mystery of human life."[7] It follows that every individual is *his own project*: also in the sense that in designing himself there are no given norms to follow. He builds from scratch, as he chooses, freely using the materials and situations of life so as to achieve his own project.

This view of man coincides with, or leads to, the philosophy of individualism.[8] Over the past centuries, individualism has become the dominant mindset of the Western world. *My* interests, *my* satisfaction, *my* happiness is the individualist's goal—to which he or she tends (even if at times unconsciously) to subordinate all else: things, events and persons. Individualism is never so powerful or so destructive as when the happiness it proposes to seek is also declaredly self-defined: "I have the right to *my* happiness—*as I understand it*; and no one can question that right or the type of happiness I seek."

For many people today, to "be happy on one's own terms" is a right and a sacred principle of living. But life itself does not always respect a person's own terms. Practical experience can hint at what may then happen. Ernest Hemingway, Nobel Prize winner and one of the great American writers of the 20th century, lived that principle out to the end. In June 1961, A.E. Hotchner, a friend and biographer of his, visited him in an attempt to pull him out of his depression and delusions. Hemingway is not quite sane; but not (at least yet) quite mad either. He can express the issue very clearly, terribly clearly, when Hotchner asks him why he wants to kill himself: "Hotch, if I can't exist on my own terms, then existence is impossible. Do you understand? That is how I've lived, and that is how I must live—or not live." A month later Hemingway shot himself.[9]

His terms were to be on top of life: writing, hunting, drinking, women. . . . When he found himself, at 62, with waning powers and the prospect of nothing (of this) to live for, his mind—and his will to live—went. Happiness on his own terms had not proved possible.

---

7. 112 S. Ct. 2791, 2807 [1992].

8. It also leads individualism to its necessary and ultimate consequence, which is to eliminate any basis for a cohesive society; cf. Appendix II.

9. A. E. Hotchner: *Papa Hemingway*, p. 328. Was there perhaps some element of anticipatory obsession in Hemingway's love for guns? In an early novel he had written of them, precisely in the context of failed lives: "those admirable American instruments so easily carried, so sure of effect, so well designed to end the American dream when it becomes a nightmare" (*To Have and Have Not* (1937), Ch. 24).

Easily achieved self-fulfillment, necessarily involving a basic self-contentedness, appears as the ideal or purpose (and even the "right") of contemporary man. Such a load of subjectivism tends to engender a "soft" anthropology. Self-contentment is a dead end for man.[10] The person who is happy with himself *ceases to grow*; he does not try to progress, to do better; and it seems that man is always made for more. The contented self is so often synonymous with the stagnant self.

"Soft" anthropologies have the effect of *reducing* man. This is true also in the hypothesis of extreme individualism which seems to leave man with the maximum freedom whose exercise is apparently not limited by any given norm and law. Personal freedom and life are reduced even in such a case, since they remain closed in on one's self. Reaching out "beyond" the self, to a happiness or fulfillment that lies "higher," is a possibility or a need that is scarcely considered.

In theory, such extreme individualism seems to offer man the possibility of dominating the world; for man alone is lord. In practice, however, the world does not let itself be so easily dominated; it proves more powerful than man. On the social plane, moreover, individualism turns life into a competition—or a war—between would-be lords. And among those in history who have seemed to be lords of their times, it is hard to find one whose life reflects any all-round fulfilment. This individualism centers the person more and more on himself. To have no worthwhile reference points outside oneself, or not to be able to follow them, involves the danger of remaining ultimately closed in on an inner core of self too poor in resources for the deeper potential of personal life.

No adequate anthropological analysis can be built around the concept of man as an autonomous or self-sufficient being. Any hypothesis of "self-sufficiency" is contradicted by the numberless needs that each person experiences in the life of both body and spirit: air, water, food, light, friendship, appreciation, love. . . . At an even deeper level "self-sufficiency" does not even remotely offer a key to the sense of *mystery* that man naturally possesses regarding life, the conviction that the world or personal life is not an absurdity, a non-sense, inevitably headed for nothingness. There is something in the normal human make-up that revolts at the idea. We are ready to laugh at absurdity or nonsense when it is presented to us as a matter of entertainment. But we have a natural repulsion toward the idea of nothingness in itself, particularly when it is offered as an explanation of the world or of personal existence. If nature, according to Spinoza, abhors a vacuum, this is even truer of man; no one likes to verify his own total or ultimate emptiness.

---

10. "'Am I happy with myself?' . . . this sort of moral puberty" (Emmanuel Mounier: *Oeuvres*, II, 525). And the more contented the self, the less it grows out of its puberty.

It is inbuilt in us to want more than the present offers. We always tend to go beyond the immediate reality, either along the easy street of imagination (wandering in dreams or in "virtual reality"); or by the more strenuous way of ambition—that challenges us to the formulation and fulfillment of practical projects.

Happiness, Evolution, Progress

We have mentioned the modern tendency to claim happiness as "a right." It is not clear that the claim is well-grounded. Among the more fundamental human rights enunciated by the United States Declaration of Independence is a right not to happiness itself, but rather to its *pursuit*.[11] This corresponds better to what can be considered one of the constants of human history, which is the desire and indeed the not easily abandoned expectation of attaining happiness—if one pursues it. Is this a mere illusion, however generalized? Or should one suppose that this longing indicates a purpose that can actually be attained by everyone?

Happiness escapes adequate definition—just as, however constantly pursued, it seems to evade a firm human grasp. Most people will readily admit to not yet being happy, or not fully so. Whatever happiness consists in, it would seem to be a good that is not achieved in any easy or automatic way.[12] Otherwise it would be impossible to explain the presence in the world of so many people who, if not unhappy, at least have the impression that the happiness they have so long desired continually escapes them. It is human nature to look for and pursue happiness. Are we progressing towards it?

A word here about evolution and progress. From a strict anthropological viewpoint, evolution, or rather "evolutionism,"[13] sells man short; it allows too little space for his life and outlook. If man (also in his spirit) is only the fruit of the unfolding of matter, he is indeed placed at the top of the visible world which surrounds him. True; but that world itself remains small. Such an evolutionary view closes man's personal horizons.

Peculiarly or not, this applies also to the belief in constant progress which, at least up to very recently, has been part of the modern mind; the conviction that humanity is always rising to higher levels; the persuasion that one is involved in an irreversible, though at the same time predominantly mechanical

---

11. "We hold these truths to be self-evident: that man was endowed by his Creator with certain inalienable rights; and that chief among these are life, liberty and the pursuit of happiness."

12. In our individualistic consumer society the ideas that happiness can either be *bought* (hard cash will automatically bring you happiness) or be procured by *calculation* (if you are smart enough you will be happy), die hard; but many who try them out find them dead.

13. By "evolutionism" we wish to designate the restrictive and more ideological versions of evolutionary theory, which make the development of the world a necessary and immanent process.

or impersonal,[14] process of improvement or growth, of a material, economic, or cosmic nature.

The idea of "progress"—that the future can be and will be better—is a strongly rooted idea of the 19th and early 20th centuries, which is being carried forward into the 21st century, though with a number of not insignificant reservations. Despite these, the philosophy of continual progress in many ways still dominates the modern conception of life. If accepted, it produces the curious result that one can be harassed by the regret of having been born—of living—in too early a stage of this upward process, since any stage previous to the final and definitive one is necessarily premature in the sense that it has not yet attained plenitude. The fullness of being human escapes every individual man of every epoch. It is not for him, but is reserved for the privileged ones who will be born in the last and perfect stage of the whole process.[15]

It is natural to hold, in opposition to this, that progress towards fullness should be a possibility for each one; otherwise, he or she is condemned to frustration. If the conditions for human fulfillment can be finally achieved only in some eventual future, then no one is offered the possibility of present or actual self-realization.

That was the psychological error of Marxism, with its message to people that it is worthwhile to live with five-year plans—for the tomorrow that will inaugurate the perfect society. But when tomorrow arrived, and the perfect society did not accompany it. . . . Not that the panorama in the Western world is necessarily more satisfactory. After so many decades of developed materialist liberalism, the signs are there that society may not hold together. Much is made of the greater sexual freedom that has been achieved; yet it is very debatable whether it has led to greater happiness. The freedom that depends on and originates from mutual trust and esteem, from respect and fidelity, survives in the family—in some families—or in isolated groups of friends. The freedom to pursue happiness is still there, but people are less and less sure about how to attain the object of that pursuit.

One of the principal parameters of progress is life expectancy. Every life-program—every aspect of human progress—seems definitively limited by the fact of death. Man is not immortal and yet would like to be. If he succeeded in defeating death, it would be the greatest progress in the whole of history, a new stage of humanity. But even then it is not sure that human fulfillment or

---

14. Christopher Dawson brings out the point that when progress is conceived as an inevitable or "mechanical" process, man himself comes to be seen as merely "part of the machine" (*Progress and Religion* (1929), Ch. 9).

15. Evolution: the fullness of existence escapes me; it lies not in the attainable present, but in a (for me) unattainable future. The dignity of "man" is not achieved fully; he is always in a process of becoming, in a state of maturation. Therefore each individual person still is and always will be "immature."

happiness would be reached. In Rider Haggard's novel *She*, the mysterious African queen has discovered the flame that constantly renews life, but it brings her less and less happiness, and in the end, destruction.

The increasing number of suicides among young people seems to suggest that in the absence of lasting happiness or of the hope of reaching it, life for many is not acceptable, much less immortality. Immortality without happiness is hell. Today more and more unhappy persons feel they cannot endure life. But are they sure, do they have any guarantee, that putting an end to life—by suicide or voluntary euthanasia—also puts an end to unhappiness? It is not possible to find a certain answer to this question.

The Importance of Meaning

Since the 1960s, modern society has fallen deeply under the sway of so-called humanistic psychology or psychologism. One of its concerns is to free us from the "historic Western compulsion" of looking for a meaning to personal life. Existence, it is said, is not to be explained but to be used, and its only purpose is "an intensely private sense of well-being to be generated in the living of life itself."[16] If at times we 'feel bad,' psychological therapy is there to help us 'feel good' again.

But can we feel good about life if we cannot make sense of it? The Viennese psychiatrist, Viktor Frankl, holds that an absolutely indispensable human need is to find a meaning to one's life. If this life has no real meaning, it becomes reduced to an ultimate absurdity. Frankl speaks of "the existential vacuum which is the mass neurosis of the present time."[17] Man is distinctive in his ability and need to "challenge" the meaning of life. As Frankl writes elsewhere, "it is reserved for man alone to find his very existence questionable, to experience the whole dubiousness of being."[18] The meaning and purpose of life—the origin and destiny of man—is a question that every thinking person must face. Only two alternatives exist:

1) man and life as absurdities, driven by instincts which lead nowhere. A world dominated by fate, or, rather, by chance, since fate implies a certain predetermined order; or

2) man and life directed toward some higher goal: toward ideas or realities which lead a person above the material or instinctive level. Order in the world, and meaning in personal and social life. Meaning too in freedom itself since, through it, man can personally aim for and achieve his goal— or fail to do so. Awareness therefore of the risk of freedom, for one cannot

---

16. Philip Rieff: *The Triumph of the Therapeutic*, p. 261.

17. *Man's Search for Meaning*, p. 131.

18. *The Doctor and the Soul*, p. 21.

really believe in any true personal freedom without introducing the sense of risk into one's life. I am free; I can choose between alternatives. I can choose well—or badly; attain my goal or miss it. In the next chapter we will examine this further.

Free, but Not Autonomous

This is the second way of conceiving human freedom. Man is a free subject, capable of fulfillment. He is free, but he is neither self-sufficient nor autonomous—in the sense of being a law to himself, totally independent of other laws. The fundamental parameters—the possibilities and limits of his being or his becoming—are a given reality. His "definition" therefore already appears as a challenge. Everyone is born as a human being; not everyone *becomes* a man or a woman in the full sense. Every person, from birth, begins to develop an image that over the years acquires (or loses) substance, clarity, definition, in which one recognizes—or fails to recognize—a truly human image. From its beginning every individual life is endowed with a basic program, but it is a program yet to be executed; it can succeed or fail.

The outline of human fulfillment which we will present rests on this premise. Man appears as a being with the inner resources to freely fulfill himself. At the same time nothing suggests that his fulfillment is an automatic process, or one that he can achieve by simply "expressing" whatever he finds inside himself;[19] for not all the possible modes of self-expression are necessarily human or humanizing.

Anthropology remains a superficial science if it is content to study the question of man's "being," without at the same time examining that of his "becoming." An anthropology of freedom, such as is proposed in these pages, must consider both; and consider moreover right and wrong ways of "being man," and especially right and wrong ways of "becoming man." It should be clear that the two concepts of "being free," on the one hand, and "becoming human," on the other, stand in delicate balance. If one is free, one may or may not *become* human, i.e. achieve the fullness of one's human potential. There may be many ways of reaching the goal of "fulfilled" humanity, but there are certainly some ways by which it will not be reached. This is the sense in which we use "right" and "wrong" in our anthropological study.

---

19. Frankl holds that meaning is found not through mere "self-expression," or as something simply emerging from existence, but, rather, by a *confronting* of existence. He rejects the existentialist thesis (of Sartre and others) that "man invents himself, designs his own 'essence.' . . . The meaning of our existence is not invented by ourselves, but rather detected": *Man's Search . . .*, pp. 100–101.

While humanity is a datum, something "given" to each one of us, it is, we repeat, also a challenge, something to be constructed by each one. Just as architecture, in studying the right ways of building a house, implicitly or explicitly indicates the wrong ways, so any anthropology that takes account of man's freedom cannot evade the issue of right and wrong ways of building a truly human life: ways by which one reinforces one's basic humanity and constructs its fullness, and ways by which one weakens and undermines it. Our humanity has a double aspect. It is not only a common foundation on which each one's life rests, but also an individual building erected by each which becomes in the end a personalized and genuine embodiment of fulfilled human living. Or a half-finished and rickety structure. Or a disfigured ruin.

So, while this is intended to be a work of anthropology and not of ethics, we do propose what we regard as a "right" approach to human living, and consequently consider certain approaches to be "wrong" (anthropologically rather than morally speaking), in the sense that they just don't work; rather than humanizing they dehumanize personal life.

Man is a being with a *destiny*, that is with a project or program to develop, a personal history to trace: the unique history of *his* life, for which he alone is responsible. He is given a set purpose to turn into reality,[20] or to reduce to failure. Man is a free subject, capable of attaining self-realization; but not by orbiting around himself, or "expanding" himself in just any way. He does not "program" himself; he is, rather, programmed—to be *human*. Only he, however, can execute the program properly. If he does so, he gives to his humanity a totally unique and fulfilled expression. Anthropology seeks to study man, so as to trace out what the program of being human—of *becoming* fulfilledly human—means.

But man's freedom also makes him capable of self-frustration—that is, of ending up as something less (perhaps much less) than human. Should we dismiss as totally groundless the fears of some people that certain contemporary scientific endeavors run the danger of dehumanizing humanity? Yet the greater danger is that individuals will dehumanize themselves.

✿ ✿ ✿

We have traced out some major parameters for our study. Distinguishing between a determinist anthropology and one which considers man to be free, we rejected the determinist point of view. True human growth posits the exercise of personal freedom. So far as the principles that govern this process of development are concerned, we also maintain that it is not a matter of "self-definition,"

---

20. "Obvious paradox: man's essence and end reside in us, not as an acquired good, but as a promise, a hope, a chance . . ." G. Thibon: *Retour au Réel*, Paris, 1946, p. 224.

nor can it consist just in a simple "response to self." It is to given realities which lie outside himself or higher than himself, that man must respond. On this depends his fully human development. He needs to "open" himself and rise "above" himself. We will try to show what this can mean.

In short, we have differentiated between a closed and reductive anthropology and one that is open. The former, despite attributing to man a freedom apparently without limits, leaves him in fact imprisoned in a life of narrow horizons. The latter, by conceiving freedom in relation with values, opens up the horizons of life. We note, without surprise, the importance which the two themes of freedom and of values possess within this anthropological analysis.

If one ask whether the differences noted here are between an optimistic anthropological view and a pessimistic one, the answer has to be carefully qualified. The view of man as an autonomous being actually turns out to be pessimistic. Its apparent optimism—man standing higher than law and open to limitless possibilities—is immediately proved false in practical life. The man who tries to fulfill himself, without laws or standards to be respected, destroys himself. He indeed places himself at the center of a "great" world—great to his imagination, ambition or selfishness—but which is really a jail whose walls ultimately close in on him. This oppressive twilight, at the end of a life lived without respect for higher values, is usually more evident in the man of action (Napoleon, for instance, or Hitler). It may be more difficult to verify in persons of less exceptional external action, or in those whose activity is mainly intellectual. Yet it can be noted in the last days of not a few artists and thinkers (Vincent van Gogh, Stefan Zweig, Arthur Koestler . . .); and more and more today in the general acceptance, as a licit personal option, of having oneself euthanized—which is simply a mode of suicide. If a person takes his own life, it is because he no longer sees any motive for living, any value in what surrounds him.

The central theme of Leo Tolstoy's *Anna Karenina*—one of the great novels of all time—illustrates how to follow "one's right to be happy" can lead to despair and self-destruction. Anna is a woman of passionate and sensitive heart; but her love is emotional, no more, and fundamentally self-seeking. She feels she can do anything for love, but not without it. She looks after an abandoned child, but admits "my heart is not big enough" to care for a whole orphanage of dirty children. While she is deeply attached to her own son, this is not enough to keep her faithful to her husband for whom she no longer feels any love. She gradually yields to the passionate attraction of a young officer; but her infidelity to her husband and son leads to a revulsion of feeling— against her love, her lover, and herself. The whole world becomes intolerable to her, existence is now hateful and she kills herself.

The mental attitude of the suicide is perfectly depicted in Anna's last thoughts and judgments: everyone (and everything) takes on a petty and senseless character, the people she sees around her seem mean and contemptible as never before; despising each other, filling their lives with empty activity, pointless interests, and stupid laughter: "Why do they speak. Why do they laugh? Everything is just lies, everything is falsehood, everything is deception, everything is evil. . . . I will escape from everybody and from my own self."[21]

Does it follow, then, that the alternative view of man—as a free but not autonomous being—deserves to be called an *optimistic* anthropology? It might be more accurate to call it *realistic*. It tends to a basic optimism, but without neglecting the presence of powerful negative elements or factors in man which can destroy him. It is an anthropology which takes into consideration both the dignity and the greatness of man—his potentiality toward everything—and his misery: his tendency toward nothing. This is the quality of true anthropology; it always offers a dramatic vision of man, never one that is banal.

We have considered distinct views of man: conceived as a being under the control of impersonal forces; or as a free being, also with the varieties that this possibility offers. We have concluded that he is free, but not autonomous. He is not capable of fulfilling himself from within, of searching, finding, creating his own standards of development with a sovereign freedom that is bound by no given limits. On the contrary, his fulfillment calls for a free response to objective values that lie outside him and above him. To fulfill himself, man, in possession and exercise of his freedom, must therefore be open to values outside himself, and be prepared to *respond* and to *rise* to them. This is the line of thought we mean to develop in the pages that follow.

---

21. *Anna Karenina*, Part VII, Ch. 31.

2

HUMAN FREEDOM

It is not easy to define freedom. Among the oldest philosophical attempts to do so there is Aristotle's phrase: "man is free when he is cause of himself." *Cause of oneself*: the formula contains real insights into the nature of freedom, but can also lead one seriously astray about its operation.

No one is an absolute cause of himself. No one causes himself to be, in a constitutive sense. Our life, our nature, our intellectual endowments, our temperament or artistic aptitudes, our free will, *are given to us*. They come with birth, they are not something we originate in ourselves. Nor, during infancy, can a child be said to be a subject of personal causality; he may be a physical cause of upsets or accidents, but is scarcely capable of actions that shape his life in any freely chosen way. But when infancy ends and we enter into a more personal possession of our faculties, then indeed—through the exercise of our freedom—we do cause ourselves to become rather than just to be. To become a better son or daughter or friend, or a worse one; a good student or a poor one; more truthful or more of a liar; more honest or more ready to cheat others; more generous or stingier; more in control of our passions or more under their domination. In this process of becoming we pass through different moments of being (one may be a sober person now, and in five years time have become a drunkard). Becoming implies new ways of being, that may themselves be temporary in nature, or settle into something stable and ingrained. In older years "becoming" seems to imply physical decline, which may nevertheless be accompanied by a balance and fullness of character never hitherto achieved.

In any case, rather than debate Aristotle's ideas further, we mean to settle for a more popular notion of freedom; i.e. 'the ability to choose between possible alternatives.' It is from this concept, without more justification, that we are going to work.

We also mean to avoid the issue of providing philosophical arguments to prove that man is free. If someone is not convinced that he is basically free, then what we write here will be of little interest or use to him. Human freedom is taken as a presupposition of the view of life we propose. Our thesis is that man is a free being and that it is in the exercise of his freedom that he develops and can fulfill himself—or not. Man is capable of free fulfillment; or of failure and frustration—also freely brought about.

The presence and operation of human freedom means that there is no such thing as automatic fulfillment for anyone. One's life, according to one's choices, can take different ways that lead to different results and destinations. One's experiences and responses can be enriching, or impoverishing. They can *open* one's horizons and widen one's understanding of values, of others, of the world; or *close* one's ambition and range of interests in on oneself, thus directing one's life down the dead end of personal insufficiency. One can grow towards happiness and fulfillment, or shrink towards misery and frustration.

Every thinking person at the threshold of life senses these alternatives: I may work out well, I may work out badly. The impression that few seem to "make it" can provoke an initial temptation to set one's sights low, so as to limit eventual disappointment at possible failure. Is it a wise precaution to act so? Is it prudence? Or faintheartedness?

The young person who deliberately aims low reduces the possibilities of his or her life from the outset. Given that, is it not better to set one's sights higher, following the natural human instinct of youth, wanting and expecting a lot from life? Yet, what about the experience of older people, many of whom give the impression of being more skeptical than anything else about what life can actually give? The life experience of many older people, if they could analyze it accurately, would probably offer two contrasting lessons. "Life did not live up to my expectations. I didn't get out of it what I had hoped. Life failed me." Or, "I didn't expect enough of life. It could have given me more, if I had started out with more courage and determination. Life didn't fail me; I failed life."

Whatever can be learned from the experiences of others, everyone must make his or her own choices; and, according to the choices made, each life will produce expected or unexpected results, some of them no doubt unwanted. Yet it does seem that the person who expects little is more likely to achieve little.

We have already stated that man is free but not autonomous. He is free but not "independent." As we have seen, he inescapably depends on so many things: light, air, water. . . He is free, though not unlimitedly so. His own capacities limit him physically and psychically. He is not free to live without food or drink or to run at 100 miles an hour or to think that what he knows to be true is false. Nevertheless, every normal person is aware of the presence of freedom in his daily life: he can get up or not, go to work or not, vary his choices, buy this newspaper or that one, etc.

Freedom and Commitment

The modern mood about freedom has become unsustainably paradoxical and, in the end, self-defeating: wanting freedom, but not wanting commitment, wanting to be able to choose, but not wanting to be bound by any choice. Such an approach cannot work; it implies a rejection of real freedom and in the end can only lead to its destruction.

Every free decision, every choice, excludes all options except the one chosen. Curiously, the inevitability of this aspect of our power to choose can become a cause of suffering for certain personalities. The French writer, André Gide, remarked, "I always found the need for choosing unbearable, because to choose seemed to me not so much to select, as to reject what I had not chosen."[1] Freedom can indeed seem a burden for those who fail to resolve the paradox of this mood.[2]

If a person is on a trip and arrives at a crossroads, he is free to continue along any one of the roads before him. It is clear that to choose one means to leave the others behind. The more decidedly he goes ahead on the road chosen, the more he departs from the other roads. If the thought crosses his mind that he is endangering his freedom in this way, that he is even losing (rather than exercising) it, he may yield to the temptation to turn back, perhaps also because the difficulties of the way are beginning to make themselves felt (every way has its own difficulty), perhaps simply because it seems more important to him to maintain—to preserve—his freedom uncompromised.

---

1. *Nourritures Terrestres*: in: Jean Mouroux, *Le Sens Chrétien de l'Homme*, Paris, 1953, p. 136.

2. Gide's mood here is close to that of his compatriot Jean-Paul Sartre. "Sartre uses the term 'anguish' to describe this consciousness of one's own freedom. Anguish is not fear of an external object but the awareness of the ultimate unpredictability of one's own behavior" (Leslie Stevenson and David L. Haberman: *Ten Theories of Human Nature*, 1998, p. 177). In theory, only people of weak will would regard their future conduct as unpredictable and hence be subject to this anguished appreciation of freedom, while the strong-willed person, sure of the direction of his or her future choices, would be free from any such anguish. In practice, even very strong-willed people at times make surprising choices which they cannot explain or which they feel ashamed of. This may turn out to be a salutary experience leading to a more modest appraisal of the strength of their will. It is not evident that it should give rise to the sort of *anguish* Gide or Sartre felt.

The ultimate consequence of yielding to such a way of thinking is obvious. Whoever allows himself to be overcome by the fear of committing himself, keeps returning time and again to his point of departure. He remains stuck at the crossroads—with a freedom that is "intact," but useless; and will thus become, little by little, incapable of any permanent and definitive choice.[3]

Fear of Commitment

There is a rightful insistence today that freedom is a particular requirement of the dignity of the person. Yet, not to want to engage oneself in any definitive decision, however noble it may be, remains a sign of freedom (an impoverished freedom, perhaps on its way to becoming totally bankrupt), but by no stretch of the imagination can it be considered an affirmation of personal dignity. To be unwilling to commit oneself to anything betrays a lack of human stature and worth. To be afraid of commitment is in the last analysis to be afraid of freedom itself. The modern philosophy of rights forgets the right to commit or bind oneself:[4] therefore it tends to see freedom and commitment as opposed.

Freedom can be overtaken by a creeping paralysis, when a person yields to the fear of any choice—since choosing involves a new situation open to what is unknown. Paradoxically, the uncertainty that accompanies every decision can then turn freedom itself into a sort of prison where, as Michael Ende illustrates in one of his stories, all the doors of choice are examined one by one, and rejected; and the person remains where he was. Nevertheless, it is clear that to refuse to choose is in itself also a choice; and leaves one equally open to the future, with that fundamental character of the unknown which it never loses. There is no way of knowing what your future holds for you. You can try to shape it; you cannot control it.

The burden of the past oppresses many people. The fear of the future can have an even more negative and depressive effect. No philosophy is adequate for facing life if it is not a philosophy also "of the future," which in some way endows the future with positive sense for *me*. The failure of Marxism illustrates how to work for an abstract future "collectivity" is not a goal that can satisfy the individual. Each one wants to be able to face a future with a personal meaning.

---

3. This applies to the realm of thinking even before that of acting. What is the point of "freedom of thought" if the mind no longer believes in *meaning*, that is, in the truth or validity of an idea or a conclusion? The thoughts that the mind is then free to think appear less and less worth thinking, for they lead nowhere. The mind wanders aimlessly. It has no "vistas," no avenues of discovery or growth. It stands at the crossroads of thought, free to choose any of the roads and less and less convinced that any is worth choosing.

4. Cf. Chesterton's remark in *Orthodoxy*: "I could never conceive or tolerate any Utopia which did not leave to me the liberty for which I chiefly care, the liberty to bind myself."

Freedom Not To Act

If it is true that freedom means the power to act, it must also involve the power *not* to act. To be free is to able to say Yes or No. "I am free to do this." But—are you free *not* to do it? If not, you are not free. Freedom implies retaining one's self-dominion in the face of alternatives. If one can only say Yes, or only say No, one no longer has freedom. Oscar Wilde made himself the object of his own irony when he quipped: "I can resist anything—except temptation." If that was really the case, then he was not free. But at least he realized it.

The most tremendous freedom man has is his power to commit suicide. Almost everyone at some time or other feels he would like to escape from life. Many people today commit suicide after a minor failure, in a situation of passing depression. No doubt that is a sign of their freedom, but it is a weak freedom unsustained by any solid system of values. There is greater and stronger freedom in the person who, in moments of stress, resists the immediate impulses of feeling, etc., and assesses more deeply what is involved in taking one more chance at life rather than in ending it.

Freedom and Motivation

A common position among determinists is to hold that man can never be really free because he is always swayed by motives. In this view, motivation *determines* a person, taking from the autonomy that a truly free decision requires. This is confused thinking, based on "the false supposition that freedom implies the exclusion of all motivation."[5] A person cannot decide between different options without having preferences; and his preferences must rationally correspond to considerations and conclusions, which are exactly what constitute motives. In fact, every decision or voluntary choice presupposes the existence of motives, to the extent that without any motive it could not be properly called a *human* decision.

There is a point which should be obvious but is nevertheless worth recalling. While it is true that every exercise of freedom—every decision or choice—must be motivated, this does not mean that all the motives which inspire a decision are necessarily univocal or unilinear, that is, all pointing in the same direction. It is the opposite which more often occurs, with pros and contras, reasons in favor of a particular decision and reasons against.

For instance, when pondering an exceptional offer of promotion in his work, a person can count a substantial increase in salary among the reasons for accepting; while at the same time, as reasons to refuse, he weighs the possible negative effect on his or her spouse's health or on their children's education, if

---

5. R. Zavalloni: *La libertà personale. Psicologia della condotta umana*, Milan, 1973, p. 66.

the new position implies changing from one country to another with a worse climate or which is less developed materially.

When there are important arguments in favor of one way of acting but also important arguments against, it seems elementary that a fully mature and reasonable person should weigh the matter thoroughly and in full depth. Yet there are many decisions where even the mature person may find it hard to make a totally detached and rational examination of all the pros and cons. Prejudices (originating in the will more than in the mind) easily lessen the objectivity of our approach and incline us to the "easy" solution or decision as if it were necessarily the best. Few people, however mature or rational, are exempt from the tendency to center on arguments favoring what is immediately convenient to them. The less mature and reflective a person is, the stronger this tendency will make itself present.

It follows that not all the motives which should enter into the decision-making process are necessarily pleasing or welcome to the person deciding. Some can annoy him, as being considerations he would much rather not have to take into consideration. But, if they are in any way solid, they should have their place in the rational process that leads in the end to a decision. The person may feel as if these reasons were being imposed on him; but this will scarcely prevent him from heeding them.

"The idea of freedom is substantially identified with the capacity man possesses to determine himself in favor of one alternative in preference to others."[6] If a person, even before having an initial contact with a matter requiring a decision, were determined to one eventual choice, he would not in fact be free. Therefore the *first* approach of a free person to any such matter must be one of indetermination.

On the other hand, if he continues to remain in such a position of indetermination or indifference, it is clear he will never come to a choice in the matter. A choice involves precisely a self-determination, a free commitment of oneself, in a definite direction. A will which is permanently undetermined is paralyzed; it is unable to choose, or it ends up making haphazard and aimless "choices" that have nothing to do with the true exercise of human freedom. "Freedom is not in fact something anarchical or irrational; it does not consist in the absence of causality or of motivation. . . . The indetermination which must be introduced into freedom has nothing in common with that other indetermination characterizing freedom of indifference, i.e. a reasonless choice, a motiveless willing. Freedom of indifference is something non-sensical."[7]

It is through a process of discovering motives that a person abandons his position of indifference, and is enabled to come to a choice for or against a

---

6. Ibid. p. 358.
7. Ibid. pp. 231, 237.

particular action, thus exercising his freedom. It is an elementary mistake there-fore to think that because a choice is motivated, it is less free. No one makes a true human choice without a motive. Actions without motives would not be free; they would be irrational, the actions of a sleepwalker or of an idiot.

Freedom and Responsibility

Motivation precedes human action; consequences follow it. The exercise of freedom cannot fail to consider the possible consequences of each choice: for oneself and for others. In fact, this foreseeing of the consequences is normally a part of motivation itself.

Viktor Frankl maintains that "consciousness of responsibility is the foun-dation of human existence";[8] and also suggests that fear of responsibility can provoke that flight from freedom which we have already noted.[9]

No sense of personal freedom can be genuine if it is not accompanied by an equally personal sense of responsibility. Since every action has its conse-quences, anyone who feels free to direct his choices along one particular way rather than another must realize that he shares in the consequences for others which necessarily derive from his free choices. If I deliberately jump a red light, I make myself liable to a fine or responsible for an accident. The more likely the consequence, the more I should foresee it, and act responsibly. The less foreseeable the consequence, the less the responsibility.

The sense of responsibility serves to confirm the awareness of being personally free. The action is mine; and precisely for this reason, I am at least a partial cause of the consequences. The person who will not accept responsibility does not understand the true scope and meaning of his freedom, is not fully in possession of it, or is perhaps afraid of it. The sense of responsi-bility also brings out the participative meaning of social life. *I* can freely produce positive consequences for the life of others . . .

Today the gravest threat to freedom may well be a generalized lack of responsibility. It has been remarked that there are few dangers greater to society than "the presence in it of people with nothing to lose." Feeling free without at the same time feeling responsible makes people destructive. A society hardly merits the name of a free society and may not long survive as one if its members are not responsible. Responsibility no less than freedom has become the test of a truly human society. And of course it is not just society alone that can suffer harm from those who think they have "nothing to lose." *They*, despite their frame of mind, do have something to lose and in that men-tal state are quite likely to lose it.

---

8. *The Doctor . . .* , p. 141.
9. ibid. xvi.

There is a widespread tendency today to speak of freedom as something we simply have (or should have), without any apparent awareness that it is also and especially something we must *achieve and secure*, and consequently something we *can* lose. In fact, the self-inflicted loss of personal freedom is one of the most striking phenomena of modern times. When we describe freedom as an "inalienable right," we are asserting a philosophical principle or perhaps staking a claim. But neither the right nor the claim is likely to be safeguarded unless I realize that the greatest threat to my freedom lies inside; it comes from myself, for it is through my own actions I can end up most irremediably deprived of freedom.

Love

When speaking of freedom, we cannot avoid referring to love, since love has every title to be regarded as the maximum expression of freedom. It is in fact only if the *free* aspect of love is stressed that its dignity is safeguarded. This ultimately means saving *our* dignity, as beings capable not only of giving or receiving love but also of understanding and appraising different *types of love*, that is, the various possibilities of loving that are presented in life, and of reacting according to our criterion of choice toward a concrete love.

The common sense of humanity has always considered love to be an absolutely necessary element of happiness. The person who does not know how to love, or who is not loved by anybody, is truly unfortunate and unhappy. If this is so, it confirms the anthropological presupposition we are following: man does not fulfill himself *alone*; he needs a complement. If he does not understand the true nature of love, if he cannot distinguish between love and its counterfeits, if he is unable to love, he will not find fulfillment.

Love involves an attraction between two persons which unites them in a desire to share major aspects of life. There is the love of friendship by which, if it is genuine, each friend not only enjoys the companionship of the other but also desires what is good for him or her. The love of friends is so characterized, but does not call for any further special commitment. Some friendships last a lifetime; others are temporary. Married love, in contrast, goes much farther. The person who marries chooses not only to love, but to do so with a distinctive love that is committed, exclusive and permanent. We shall take a closer look at this later on.

"Love is a centrifugal tendency that moves from inside to outside, but which needs an external stimulus to begin its movement. Therefore loving someone means coming out of oneself and being prepared to share. To be loved is to be treated as an exception, with special consideration."[10] When love

---

10. Enrique Rojas: *Una Teoria della Felicità*. p. 92.

is reciprocated, we can speak of two freedoms that meet in a movement toward mutual gift and acceptance of each other.

To fall in love means to realize that one is incomplete, and cannot be whole or happy without the loved one.[11] And to *want* to fall in love, even when one does not yet feel attracted to any concrete person, is equally a sign of the sense of incompleteness.

To fall in love produces a number of paradoxical consequences. The person who begins to love can no longer feel self-sufficient.[12] His need for someone else is experienced in too deep a way. But this very dependence opens the person's horizons as the conviction grows that life promises even more than he or she had first sensed. Gordon Allport, former Professor of Psychology at Harvard University, writes: "Hitherto self-sufficient, the lover finds himself no longer so. The welfare of another is more important than his own. In this way"—Allport adds—"*the self is extended.*"[13] The importance of this last conclusion cannot be exaggerated. When a person loves, the closed circle of the individual is broken, opening not only toward the person loved but, if the love is real, toward the whole outer world.

For the lover, life begins to move around a new center of interest. A person on his own can be dogged by the sense of being a poor specimen of humanity, but if he loves and is loved, the conviction springs up that his life has become endowed with extraordinary richness. Love can be the only way out of that narrow and obsessive self-awareness which is the wretched prison of many. One of George Eliot's characters reflects: "Nothing but complete and intense love could have initiated me into that enlarged life which grows and grows by appropriating the life of others; for before, I was always dragged back from it by ever-present painful self-consciousness."[14]

Life and the world take on new radiance for the lover: "love does not make one blind but seeing—able to see values."[15] A sign of true love is the new joy toward life that it induces. "The enthusiasm that love awakens is capable of renewing even what seemed totally sunk in inertia. Love gives meaning to life. The human being who discovers genuine love is often said to have been reborn, to have changed, or to have recaptured the meaning of everything. Without love it is as if a decisive and harmonizing component

11. Cf. R. Yepes: *Fundamentos de Antropología: un ideal de la excelencia humana*, Pamplona, 1996, p. 273.

12. The self-sufficient person has never known, or has long forgotten, what it is to love someone else. To fall in love, perhaps against one's deliberate will, can release him or her from the trap of self-sufficiency.

13. G. W. Allport: *Personality: a Psychological Interpretation*, p. 217.

14. *The Mill on the Floss*, Bk. VII, Ch. 3. I confess that the notion here of "appropriating," with its one-sided and individualistic overtones, leaves me less than content. Better if it had been expressed as "opening up to and assimilating."

15. V. Frankl: *The Doctor . . .* , p. 107.

were missing in this puzzle of life and happiness, a component capable of leading the person to make sense of the maze of contradictions in which each of us seems caught."[16]

Love and Freedom: "Free Love"

Don Juan, the hero-villain of plays, novels, and poems, is the prototype of the unrepentant libertine. The original Spanish legend tells how he seduces a girl of noble family and then kills her father, who tried to avenge her. Later, seeing the funerary statue on the father's tomb, he mockingly invites it to dine with him. The stone ghost duly arrives and, coming to life, seizes the defiant Don Juan and drags him down to hell.

The 17th-century dramatist, Molière, is among the best known of those who put the story on the stage. As a good Frenchman, Molière has Don Juan explain his *philosophy* of "free love." He feels he will "lose" his freedom in a committed love, and is not prepared to place his heart under such restrictions: "I love freedom in love, and I could never resign myself to enclosing my heart within four walls."[17] There is a strong modern tendency to echo or absorb this idea of Don Juan; but those who do so show that they have failed to understand true love or to find it. Real love reasons differently. The heart in love wants indeed to be bound to the other: but does not thereby feel *enclosed*, but rather open—to everything and everyone. Konstantin Levin, one of the main characters in Tolstoy's *Anna Karenina*, goes to a stag party the day before his wedding. His friends there pull his leg—that he is about to lose his freedom. He accepts the charge, turning it into a claim of happiness: "Just the contrary: I am happy at this loss of freedom."[18] What the person in love fears is not the loss of freedom but the loss of love. It is not so much that love is seen as a greater value than freedom, but rather that freedom "feels freer" in choosing to love.

This "freedom of love" must be understood also in order to clarify the relationship between love and feelings, or (as one goes deeper into the analysis of love) the relationship between feelings and will. It is true that love is normally accompanied by feeling. But, more importantly, it is always—if it is authentic—an operation of the will:[19] "therefore it can be corrected, increased, perfected. This conclusion is not in fashion: nevertheless it is based on reality. If love were only a feeling, an inner sense of the variations of joy or exaltation, etc., one would have to say that love goes and comes as it wants, that we are not free in its regard, since it overpowers us and we can do nothing to defend ourselves from it."[20]

---

16. Rojas, op. cit., p. 92.
17. *Dom Juan*, Act III, Sc. 5.
18. *Anna Karenina*, Part V, ch. 2.
19. Cf. Thomas Aquinas, *Summa Theologica*, I, q. 41, art. 2.
20. Rojas, op. cit., p. 94.

If love were no more than a feeling, then those would be right who hold that once feeling has disappeared, love has necessarily gone with it. This modern argument is often the cloak of selfishness. Others may have no claim on my good feelings, nor may I be able to summon them up, since feelings are seldom forthcoming as one wishes. But I can always give good will, all the more so where good will is due; as, in humanity if not in legal justice, it is due to all my fellowmen. A society not prepared to accept this principle gradually becomes inhuman. Now in many situations love, in the precise sense of wishing well to another, *is due in strict justice.*[21] Thus parents have a duty to love their children, just as children owe love to their parents; affection that is "felt" may dwindle or disappear, but love—as Aristotle defines it: "to love is to wish good to another"[22]—can and ought to be maintained. We will return to this in our chapter on marriage.

A strongly felt attraction toward another can be easily mistaken for an outward-going and truly donative or self-giving love, whereas all it may want is its own satisfaction, without being prepared for any commitment that could break the bonds of attachment to self—a necessary condition if one is to experience the liberating openness of true love. "Love can assume a debased form in which all the powers of devotion are bent to serve the ends of a limited ego. That debasement springs from timid self-defense against the shock of the greater, deeper world that can be entered only by the one who truly loves."[23]

Limited egos often imagine themselves marked out for great destinies. But they may be incapable of passing from the petty world of virtual greatness to that real self-giving love without which a person never truly grows. Henry James' polished characters are almost all painfully small and egotistic, though few seem to realize it. This lends all the more interest to his well-known story, *The Beast in the Jungle.* There he shows how a vain and mindless obsession with being called to "something great" can enclose a man within himself, thus making him blind to the one love which could have been his and which, as he understands too late, might have filled "the sounded void of his life."[24]

---

21. That love may at times call on the individual to subordinate his needs and interests (and especially his emotional requirements) to those of others, is simply unacceptable to modern psychotherapy. "'Love' as self-sacrifice or self-abasement . . . strike(s) the therapeutic sensibility as intolerably oppressive, offensive to common sense and injurious to personal health and well-being. To liberate humanity from such outmoded ideas of love and duty has become the mission of the postFreudian therapies and particularly of their converts and popularizers, for whom mental health means the overthrow of inhibitions and the immediate gratification of every impulse": P. Lasch: *The Culture of Narcissism*, p. 13.

22. *Rhet.* ii, 4.

23. Joseph Pieper: *Leisure, the Basis of Culture*, p. 74.

24. *Selected Tales of Henry James*, pp. 219–267.

Doing Someone Else's Will

Understanding how love and freedom relate can also help to dispel many frequent but mistaken notions about the relationship between freedom and obedience: the idea, for instance, that to obey—which implies doing someone else's will—means to renounce your own will, and reveals an immaturity of character by which you let yourself be placed in an alienating situation of inferiority and dependence.

But is this always so? Is immaturity shown by the team player, or by the soldier who follows the indications of his captain? Coaches of sports teams frequently discard talented players because they find them too *immature*—too self-centered or too preoccupied with their own "independence"—to fit in with others.

An enforced commitment (for instance, that of a slave to his master) is degrading and does violence to freedom. A commitment inspired by love is uplifting and allows a constant exercise of freedom charged with a sense of fulfillment. Here it is not even an adequate analysis to say that love makes it easy to "do someone else's will." Behind this, there can still be the idea that a commitment calls on a person to *renounce* his own will. That is not so. In a certain sense, it could not legitimately be so; for no one can be called on to abdicate the exercise of his will without thereby giving up one of his titles to full humanity. The fact is that a commitment is a determination of a person's *own* will. I do not "abandon" my own will to do someone else's. I *exercise* my will—for good and personal reasons—in choosing what someone else has also chosen. Here there is not absence, but rather a stronger presence, of personal choice. *I* will to make someone else's will my own.

There can be opposition between two wills, or there can be perfect, mutual, and willed identity. A person in love wants to do the will of the loved one: he *wills* to do it. The other person's will is what his will yearns for; he comes out of himself so as to find what he wants.

True love, while wanting to be united to the other, not only respects him or her, but is uplifted and opened out to other people and to all values. When the opposite occurs, love has been more egoistic than real. A classic example is offered by Emily Brontë's *Wuthering Heights*. Heathcliff's love for Catherine, just as hers for him, is not reciprocal and donative love that can unite them in a participative way. It is possessive love of the other, over whom each feels a total and even bitter claim. So too, it has no purifying effect on relations with others, but leads only to increasing rejection and hatred.

In *Anna Karenina*, as we noted earlier, the final reflections of Anna herself show how everything and everyone appear as hateful to the person whose last sense of love has died. Konstantin Levin offers the counterbalance to Anna. In chapters 14 and 15 of Part IV of his work, Tolstoy gives a fine portrayal of how, to the person who has just fallen in love, everything and especially everyone appear to be endowed with a new aura of goodness. Towards the end of his other masterpiece, *War and Peace*, he shows Peter Bésoukhow with that same new appreciation which the lover acquires: "the radiance of his soul, throwing its light on all who came in his way, enabled him to detect at once what there was of good or kindness in each."[25] Are these just subjective impressions induced by a certain state of mind, or are we really dealing with a keener positive perception that love indeed gives that ability to "see values" which Frankl notes? Whatever the answer, it does seem that the opening out from self involved in true love, enables a person to see not just the loved one but others too with new appreciation, while the absence of love darkens and warps a person's outlook towards life and his fellow creatures.

To be bound by love to someone else can give a needed sense of completion, and a new happiness. It is true that the bond with the other links you also with his or her sorrows, and so enlarges your possibilities of suffering. However, while allowing that Freud is therefore correct when he says, "we are never so defenseless against suffering as when we love,"[26] it must be added that this new capacity for *com*-passion is also a personal enrichment.

The essentially *volitional* aspect of love—the irreplaceable role of the will in all genuine love—has special importance in the evaluation of certain statements which are not infrequently heard: for instance, "I *cannot* love this person. . . ." This may be a handy formula which in the end simply means, "I am not prepared to make the effort, if not to love, at least to accept or forgive him or her." One can allow that acceptance or forgiveness may be difficult in such a case;[27] but then it is a difficulty, not an impossibility, which one is faced with. This can also be true in the case of an apparently opposite affirmation: "I cannot *help* loving this person," used perhaps as a justification for a relationship that is considered immoral (love for someone already married; certain ways of expressing love in extra-matrimonial relations, etc.). Unless a person knows how to govern love, he or she cannot claim the power to love and will not be capable of persevering in love.

Love has many types, and many counterfeits. In the end, it is the most definitive measure of personal worth, for the person is most genuinely revealed in the kind of love he is capable of: "each one is worth what his love is worth."[28]

Freedom and Authority

But how can human freedom be preserved in the face of the massive and impersonal business or political forces of the modern state which so dominate

---

25. *War and Peace*, vol. III, ch. 50.
26. *Civilization and its Discontents*, p. 82.
27. Being unable to overlook or forgive is a clear though frequent sign of psychological immaturity, and can totally block a person's growth in humanity. Vindictiveness makes a person live in an enclosed world. Few things so obsess and impoverish the mind as the "I'll get even with them" mentality.
28. "Talis est quisque, qualis eius dilectio est": St. Augustine, *In Ep. ad Parth.*, II, 14.

the individual? Is there any way of keeping a sense of freedom when the individual is enmeshed in the legal restraints of modern life? Yes—if the laws correspond to justice, and if people have been grounded in love for justice itself, considered as a basic inter-personal value on which the whole of social life needs to be built.[29]

Social or legal authority suggests "rules"—rules and regulations which, by inexorable tendency, seem to multiply indefinitely. The hankering after an existence free from institutional or corporate regulations underlies many currents of modern thought. Popular works of social criticism[30] argue for a new way of life that will be more spontaneous, more natural, more unregulated. To a large extent, this radical reaction is understandable. Modern man is so exasperated at having so long had to obey soulless forces—government, business corporations, etc.—so fed up with being regulated, that he now does not want to have any rules or to obey anyone other than himself.

Nevertheless, both social and personal living need rules. The completely unregulated society tends to disintegration: and so does the unregulated self. "Obeying self" often means following the whims of the moment; and that too tends to be soulless, or soul-destroying. Not a few of our impulses can enslave us more than any bureaucracy or police force, and alienate us from others.

A society seeks to protect itself with equitable rules, and with some system of enforcing their compliance. An individual needs to do something similar in his own inner life, i.e., in that mixture of mind, will, passions, and prejudices which, if not harmonized and molded into some sort of unity, gives rise to growing interior chaos. Self-dominion is no easy matter; yet if a person cannot rule himself, something else or someone else will.

Freedom, the sensation and the reality of personal freedom, does not depend on having no regulations, no directions, no goals—just drifting—but on *self*-regulation in the search for worthwhile values, and in the free choice and steady ability to respond to those values.

❂ ❂ ❂

"The power to choose is at the service of the power to complete yourself. . . . Each person is a reality given and a reality to be achieved."[31] What matters is not so much what you choose, but who you become as a result of your choices. This is not to say that what you choose is unimportant. On the contrary, the *value* of what you choose, just as the value of what you love, has a decisive bearing on the personal worth that you acquire as a result of your choices. So we pass on to consider the question of "values."

---

29. Cf. chapter eight.
30. Such as, for instance, Charles Reich's *The Greening of America*, New York, 1970.
31. Mouroux, *Sens Chrétien* . . . p. 131.

3

VALUES

Freedom and Preferences

It is among options that freedom is exercised. When choosing one thing rather than another, a *preference* is shown. I choose this because I prefer it to that. The idea of "preferences" opens up the whole question of values.

To exercise a preference means to act according to a scale of values: one chooses this because the choice seems better than the other option(s). Life is a constant making of choices and revealing of preferences. The person for whom golf rates high in his or her scale of preferences goes to play golf at every opportunity, whereas someone with different values plays tennis or listens to music or visits friends. A person buying a house or an automobile exercises his choice according to his preferences, trimmed down by the possibilities of his bank account.

The exercise of free will can therefore be described as a response to values. The fact of having options, of being able to choose, shows the existence of freedom but does not gauge its dignity. What is the value of freedom if it is faced only with alternatives that are scarcely worth choosing? The scavenger rummaging through a pile of garbage also has his freedom, but what dignity is there to it?

So the question of values enters inevitably into any consideration of freedom, for the value of freedom itself is necessarily measured according to the value of what you can choose. There is no comparison between the concession of the free choice of whatever you want in the supermarket of a small town and the same freedom inside a jeweler's in a capital city. Or on another level, which is a better exercise of freedom: to become rich by telling lies, or to remain poor by preferring to respect the truth?

A person's free choices are the best mirror and test of his values. Even in the decision to commit suicide—which appears as the most definitive proof of the absence rather than the presence of values—there can be found a certain confirmation of this. If a person takes his life, it is not because death has more to offer but rather, so he thinks, because life has nothing to offer. He has reached the bottom of the scale, and "prefers" death because there are no values left in his life. There is nothing to "go up to"; he prefers or hopes for nothingness, even at the risk of actually "going down."

Sartre[1] held that freedom is the *only* given value (and that by it man "creates his own values"). This proposition does not hold water. Freedom is not so much a value as a means by which a person can enrich himself with values, or impoverish oneself if his choices actually undermine his values and introduce "anti-values" into his life. A simple ability to choose has little title to be regarded as a value if the field of choice covers nothing worth choosing, or if the chooser has been so conditioned to choose that his choices *diminish* his life, or if he is afraid of committing himself to worthwhile, but perhaps difficult, choices that can enrich it.

But, what is a "value?" A value could be defined as an aspect of a reality that makes it seem attractive and desirable, or—and we are going up a scale—worthy of admiration. Alternatively, we can say that values are elements or goods that enrich life. This can be grasped at once on the material level. Food is a value, and so is clothing. A minimum of healthy food is essential at all latitudes to stay materially alive; the essential nature of clothing will vary the farther north or south we go. Food and clothing, then, are basic material values. There are other values that, without being essential, make important aspects of life easier and more pleasant: good housing, a healthy climate, appropriate medicine . . .

Life appears as more attractive, the more it is enriched by values and especially by values of better *quality*. Most people welcome the possibility of eating in a good restaurant or of wearing shoes of top-class leather. When a person *has* more or better things—houses, cars, vacations—his or her life undoubtedly seems richer, fuller, and more fulfilled.

However, not all enriching goods can be bought. Some are possessed constitutionally: exceptional physical strength, for instance, or a fine musical ear. Others are acquired by effort, as when someone becomes an Olympic champion, a concert guitarist, or a master of several languages.

---

1. Jean-Paul Sartre (1905–1980), the best-known exponent of mid-20th century existentialism.

You can buy an Olympic medal if you *have* enough money. But you can win it only if you are in top physical form. To have sufficient money is enough in order to acquire a real museum of old medals; but you cannot win a medal without *being* an exceptionally gifted and trained type.

There are other values that do not consist in material goods or in bodily capacities, but in simple interior aptitudes. To possess a sense of humor or a good memory, to know how to reason well, to have special talent for mathematics or philosophy, to enjoy a strong aesthetic sense or natural appreciation of beauty, to be endowed with strong willpower and self-control . . .

So, while one can grow in *having*, one can also grow in *being*. One can even grow in what one has, *without* growing in what one is. The latter—to grow in what one *is*—seems to be more decisive for measuring the value of a life. One person may *have more* money than another, and at the same time *be less* wise or truthful or generous. What we begin to note here—the difference between "having" and "being"—has no small importance for our study. The fact is that what most distinguishes man is not his capacity to possess or appropriate material values, nor even to be well developed physically, but his power to assimilate values of the spirit. As a person assimilates them, becoming the bearer of spiritual values, his life grows from within.[2] His outlook and perspectives expand. A blind man can be someone of extremely broad interior horizons. A beggar can be richer than a millionaire in artistic understanding or in appreciation of nature.

Appreciation

Chesterton insists that the aim of life is appreciation. Therefore there is no sense in not appreciating things, and less sense still in having more of them if you are unable to appreciate them.[3] It is much less what a person can buy or have, than what he can appreciate, that makes him humanly rich.

Since material values belong less intimately to the person—remaining at the surface or periphery of his existence—they are more easily lost than spiritual values. A thief can deprive me of my car, but not of my knowledge. Spiritual values, being more intimately assimilated, sink deeper roots in the person and are lost or uprooted with greater difficulty. It is easier to lose what I have than what I am; nevertheless, the latter can also be lost.

Other reasons too indicate that the way of human development lies in the acquisition of goods of the spirit rather than those of matter. If the fullness of human life is to be calculated according to the number and quality of material

---

2. "I begin to achieve fulfillment as a person only from the day in which I dedicate myself to values that raise me above myself": E. Mounier: *Rivoluzione personalista e comunitaria*, p. 94.
3. Cf. G. K. Chesterton, *Autobiography*, p. 333.

goods each one possesses, it is clear that, given the limited amount of these goods, not everybody could develop a full human life. In fact, since any individual material good can be possessed only by a single person, the development of humanity—if measured in exclusively material terms—runs the danger of being seen as a competition in which other people appear as rivals for the same non-shareable prize, as competitors whom each one would like to see drop out of the race.

It is different when personal realization is understood in terms of the acquisition of spiritual values. Spiritual values cannot be monopolized by a few individuals; they can be held by all. They permit limitless participation, and do not decrease when somebody obtains them. They spread "ownership"; but do not alternate it, passing just from one owner to another. In communicating a piece of good news to a neighbor, a person is not deprived of the news, but rather feels the increased satisfaction of having shared it with someone else.

When the search for material goods is a dominant ethos in a society, it tends to breed envy and separation among that society's members; whereas the more people have been reared in an ethos which inculcates the primacy of spiritual values, it is easier for them to pursue common goals in harmony.[4] Only an educational system which emphasizes such values will focus attention on the deeper meaning of democratic equality and rights, prepare young people to understand better the factors that make for social harmony, and tend to the preservation of true democracy.

Spiritual values are not consumed when they are "used" by someone who incorporates them into his own life or communicates them to others. Not only are people enriched by means of values, but we can even say that the values themselves are in a certain way enriched, at least in the sense that they increase in extension and effectiveness through the new "incarnations" given to them. Along the same line, we can say that each individual life leaves a stamp on the world, marking the lives of others strongly or weakly, positively or negatively . . .

When we possess and appreciate a value, there is always the desire to know and possess it still more. A person who acquires a taste for music is

4. Some people would see in a "value system" a possible replacement for a "moral system." This viewpoint confuses notions. A "value system" implies an order of goods, whether subjectively or objectively appreciated, whether derived from reason or faith or both. In itself it does not enter the field of morals, though it may lead to it. A "moral system," which must accompany any belief in free choice, implies the possibility of acting "rightly" or "wrongly," for or against a person's own system of values (however subjectively these may be held). If, say, friendship or sincerity forms part of a person's "value system," it takes only elementary self-awareness to realize that he can treat the value as it deserves, i.e., as he *ought* to; with that one passes from the mere intellectual awareness of something to be valued, to the moral awareness of how it can be treated well or badly, rightly or wrongly. If one has no sense of duty towards one's values, no sense that one should be a reliable friend or a sincere companion, then one cannot claim to possess any real "value system" at all.

motivated to increase his musical knowledge or talent. The tendency is toward fuller possession. We are led on to want perfection (even the man whose value is money wants more).

Moreover, appreciation of a value, especially if it is of a spiritual nature, normally opens us to a greater appreciation of other spiritual values. Whoever admires truthfulness or sincerity is better able to appreciate trust and understanding, along with all the other elements that go to make up friendship. This is logical since spiritual values, more directly rooted in truth and goodness, have a necessary interconnection that goes far deeper than any possible connection between material values.

Scale of Values; Criterion

We have said that the value of my freedom depends also on the value of what I can choose. But it equally depends on my ability to *evaluate* what I can choose. I may be surrounded by nothing worth choosing; but I may be surrounded by things worth choosing, without having any appreciation of their value. The American Indians who exchanged gold objects for tawdry colored beads offered by the first explorers may have felt they made a good exchange. No doubt the explorers thought they had made a better one. It is a pity if we are exploited by others. But it is also a pity if, having riches or values at hand, we fail to recognize them, or freely choose inferior ones to those that objectively are worth more.

Values themselves are not all worth the same, but stand in a certain hierarchy (when everything appears of equal value, then a person loses interest in choosing: "it's all the same to me"). Unless one has a "scale of values," one does not have values at all. A scale of values implies a criterion, a basis or standard according to which we judge between what is worth more and what is worth less, weighing the positive and the negative aspects of each choice.

A hierarchy of values exists, a scale in which certain values are worth more "in themselves," while others, although being real values, are worth less. It is true that any attempt to assign a particular position on this scale to concrete realities or experiences easily provokes different opinions: yet it should in any case stimulate a deepening in personal reflections. Which, for example, is superior as a value: economic wealth or physical health? Each one can ponder what choice he would make before the alternative: a multi-millionaire with chronic bad health or a middle-income person who never suffers from even a headache. Or, on a different level, what answer to give to the question proposed in a professional forum: "is it rational or neurotic to sacrifice one's life for one's child?"[5]

---

5. *American Journal of Psychiatry*, vol. 138, 1981, p. 439.

If education is to prepare young people for life, it must help them develop discernment, i.e., the critical ability to assess their choices in terms of values. Students who go through a school system that does not develop their critical sense are more likely to shape their later choices according to commercial, political, or ideological slogans, rather than to any properly thought out standards of their own.

Relativity of Values

Nevertheless, it remains true that what is a value for one, because he sees special meaning in it, may often be of no value to another, because it lacks meaning for him. A visit to an exhibition by a contemporary artist may be an exceptional experience for one person, and a total waste of time for another. Meaning or purpose is at the heart of a value. What has (or appears to have) no purpose, has no value, at least to the person considering it so. Life is the greatest example. A life without conscious meaning fosters the impression of a life without value. No impression can be more dangerous.

We have already referred to suicide. However, even though one can hold that very many persons today experience a life lacking in any sense of deep meaning, the suicide rate (which is extremely low; about 12 or 13 per 100,000 in the U. S. A., with some developed countries somewhat higher, and emerging countries considerably lower) seems to indicate that the hope of finding "a better tomorrow" is a strong factor in normal human life. In the last analysis, it is not the person who just lacks values, but the one who lacks the hope of having any, who is drawn towards the nothingness of despair.

Jean-Paul Sartre, as we have seen, suggested that each person should "create" or "invent" his or her own values. This is really to hold that there is no objective value or meaning to anything in life. As he liked to do, Sartre expressed himself in a provocative, attention-getting way: "To say that we invent values means nothing else but this: life has no meaning *a priori*. Before you come alive, life is nothing; it's up to you to give it a meaning, and value is nothing else but the meaning that you choose."[6] Let the reader decide whether Sartre's formula is likely to lead to a life of real richness, or boils down to a catchphrase which, if followed, leaves life bereft of any true meaning or value. It is hard to see how freedom considered as a completely irrational power can yield any other ultimate result.

An idea running through much of popular modern psychology is that, to grow and to be oneself one should be ready to try everything since every new experience adds something to the individual's personal character.[7] In this view,

---

6. Cf. *Existentialism*, Philosophical Library, p. 58.
7. Cf. *The Greening of America*, p. 394.

it matters little what one chooses because there is in fact no standard by which one can or should choose.[8] In fact, the reasoned evaluation of events and possibilities is an approach to be scorned. Subjecting yourself to "experience" rather than trying to dominate it is the best way of meeting human needs. And so, the ideal for personal fulfillment is to live "in a never-ending state of tentativeness and uprooting."[9]

This idea merits a brief comment or two. Not every new experience adds something positive to a person's character. Many experiences add a negative factor which, by closing the person in on himself, thwarts fulfillment. It is not a question of "dominating" experience, but of being open to those experiences which enrich and rejecting those that may indeed attract but impoverish. "Never-ending uprootedness" . . . ? Is fulfillment in life a matter of letting down roots, or of tearing them up?

We can certainly speak of "greater" values and "lesser" values. Is it possible to speak of "true" values and *false* values? Whoever one holds that it is will probably go on to say that the latter—"false" values—are not in fact *values* at all. But, is there any objective standard by which such a fundamental difference can be justified, or is it simply a matter of personal taste and preference? We leave the question unanswered, at least for the moment.

A solid foundation for the dignity of individuals is laid only when each one manages to establish an attitude of openness and receptivity toward values, above all toward truth and goodness, thus acquiring the capacity for both personal self-enrichment and a worthwhile social life.

Response to Values

Values fulfill us by drawing us up; our mind *rises* to them and accepts them at a higher level. But our will too must respond to the attractions—or to the demands—of values. Again it seems that we must somehow be drawn out of ourselves, in order to fulfill ourselves.

The response to values should ordinarily be one of pleasure, joy, admiration, to the point that—in the case of a really exalted value—one can speak of an ecstatic reaction (ecstasy properly means going out of oneself). There are values capable of asking and obtaining the very gift of oneself: freedom, the family, a nation's independence or identity . . . ; and there are people who are prepared to die for such values. Whoever does not have a value in his life for which he thinks it is worthwhile to give that life itself, has a life poor in values. To say that something is worth dying for means that it is worth living for. To

---

8. The "criterionless-choice," as Alisdair MacIntyre puts it: *After Virtue*, p. 202.
9. *Greening* . . . , p. 89; p. 398.

say there is nothing worth dying for, implies that what we are living for is also worth nothing.[10]

While we would all like to find perfect values, they rarely occur. As a rule, our experience of values is partial, either because the capacity for appreciation which we ourselves possess is insufficiently developed, or because the values we encounter are limited, since even higher values are so often expressed in practice in an imperfect form; mixed, that is, with defects.[11] Hence the importance of knowing how to identify and appreciate the aspect of value in individual things or situations, without being blinded or hindered by the presence of defects on the one hand; and, on the other, without losing the discernment of what is defective. Such discernment or criterion is also a sign of a sense of values.

Values call for adequate response. To be able to respond duly to each individual value shows discernment, maturity, and depth. Such a response calls for an ability to distinguish between values, between those that really are values and those that are so merely in appearance; and, among the real ones, to know how to gauge those that are of greater worth, since not all values are equal, nor should a person respond in the same way to all. Some are superior (they are worth "more") and others are inferior (they are worth "less"). It is a matter of criterion: and, we repeat, of developing both receptivity and a capacity for response.

To respond with too much enthusiasm to inferior values can indicate superficiality, but is not normally very harmful. Is it a defect to be crazy about football? Some no doubt think so. But this also can be a superficial judgment. When all is said and done, being a Dallas Cowboys or a Green Bay Packers fan can compensate for the stress of a very demanding professional occupation.

It is worse to respond insufficiently to great values. Whatever the reason—shortsightedness, lethargy, selfishness—the person who is not open to a true value remains without enrichment. Such a lack of response can happen without any personal fault; for example, when a defective or inadequate response is the consequence of a lack of formation, the capacity to appreciate such values simply not having been developed. Education is defective insofar as it does not open up a person's horizons to different values and, if possible, to the awareness of a valid scale of values and to a taste for the more enriching

---

10. Here we might recall the modern concept of freedom noted earlier and the dangers of freedom in a world without values. If you lose respect for all the things you can choose, you lose respect for your own freedom; it becomes worthless to you. And once you have lost respect for the power or value of your own freedom, you lose respect for yourself. If you can choose nothing of worth, you are worth nothing. It is a view of self and a world view that makes for the suicide or for the terrorist; or for both put together.

11. Despite the many cases (falling in love . . . ; the simple acquisition of a new car) where a first impression—which however does not last—is of having found perfection.

ones. Young people are not naturally apathetic; they have an innate capacity for wonder that, if developed, is a powerful enrichment and ought to be a source of enjoyment in their future lives.[12] It is questionable to what extent most of modern education communicates enthusiasm for values, or even the capacity for simple admiration. If that is lacking, then people easily become bored and incapable of enjoying the ordinary things of life.

While the desire to find "perfect" values seems innate in us, this can create a problem if a person's expectations prevent him from seeking "partial" values, so as to recognize them and take an interest in and respond to them.

Here there is the danger that usually accompanies discernment or critical spirit. There are people who know how to appreciate great works, but are not able to discover *anything* in an intermediary or mediocre work or situation containing values which are not evident or fully perfected, since they are intermingled with defects. It is always a limitation if a person is capable of responding to what is exceptional, but not to what is ordinary.

There is still another possibility of which special account should be taken: that of responding *negatively* to real values, and rejecting them. Such a reaction can derive from malformation which not only prevents the person from seeing the value as it is, but leads him to judge it as an anti-value. But it is also true that one can possess the capacity to see and understand a value, and yet not be willing to do so because of the practical difficulties this could involve. When such a thing happens, it ordinarily derives from some rooted prejudice, and may be a (possibly unconscious) defense mechanism of a lifestyle the person does not want to change.

We repeat that the desire to find perfect values is completely human. In fact, a lack of humanity is shown by whoever does not have some desire of perfection, whether in knowledge or beauty, in joy or happiness. However, perfect values—outside of God—do not exist; great and even exceptional values, do. Anybody would expect that the response to a great value—even though it is not perfect in every aspect—should arouse an appreciation, an admiration, a response that is also great, in whoever contemplates it. It is not always so; at times, in fact, there is a reduced or even negative response to great and evident values, and this can happen in the case of a person with full capacity to appreciate the wealth of that value. There is something particularly intriguing here, precisely because this phenomenon is relatively frequent. We will return to it.

All true values should attract. This does not mean that you can speak of a moral fault (although you could posit an aesthetic limitation) in the case of a

---

12. The capacity for wonder is never fully developed unless in some way it carries with it a capacity for anger—whenever one sees a truly admirable value despised or mistreated. Indignation in such cases arises from admiration, as the logical—and, indeed, desirable—reaction to the debasement of values (all the more so if this leads to the exploitation of people).

person who is not attracted by, say, classical music or baroque architecture. Nevertheless, there are other values—truthfulness, for example, or respect for other people's property—towards which no one can remain indifferent without showing a moral defect. In such cases, values and conscience stand in a particular relationship.

A person can be "blind" to values, incapable of seeing or discovering them; it is a defect that seems to reside in the intellect. A person can also be "deaf" toward them, being completely insensitive to their call; a defect rather of the will or the capacity for feeling. Mere appreciation of a value, which can remain at the stage of simply receiving it into oneself, is easier than response to the value, which always calls for a certain going out of self.

Deafness (more than blindness) to values seems connected to a free attitude of the subject who closes in on himself and "shuts his ears," so as not to feel any call that might disturb the sense (the illusion?) of a good conscience, and especially so as not to let himself be led where he does not want to go.[13] It is a curious resistance which the individual offers against the natural call that values—and precisely those that are greatest and most enriching—address to every person who wants to *be of worth* in life. This danger of remaining blind or deaf to values that one does not want to see or respond to is a primary and mysterious threat to human growth; again we will return to it.

A major value—without which a personality always remains incomplete—is a sense of humor, the ability to see the comic aspect of what is incongruous or absurd. This quality is an important aid to riding over the contradictions of life without excessive annoyance; and so it fosters a healthy optimism. While it is of course a great source of enjoyment as well as peace, few people possess it in full measure. The worst defect is not to laugh too much at what is not so funny, or too little at what is, but not to be able to *laugh at yourself.* Few people can sincerely join others in being amused at their own mistakes. This reluctance to see yourself objectively is a limitation which is not easily overcome. The point is finely made by Jane Austen at the end of *Pride and Prejudice.* Elizabeth Bennet's prejudices have been dispelled, and Darcy's pride overcome—though not yet completely. Darcy tells Elizabeth how she has been for him the means of salutary humiliations. She realizes that the process needs to continue, but gradually: "She remembered that he had yet to learn to be laughed at, and it was rather too early to begin."[14]

"Value judgments" are considered unwarranted today, at least when they imply an ethical assessment of personal conduct. Yet people apply value judgments constantly to *material* things—this car is "more comfortable, but more expensive"—and so can weigh the effect of possible choices on their bank

---

13. Cf. J. de Finance, *L'Affrontement de l'autre*, Rome, 1973, p. 273.
14. Vol. II, ch. 16.

accounts. Advantages are often accompanied by disadvantages. Does no one ever do the same when faced, for instance, with the temptation to tell a lie to a colleague? I may deceive him; but he may eventually find out, and I may lose his esteem. Or, applying a slightly different and apparently more interior criterion: he may never find out, but *I* may lose *my* self-esteem, thus going down on my own scale of values.

To pass value judgments on yourself but not on others, may show a high (perhaps an exaggerated) degree of humble exigence toward yourself and of understanding charity toward others. But it could also reflect such an absorbing preoccupation with yourself and your self-image that it leaves no time or interest to care about others. In any case, it seems to show a skepticism regarding the importance—for the fulfillment of others and the achievement of a more human society—of certain norms of behavior; or at least a selfish indifference regarding the operational presence of such values in the life of others.

4

CONDITIONS FOR FULFILLMENT

The human person is not self-sufficient. In order to live—and more particularly, in order to attain the self-fulfillment which is the purpose of life—no one possesses or finds in himself all that he needs. External elements are necessary: air, light, nourishment. . . . All these things, which sustain and help the person to develop, are *goods* or *values* for him. He has to be open to receive these "goods." The consequence of refusing to eat or to breathe is to lose his life. The same holds for the sick person who fails to recognize and take a medicine necessary to cure him.

To develop our body, we must be open to material goods; we need them, even while we should be aware that they are of an order inferior to ourselves. To develop our spirit, one must be likewise open to spiritual goods—which we more particularly designate as *values*.[1] Material goods are also values, but of a secondary order, for they cannot be really assimilated into ourselves.

At the end of the day it is myself and what I am inside that I have to live with; it is not what is around me. I can turn my back on what is outside and

---

1. We pass over the question of whether these spiritual goods are to be considered higher or lower *than the human spirit itself*, simply noting that if we hold them to be above man, we can then say that man grows physically by assimilating what is lower than himself, and grows spiritually by assimilating what is higher. The first process arrives at a maximum point, and afterwards goes into decline; the second can always progress.

get away from it, but I cannot get away from myself. When one is deprived of all I have (the moment will come), it would be pitiful to find that *it was all I was.*

We will center our attention on spiritual values and on the two complementary dispositions or attitudes needed to be enriched by them: opening (looking out) and assimilating (receiving into ourselves):

- opening; toward new horizons and higher values. The outlook of the mind is enlarged; it especially grows in capacity for appreciation and admiration. A mind in search of higher values and positively open to them is the first condition for personal growth. Paradoxically, the more the mind can "lose" itself in contemplation of these values, the more it grows.

- responding and assimilating, by accepting within ourselves; letting ourselves be filled by what is greater or more admirable. Man cannot grow and come to be truly great except in the discovery of what is greater than himself, and in the readiness to make it his own, incorporating it into his personal life, whatever the efforts this may require.

Openness to Values

Openness of mind. The person with narrow or closed horizons cannot grow or develop; he lacks space. The same happens with the one whose gaze is fixed too low, seeing just what lies below him with no reference to anything above. Broad and open horizons are essential. The qualities of the intellect are put to the test here: the purity, clarity, penetration, and height of one's intellectual outlook, and one's mental receptivity.

The self-development of each person is conditioned by the ability to discover and appreciate values. The greater his ability to admire authentic values, the richer and more fulfilled his life can become. For both Aristotle and Thomas Aquinas, our human capacity for knowledge has a necessary relation to our power of admiration. Since admiration is a form of love, the capacity to know things, seeing their true value, also depends on the ability to love. Without love a person can remain blind to values. Viktor Frankl's comment, "love does not make one blind but seeing—able to see values"[2] comes to mind here again.

If education consists particularly in drawing out[3] a person's capacities for appreciating all the aspects of life, the question of values assumes a primordial role in the whole of education; and no educational system can escape being appraised and criticized according to the scale of values it proposes or communicates.

---

2. See ch. 2.
3. Education comes from "e-ducere," which means "to bring out."

Acceptance and Assimilation of Values

If a value is to play its part in the process of personal fulfillment, a first condition is to understand and appreciate it. But if it is to help us to grow, mere intellectual understanding is not enough. Along with being appreciated, the value has to be accepted and assimilated. Otherwise it remains just something known from the outside, and is frustrated in its potential to enrich us within. Here the challenge is to the will: to choose and accept, to respond and to grow.

With my mind I have the capacity to discover values (in the authenticity or truth shining in them). And with my will I can respond to them (in the good they possess)—coming out of myself toward them; opening the way so that they can enter into me and, through assimilation, become mine.

This assimilation, however, is not like the physical assimilation of food, which occurs through a process involving absorption on our part of the material value, to the point of destroying it (and so it ceases to exist in its original form). Man is nourished by consuming, absorbing, and changing food, water, oxygen into himself. Spiritual values, as we have seen, are not consumed; they are not changed. They are communicated to man, enriching him without losing anything of their own reality or existence. Spiritual values have an inexhaustible communicability with regard to all those who are open to them.

To have an "open mind" is a good initial attitude in approaching any question. However, the mind cannot remain indefinitely open; it must close—around the truth—incorporating it to itself, just as the open mouth must close on and swallow the food that is to nourish the body. The healthy mind is not only open to truth, but searches for and *embraces* it, once found. It has a natural hunger for truth, in which it finds its nourishment. There is no limit to the nourishment which the healthy mind can draw from the truth, provided it realizes that certain truths, which initially seem tough and bitter to the palate, only yield their substance, good taste, and nourishment to those who are prepared to bite into them deeply, chew them over, and digest them thoroughly.

A person who cultivates a mind that is satisfied with "soft" truths— subjective, partial, and circumscribed truths—will move in a confined intellectual world, of undemanding and unpromising prospects. He will not have great ideas (he will tend not to let himself have them) or great projects, except in the imagination. Perhaps he will lose that intimate conviction which is naturally present, consciously or not, in everyone: that we are made for more— for broader horizons, for more knowledge, for greater goodness. In Pascal's words, "Man infinitely surpasses man." He is capable of conceiving and desiring great things, and greater things still. He has an innate tendency to rebel against philosophies which present human life as inherently constrained by definitive limits.

Values of this type cannot be truly assimilated in a life without enriching it interiorly. A necessary condition for this enrichment is that the subject not only opens himself but lets himself be drawn outwards and upwards in a way that broadens and heightens the reach of personal life. In this process the person acquires greater understanding of his own uniqueness and dignity, not as a source of values, but as someone capable of knowing values—as a real "connoisseur"—as well as of truly *embodying* them.

It is interesting to note that there is a certain two-way aspect to this process. The person is enriched by the value; and at the same time he gradually gives a new character and, so to say, a "new life" to the value, *personalizing* it in a particular human expression, and thus broadening its area of influence or effectiveness. We could add that every "incarnation" of a value personalized in this way, possesses something totally singular and unique, and so constitutes a sort of new "creation."[4]

Here the paradoxical mode of personalist fulfillment can be more fully grasped. The self gradually becomes aware of its identity, not as center of the universe, but rather as observer and spectator, enthusiast and lover of the world, the contemplation of whose wealth becomes the key to personal enrichment. The self forgets self and stops contemplating itself, so as to contemplate. . . . It is a process of enrichment, not by possessing the world in its material aspect (having more), but rather through letting oneself be enriched by values in one's own personal existence: being more.

To accept a spiritual value is not merely to appropriate it, and less still to subordinate it to oneself. One can never "take in" a true value without in some way coming out of oneself toward it, admiring it, and respecting it in its peculiar nature. This respect for what a value is in itself must always accompany true appreciation; as must the awareness that no one can seek to relate to it as exclusive proprietor, since others too can participate in its appreciation. In fact, the more truly one appreciates a value, the more one will want others to appreciate it also.

Every choice, we have emphasized, involves a commitment. In regard to material values, we have also considered how the choice of one object—this car model rather than another—means the exclusion of other choices (at least for the moment). This is not necessarily so in regard to values of the spirit. We can potentially choose all spiritual values at one and the same time.

Something further should be noted. In choosing a material value, we commit ourselves only in the sense of excluding other possible choices. We are

---

4. This is at times strikingly illustrated in the field of musical performance. The "Triple Konzert," for violin, piano, and cello, is a relatively minor piece among Beethoven's works; yet under the direction of Herbert von Karajan, it takes on a new vigor and brilliance that possibly surpasses Beethoven's own conception.

not bound by any special commitment to the *object chosen*, or by any particular call to respect it. We may put our money into the object, but we are not
bound to "put ourselves" into it. We may come to regret the choice, feel let
down by what has been acquired, and dispose of it—e.g., sell a car—without
any sense of having "let down" the material value itself. It is not so with a
spiritual value, at least of the higher order. A choice of a value of the spirit
calls for a commitment on a different level: a commitment into which we do
"put" or "give" ourselves, in such a way that it is possible to speak of a certain
reciprocity of giving and receiving. We can say that on this level a value does
not "give itself" to the person, so becoming his, unless the person in some
way reciprocates with the gift of self. The truth only gives itself to the mind
that gives itself—commits itself—to the truth. There is a lack of depth in the
spiritual value chosen—or in the choice we have made—if we do not sense
ourselves committed to it.

Real friendship, for instance, cannot be bought. It is a value you can only
acquire and retain by putting something of *yourself* into it. A measured or
calculated friendship, where one is careful to put little of oneself (of time, of
readiness to understand, to yield, to help . . .), is a poor sort of friendship that
is not likely to last. As we will see later, this applies much more still to that
very special form of friendship which is marriage. Selfishness and calculation
are main causes of broken friendships and unhappy marriages.

There is a principle here that applies in a broader and even more fundamental sense to happiness itself: a principle which underlines the whole
thought of this book. There is no such thing as calculated happiness; nor
can happiness itself be bought at a price. It is a gift and can only be received
as a consequence of a gift: giving yourself to—looking up to, respecting, and
loving—what is worthwhile. Therefore the search for happiness resolves
itself first and foremost into a search for realities (things or, better still,
persons) worth looking up to and loving: into a search for true human and
spiritual values.

Not all spiritual values are of the same order, nor do all call for equal
commitment. But some at least are of such quality and importance that they
can be properly considered as of higher value than one's self; recognized, that
is, as of greater worth than one's own life. As we suggested in the last chapter, a
person who has no cause or value in life which he is prepared to die for, if
necessary, lacks the presuppositions for self-fulfillment. "I could not love you
so much, did I not love honor more."[5] If there exists no value higher than the
value I place on my own life, if there is nothing for which I consider it worthwhile to give my life, what basis is there to the value which I attribute to this
life of mine?

---

5. Richard Lovelace, *To Lucasta*.

There is no suggestion here that one must not love oneself, and less still that one must despise self. The point is rather that, to be oneself, a self worth loving, one has to love values worth more than oneself. One needs to feel oneself made for great goals; and to pursue them with all one's strength. Life then appears as a fascinating contest in which the most is achieved by whoever is most capable of leaving self-centeredness behind, in pursuit of values whose attraction lies in what they are in themselves more than in any pleasure or utility they may offer to me. Self-fulfillment is simply not possible without an increasing forgetfulness of self. "Paradoxically, 'self-expression' requires the capacity to lose oneself in the pursuit of objectives, not primarily referred to the self."[6] The French philosopher, Emmanuel Mounier, insists on the paradox: "True will is an open force that tears a man from himself in order to center him on an external and higher end, which is at the same time deep-rooted in his intimacy."[7]

A person's worth, then, depends on his capacity for appreciation and admiration, and on what and whom he really appreciates and admires. In this sense we can say that a person is worth what his values are worth. If these are elevated and true, the appreciation he has for them reveals more particularly his worth as a person. And yet appreciation and admiration alone are not enough. In the end his worth depends on the respect he nourishes for those values, and even more on his dedication to them: the extent to which he is prepared to serve or save them. Subjectively at least, the ultimate test of the values with which a person senses his life to be enriched is his readiness to give that same life for those very values.

A faith without martyrs, or a nation without soldiers who have died for a common cause, does not offer or does not inspire any real value. The individualist is always tempted to reject "common causes," and to reduce *his* values to a measure that fits the type of life he wants to program and build.

The attitude which no longer sees a value in patriotism—above all in its extreme expression of giving one's life for one's country—is spreading today. Logically enough, the idea of sacrificing *one's self* appears as the ultimate alienation and anti-value to whoever claims full dominion over his own existence and wants to be author of his own identity. Once one thinks oneself self-sufficient or capable of absolute self-fulfillment just with one's own interior resources, one's "I" necessarily takes on the character of central and supreme value. Then, to sacrifice one's life, so lapsing into extinction, for any other cause than one's own self, presents itself as an absurd action which perhaps could even be called "unethical," inasmuch as it implies preferring a lower value to the one truly supreme value.

---

6. G. W. Allport: *Personality: a Psychological Interpretation*, op. cit., p. 213.
7. *Oeuvres*, II, Paris, 1947, p. 458.

Yet is there not something inherently contradictory and self-defeating in this existential outlook, when many who embrace it are also proponents of the right to suicide or euthanasia? That very life which I will sacrifice for nothing—because nothing is more valuable to me—can become so valueless in my hands that I will destroy it. What, then, was the real value of what I have destroyed?[8]

Ambition and Human Stature

A reference to ambition, in the context of values, is in order here. To want to be great is a sign of health. But it should be a genuine "*being* great," based on the possession of values and qualities that are of true worth and on the achievement of worthwhile goals. Not a few 'successful' persons have very stunted personalities, "choked with ambition of the meaner sort."[9]

Physical endowment (good looks, great athletic ability) can give a certain "fame of greatness" in the sight of others; but it does not tell much about the person. In sports, for instance, being a "good loser" tells much more of an athlete's human worth than does physical prowess.

Some people don't want to *be* great, seeing greatness as beyond their reach or as simply demanding too much effort. But most people would like to be *considered* great, even if it is a greatness without real substance. Of course this is vanity, which logically enough is a dominant modern defect, since the temptation to draw attention to "self" is inevitably stronger in the absence of any other focal and higher point of interest.

An impression or appearance of greatness can be built up on deception. History offers many examples of clever people who lied or cheated their way to fame or fortune—such as the 18th-century Baron von Münchhausen, genius of the "tall story," or Hans van Meegeren who, between 1936 and 1942, created and sold seven paintings as genuine works of the 17th-century Dutch master, Jan Vermeer.

Strictly speaking, vanity was not van Meegeren's main motivation. He put his considerable talent to use in order to draw profit (and not other people's attention) to himself, being quite happy to remain hidden behind someone else's name. Most people, however, the talented and the not so talented, like to be the center of attention. The talented easily enough find themselves objects of popular praise, no doubt a pleasing if passing experience. The less talented,

---

8. The problem of course extends much beyond these doubts. To the question, what was the real value of what I have destroyed, another question might reasonably be added: have I really destroyed it? Or could it be not only that my own subjective system of values has proved too fragile for life itself, but that I have perhaps consigned my existence to another dimension where the determination of values totally escapes my subjective choice?

9. Shakespeare, *King Henry the Sixth*, I, Act II, Sc. 5.

with little or nothing to offer, have to find other ways of drawing some lime-light to themselves.

Certain prominent figures in the arts of the 19th century (Byron, Shelley, Baudelaire, Gauguin . . .) seemed to find gratification in flouting the accepted social standards of their time. In an age of settled conventions, they managed to attract quite a bit of scandalized attention; an exercise, one feels, probably characterized by a strong element of adolescent "showing off." Much the same might be said of some pop-culture leaders today who seek notoriety by flying in the face of conventional or "Establishment" values. Psychiatric and psychological experts classify this sort of superficial narcissism or attention-seeking histrionics in many ways. But, classifications apart, our current world makes this antisocial exhibitionism appear, ironically, as pathetic even more than pathological.

The urge to draw attention to self has always been a strong tendency and generally a foolish one. Today, in the almost total absence of worthwhile values, it becomes especially inane, leading some people to do things that might have made them appear shockingly nonconformist to former generations but today simply make them look silly. Foolishness usually precedes and always follows on the loss of normal values.

Nothing is really freakish in a world without any standards. It is useless trying to be nonconformist where there are no common norms to non-conform to. The fact is that a generation without values, incapable of real admiration, in constant search of new sensations that will keep it momentarily amused as it enthusiastically chatters about nothing, is not easily impressed.

In any case, if you have *no* scale of values, there is little point in professing to despise the values of others. There is less point still in trying to violate them. The contempt behind such "violations" would seem to be directed not so much at particular values (one believes in *none*) as at particular persons. Such contempt may be a sign of envy, but certainly not of independence; it rather suggests an inferiority complex disguised under the appearance of a silly nonconformism.

To want just to *feel* great—picturing yourself at the center or summit of reality—lends itself to artificial constructions and can produce pathological results. Its effect does not of course decrease reality itself, but it does reduce your personal horizons. So you remain with a diminished ability to see the full scope of reality, admitting as real only what falls within a limited range of view. Alice had to become small if she was to experience living in Wonderland. . . . Those who cannot appreciate and warm to others are lacking in an absolutely basic element of human stature. So Chesterton rightly distinguished between "the great man who makes you feel great, and the great man who makes you feel small."[10]

---

10. G. K. Chesterton: *Charles Dickens*, Ch. 1.

Chesterton himself was an outstanding example of the first type. Interested in every single person he met, he mused in his Notebook: "I wonder whether there will ever come a time when I shall be tired of any one person."[11] In his conversation he would take up with enthusiasm some apparently minor idea a friend or acquaintance had put forward and draw out incredible riches from it, in such a way moreover that the riches seemed to have sprung from the mind of the original speaker.[12]

At the other end of the scale stands the very clever person who maintains his superiority by never admitting the significance of the ideas, qualities, or achievements of others. Consciously or not, he manages to protect his own greatness by ensuring that others seem small—at least to him. This is the sad pity about being proud: if you come into contact with something greater than yourself, pride makes you incapable of admiring it.

In any case, it remains difficult to say what makes a person "great." Many historical "Greats"—Catherine the Great, Frederick the Great—may not necessarily have been "great *persons*." What makes someone great is not what he or she does externally, but what motivates them from within.

Support for this view could probably be drawn from a psychological study of history. No one would deny that Alexander, Julius Caesar, Napoleon or Bismarck were men of great talents, and must be counted among the outstanding figures of history whose lives profoundly shaped the course of world events. But how was the *person* of each shaped by his own life? History bears witness to Napoleon's military and administrative genius, and to his power to inspire men. But history also bears witness to his colossal pride, his overweening vanity, his nepotism, his unfailing tendency (precisely because he believed *in himself*) to blame others for his misfortunes, his contempt for men—using them, using them, using them—his inability to trust or to make friends, his total isolation.

Would it be just to say that Napoleon had great talents which he used to do great things, without being made great himself by his achievements? In his last years at St. Helena, removed from the field of conquest and administration, he appears as a man of few interior resources for his personal life—reduced to daily boredom: "ennui, ennui, grand ennui," as one of his companions described their existence.[13] Yet the experiences of others, such as Aleksander Solzhenitsyn or Viktor Frankl, show that exile or imprisonment can reveal or create interior resources which might otherwise have never come to light.

---

11. Cf. Maisie Ward: *Gilbert Keith Chesterton*, p. 58.
12. Cf. Ward. ibid.
13. Cf. J. M. Thompson, *Napoleon Bonaparte*, p. 392.

Bismarck, the "Iron Chancellor" and forger of the 19th-century German Empire, was an extremely proud man, though free from vanity. What he cared for was his own esteem of himself; he despised being swayed by what others thought of him. He rightly summed up the effect of vanity, describing it as a mortgage to be subtracted before one arrives at a person's real worth. What Bismarck did not realize is that pride too is a mortgage on personal worth. It has been said of him that he made Germany great, but Germans small. Without judging at what moral cost (or at what cost in terms of human lives) he made Germany great, one can wonder if the cost to himself was to remain interiorly small—despite his place in history.

As a young man of 23, he had written, "I want to make only that music which I myself like, or no music at all." In fact, he refused to enter cabinets or ministries until, at the age of 47, he was called to be Chancellor of Prussia on his own terms, with absolute power to play the music he wished. And for 28 years until his fall, Bismarck played his music.[14] Perhaps his music satisfied him. Did it *realize* him?

In the end, we repeat, the greatness of a life is measured not by the external record it offers, but by what it has made the person become inside.

✹ ✹ ✹

Our line of argument, then, is that man is free, seeks fulfillment, yet is not self-sufficient. He is not capable of fulfilling himself from within, on the basis of his own interior resources alone. He is able and needs to go beyond his own inner world, to encounter and identify values, to open to and accept them; and so incorporate them into his own life and in some way make them his own. What should be the interplay of his interior faculties in achieving this?

---

14. Cf. Erich Eyck, *Bismarck and the German Empire*, p. 57.

5

INTELLECT, WILL,
AND FEELINGS IN THE
PROCESS OF FULFILLMENT

The adequate assimilation of values depends above all on the intellect and the will. Let us resort here again to a parallel with how the body works. Just as the feet must be fit for walking (and need exercise to do so), and the eyes for seeing, and the mouth or the stomach for feeding—and if they are not healthy or adequate, a person will suffer in his physical life—so the intellect and will need to be exercised and developed in a way consistent with their purpose. Otherwise they may not develop; they may end up in a warped condition and with an altered operation whose effect is to hinder rather than favor a person's fulfillment. The person who tries to feed his body with anything and everything can die of poisoning, or at least become chronically undernourished as a result of an inadequate diet. So too, the real development of the spiritual faculties requires healthy and proper nourishment.

A person has to exercise, develop, and mature the mind and the will. They need to be fed with their own distinctive sustenance, and be safeguarded against what can undermine or damage their proper operation and the psychic health of the person. Truth is the nourishment of the mind; goodness, that of the will. These are fundamental principles which we will briefly try to justify and illustrate. Their full understanding and acceptance can only come about as a result of further reading, and above all of further personal reflection on the part of the reader.

Working from the basic principles enunciated, let us outline what is involved in this need to form and develop intellect and will.

The food of the mind is truth, a food which it naturally seeks. All relativisms and skepticisms notwithstanding, it is practically speaking almost impossible to deny this principle. Everyone considers—and uses—the mind as an instrument for pursuing and reaching the truth, at least in certain concrete areas of study: mathematics, physical sciences, etc. In fact, to discriminate between truth and falsehood is the recognized function of the intellect. Truth is the value that the mind looks for.

Man is constantly seeking truth. Scientifically established truths are a condition of progress in all areas of applied technology. The everyday existence of the individual depends on a grasp of many elementary physical and experiential truths (an electric cable can take a person's life; so, each in its own way, can contaminated water or thin ice). Truth in communication is a condition of any social life with a minimum of mutual trust or confidence—which can only exist to the extent that one is convinced that people in general do not lie, or that newspapers do not deliberately spread false news. All of these can be described as "truths of life," at times even as truths of survival.

We are used to applying a "true or false" criterion as a means of testing or improving people's knowledge of mathematics, physics, geography, history, civics, etc. Those who cannot distinguish true from false are poorly qualified to protect and develop their own life, and utterly unqualified to guide others—if that is also their mission. This is particularly evident in the directly physical field. Serious harm can be done by the parent or teacher who does not know that electricity is dangerous or that exhaust fumes can kill. These are objective principles or true laws not just of physical growth but of survival that, if known, protect the life of the body. People, especially young people, do not normally know these truths by instinct and so need to be taught.

How far can one apply the true/false criterion to values, especially to values in behavior? Are there psychic or moral laws or principles that should guide the process of self-fulfillment, fostering the health of our spirit or even safeguarding what is necessary for its "survival?" "Selfishness narrows our mind and sympathies"; "Jealousy stifles our response to values"; "Racist propaganda breeds intolerance"; "Pornography can lead to obsession and an inability to love." Are such principles valid? Are they important? Are they true? Should they be *taught*? Can they simply be dismissed as pertaining to the ethical or moral order, and therefore not to the field of anthropology? Or should they too not be regarded as valid anthropological guidelines for the achievement of true human fulfillment? We do not intend to debate these questions here. We leave them among other points to be pondered by the reader.[1]

---

1. One particular consideration may be helpful. We readily enough accept that a person's awareness of the material world may be defective and that this is a handicap capable of causing him serious

Formation of the Mind; Recognizing the Truth in a Value

Since values are our focal point of interest, we hold that the mind should be formed so that it is an effective faculty for discovering genuine or true values: distinguishing between those which are worth more and those which, being inferior, are worth less (as noted earlier, one needs to have a scale of values, because not all values are of equal "value"), spotting and being able to resolve possible conflicts between certain values, discerning, when necessary, what is a true value from that which, perhaps despite appearances, is not.[2] All of this enters into the process of forming the intellectual faculty; and to the extent that it is accomplished, the man or woman "of criterion" emerges.

The power of the intellect varies greatly from person to person. Some minds are quick, others slow; some deep, others superficial. The speculative mind can be distinguished from the practical. Some minds seem more suited for a particular field: mathematics, business. . . . Intellectual qualities combine in the most varied ways. A person with a slow mind can have the ability to reason deeply (if he works at it), while another may have a quick understanding that remains on the surface of things. In any case, the simple fact of being very intelligent is not enough to guarantee a person's fulfillment. A first-class intelligence can be used by a criminal to plan a robbery, a murder or an act of terrorism . . .

The mind has its enemies: lies or deception from without, by which a person of little intellectual perception is convinced by a wrong (although perhaps cleverly presented) argument to embrace false theoretical or practical principles in life (racial intolerance, social discrimination . . .); lies from inside or self-deception by which a person, out of selfishness or pride, "re-makes" or models a "truth of one's own" that is easier to assimilate.

In the last chapter we said that there has to be a capacity for digesting truth, even truth that is unpleasant. With relation to "unpleasant" truths, there also has to be a *willingness* to digest them, and if necessary a determination to do so.

---

harm, as in the case of the child who ignores that a live electric wire can kill. But the defect of perception may be the fruit not of simple ignorance but of a deranged mind. Only a crazy person thinks that he can stand in the way of an oncoming express train and stop it, or that he can pass through a blast furnace unscathed. An unbalanced mind easily "gets things wrong." If this can happen with regard to material realities, are there any solid grounds for holding that it cannot happen with regard to "values?" May there not be universal rules of survival in the realm of the spirit also, or is it a matter of indifference if one turns aside from any quest for objective truths or norms regarding conduct and concludes that all forms of behavior are equally valid for genuine human fulfillment?

2. To love is a value. So is fidelity to a commitment freely taken. If a person has *committed* his or her existence in a love which should be faithful and exclusive (like that of marriage), then the possibility of an alternative love becomes a threat to that fidelity.

One can spit out such a truth at the first taste of unpleasantness, refusing even to consider if it is nourishment for the mind. One can begin to discover its unpleasantness after having swallowed it, and then refuse to assimilate it.[3] But an undigested or half-digested truth of this nature does not easily pass out of the intellectual system. It remains; and, even with renewed rejection, it tends to remain—with little or no interior profit; just an uncomfortable feeling of something not properly assimilated.

Nevertheless, its continuing presence inside justifies some hope that the person may one day make up his mind to accept and absorb it, along with its demanding but beneficial consequences.

There is also skepticism or intellectual distrust which leads a person to an attitude of habitual doubt or uncertainty toward everything—producing a paralysis of thought that is a manifest handicap for life.

Truth attracts the mind; however, it never makes a forced entrance. The way in needs to be open—not blocked by bias or inertia. And there must be a positive disposition to welcome truth. It is necessary to be on special guard against prejudice, which becomes operative whenever an already formed judgment is allowed to determine in advance the consideration of a question, in such a way that this pre-judgment effectively excludes any alternative proposition from gaining access to the central tribunal of the mind.

Formation of the Will; Choosing the Goodness of a Value

The function of the intellect is to allow us to discover the truth: i.e the real essence (and not the first impression or the mere appearance) of things and ideas. Thus we can acquire information in order first to distinguish and so to be in a better position to choose: "this is good; that other option is not so good, or perhaps is actually bad." This is what is meant by having criterion.

Acting calls for choosing. Now, our existential choices are seldom the simple result of a detached intellectual appraisal (whereby we understand that a proposal is clever, or that a way of acting is not honest); our decisions tend to correspond even more to subjective and interested motivations. This job suits me better than the other; I prefer to go out with X rather than Y because I like him or her more.

So, we normally choose on the basis not merely of the truth ascertained but as much, or perhaps even more, of the *goodness* seen (or thought to be seen, or *wanted* to be seen) in the object proposed for a possible choice. The election or final choice depends on the will, whose tendency is to adhere to

---

3. The failure to assimilate a truth that one has "swallowed" can of course be unintentional, as often happens in the case of rote learning.

what presents itself as good. If the nourishment of the mind is truth, that of the will is goodness: nourishment that the will also seeks in a natural way.

In human choice the action of the will is of course not by any means just of attraction or acceptance. It is also of rejection. This is so in the elementary sense already noted, that each concrete choice involves the rejection of all the alternative choices present at least at that moment. But it may also be so in the much more important sense that the will can quite deliberately reject a possible choice, even though the person is strongly attracted towards it.

Human fulfillment, then, appears as an intellectual-volitive process in which the discerning mind penetrates to the truth of values, and the upright will is drawn to the goodness they contain.

The matter would be straightforward and uncomplicated if the mind always distinguished the truth of situations and values with accuracy, and the will were always unfailingly drawn by the real goodness that is discovered there. Unfortunately, experience teaches us that things are by no means so simple in reality. On the one hand, our mind is often slow to recognize the truth. But, even more importantly, at times it goes astray in its reasoning and takes to be true what is in fact false, or as right what is in fact wrong.

These errors of the mind have an effect on the will. A likely consequence is that the will is mistakenly drawn to prefer some inferior good or value to one that is greater. But the complexity of the matter does not rest there. The fact is that even though the mind may be quite clear and certain in its judgment of what is a true and right value, the will can nevertheless choose in contradiction to the mind, making a wrong choice—wrong, that is, from the standpoint of truth. In other words, the will can take over or "hijack" the mind somewhere along the process of discerning what is true and good. There is something here that merits closer scrutiny.

Interrelation Between Mind and Will

Existential decisions—the choices that shape a life—ought to proceed from the intellect, committed to its task of discerning the positive or negative value that every reality or possibility offers; and from the will, freely attracted by the good that is presented to it. Reasonably enough, then, one can ask whether the mind and the will carry the same weight in each decision, or whether one of the two is predominant.

It is often maintained that the mind plays the principal role in the elective process. This view tends to describe the will as a *blind* faculty which necessarily chooses what the intellect sets before it as a value or a good. This may be an over-simplification, which fails to correspond to the complexity of the human operation. Each human decision is after all to be attributed ultimately not to the faculties—intellect or will—but to the *person* who thinks and wants. The mind influences the will; but the opposite is also true. And perhaps more attention needs to be paid to the decisive role which the will can play in the evaluations made by the intellect.

The process of fulfillment is not mainly intellectual in character; it is also voluntary. In fact the will's response is probably the more critical aspect of the process. One cannot love what one does not know; but one may *not* know what one ought to love. One can even *want not* to know what one ought to love.

"Easy" and "Difficult" Truths

An underlying point needs to be considered here, and perhaps it could be best expressed as follows. There exist "easy" truths—so elementary and obvious that the rudest mind can grasp them immediately; and perhaps also so pleasant to learn (the young girl who discovers that boys think her pretty) that there is no resistance to their acceptance. There also exist "difficult" truths; and this too in various ways. The difficulty can be no more than the jolt given to vanity, as when a girl's pleasant self-image is upset by hearing that someone else is considered particularly attractive. The point is made with quiet humor by Margaret Schlegel, protagonist of *Howards End*: "You know—at least, I know in my own case—when a man has said to me, 'So-and-so's a pretty girl,' I am seized with a momentary sourness against So-and-so, and long to tweak her ear. It's a tiresome feeling, but not an important one, and one easily manages it."[4]

The difficulty, which is not always so easy to manage, may have nothing to do with the emotions but be of an exclusively intellectual nature—in the sense that a special effort of the mind and perhaps special intellectual penetration are required if the truth of a matter is to be discovered or understood. The solution to the difficulty may seem important to the person (say, as a step necessary to progress in scientific research); or may be of little real interest to him or her (finding the right answer to a crossword puzzle, for example).

But there are other "difficult truths" whose peculiar difficulty presents itself not to the intellect but to the will. This can occur when the truths in question—if faced up to and acknowledged—involve practical consequences which the will may be reluctant to accept.

Truth always moves man. It does not however always move him to pleasure, because some truths are unpleasant. Then it is easy not to want to face them.[5] There is no great change of perspective in adding that "difficult goods"

---

4. E. M. Forster: *Howards End*, Ch. 19.
5. "People can even run from the truth as soon as they glimpse it because they are afraid of its demands" (John Paul II: *Fides et Ratio*, no. 28).

equally exist: "goods" that contain some deep values which also attract the will but whose attainment requires no small effort; for instance, because it demands resisting a strong impulse. Our will needs to be vigorous because it must often not only choose good but also reject evil, above all attractive evil.

In the world today there are many people who, it seems, sincerely consider that abortion injures no one, and is indeed a human right. How do they not see that the being in the womb is a new individual, belonging to the human species? Without wishing to make general judgments, it is hard to avoid positing as explanation that, at least in some cases and maybe unconsciously, they *do not want* to see it; or, perhaps more exactly, they *want not* to see it. The scientific-biological demonstration of the separate human life of the fetus is beyond question. But what most probably happens is that when these scientific reasons are about to come up for intellectual consideration, it is the will which shifts attention in another direction. It is the will—the "*persona volens*"—which does not permit continued reflection along a way that could lead to unwelcome and therefore *unwanted* conclusions.

Normal sexual-conjugal intimacy is a physical good and also a human and ethical good. There is no difficulty in explaining the physical good—in its human sense of giving privileged expression to the uniqueness of matrimonial love—and in justifying the choice of this good by an act of the will; always provided the ethical good is respected. An extra-conjugal sexual relationship can present itself in the guise of a physical good, but not of an ethical good. As a consequence the tendency—the temptation—can arise to look for "reasons" to make the relationship ethical; and to let oneself be convinced by these reasons. Here enter questions of the disinterestedness, sincerity and truthfulness of the "intellectual look."[6]

This is why the relationship between "mind and truth" cannot be considered without reference to the intimately connected relationship between "will and good." Whoever does not want to see the truth will never see it.

No analysis of the calculations and choices that enter into human decisions can neglect two powerful factors which easily make their presence felt: the pride of the intellect, capable of disfiguring the good it presents to the will; and the selfishness of the will, capable of preventing the mind from recognizing the truth.

---

6. "To love is to contemplate [something inasmuch as it is beautiful]. There is a great difference between the act of loving and the act of the will which a man adopts towards something which he considers useful or instrumental; this latter act is one of *interest*. It can be defined as *the desire to have something as a means to another*. The interested look contemplates things not as they are in themselves, but as a means towards other ends. The interested look, if it is not at the same time benevolent, tends to instrumentalize the object sought and to subordinate it to the ends of one's own activity extrinsic to the object. Interest in this sense implies an *instrumentalizing* look, a look, in other words, lacking in love": R. Yepes: *Fundamentos de Antropologia* . . . , pp. 202–203.

Here we must add that it is not possible to refuse to adhere to truth-goodness without compromising one's own integrity and very identity. The inherent power and intimate authority of the truth send a powerful call for acceptance to all that is best and most honest in man. To withhold one's adhesion is to shake one's values to their foundation.

In the end, each becomes what he has chosen; in this sense, man forms himself. But to form ourselves truly (and not to deform ourselves), there is need for coherence: i.e. conformity between values and behavior. Lack of coherence occurs when "a person's encounter with truth is weak, because it does not go far enough to inspire his conduct."[7] This will inevitably happen to people who grow accustomed to examining matters in a superficial way, without wanting to reach a deeper judgment about the value of things and events. It will happen just as much to whoever thinks of "assimilation" of values as a merely mental process. The greatest values will not enrich us unless we let them shape and—where necessary—*change* our behavior as well as our outlook.

These considerations confirm that fulfillment is fundamentally more an interior than an exterior matter; it must be appraised with reference to the personal inner life of each one. It is according to one's response to values that the question of whether one has found fulfillment in life or not must be resolved.

This could naturally lead us to consider the subject of virtue. However, as we have said, our purpose is to raise questions rather than to offer answers; this is especially so in the field of ethics. So we will just note here that virtue implies orderly growth in effective capacity for values: capacity to know truth and to choose or do good. The moral dimension of choices or actions matters, because without an ethically positive response to values a person ceases to grow.[8]

Affectivity in the Process of Personal Growth

Personal life would never be fully human if it were exclusively intellectual and voluntary. The development-fulfillment of the person does not depend only on the mind and the will, and their healthy interaction. Another factor sways or influences our choices; that is "heart" or, more precisely, feelings. Man is not pure intellect or pure will; he is also made up of emotions and passions. In many situations, the first movement towards acting that a person undergoes, even before any intellectual evaluation of the action itself or any freely willed choice in its regard, may be one of fear or pity or anger.

"Affectivity"—that emotional reaction which involves body and soul together—needs to find its proper place in personal growth, for it forms an integral part of the dynamism by which the human person develops.

---

7. R. Yepes: op. cit. 147.
8. Cf. L. Polo: *Presente y Futuro del Hombre*, p. 200.

Kant, at one extreme, and Hegel at the other, considered feelings a weakness. Today we are more aware of their importance; yet the rehabilitation of the emotions also runs the risk of failing to grasp the necessary synthesis and integration of the principal elements conforming the human "psyche."

It is certainly true that neither the mind alone nor the will alone can achieve human fulfillment. But neither can affectivity-feeling on its own. The three should go together; in proper order and interrelation. Affectivity is not higher or more trustworthy than the mind or the will. Nor is it (despite some psychological theories) a third faculty in its own right, on the same level as the intellect and will. It is true that both mind and will can be in an unhealthy state; and then a person's affectivity might seem to remain the only resource or support. But it is a deceptive and precarious resource: "because if the intellect has failed, if the will has failed, how can one expect affectivity to succeed? Isolated affectivity is to be trusted very much less than the two human faculties just mentioned; it is more a passivity than a type of power. . . . What happens quickly when one tries to live on the basis of feelings, is that these recoil on coming into contact with the rigidity of reality, and the result is total disorder. Paradoxically, in an elaborate world of instrumental organization, the affective person goes adrift and dissolves."[9]

Pure rationalism can be cold: farsighted perhaps, but incapable of the necessary practical sacrifice to motivate itself and to inspire others. Voluntarism too can be merciless: deciding and executing without principle or respect for the rights of others. Pure emotionalism can leave a person at the mercy of feelings and of the ability of skilled practitioners to take advantage of these feelings (modern publicity thrives on the predominant cultural sentimentalism). Paradoxically, too, it limits one's capacity to appreciate other people and to respond to their values or needs. It is good to feel with others in their sufferings, and thus to be moved by compassion. Today, however, it is not infrequent to come across people with a great capacity for compassion, but without the willpower and persevering generosity to turn momentary compassion into any enduring help to others.

To go wherever your heart leads you, is in the end to be led this way or that by passing moods of sympathy or antipathy. Those who make this their philosophy easily fool themselves into a comforting conviction of being warm-hearted, while in fact they are circling more and more tightly around themselves, becoming less capable of any lasting loyalty or service to others and equally powerless to explain the ultimate loneliness into which their life leads them. The perceptive reader will discover in Susanna Tamaro's *Follow Your Heart*[10] an attractively drawn portrait of this type of self-deceiving and fundamentally unattractive character.

---

9. L. Polo: op. cit. p. 79.
10. *Va' dove ti porta il cuore, Milan*, 1990.

Affectivity is healthy when it responds adequately—in its own proper way—to the values present in every person and situation. Its response will be inadequate if it is not the result of a mature intellectual judgment; and will be inconstant if it is not sustained by the generous determination of the will. So, even allowing for the special importance of affectivity, it will only play its due place in human development under the guidance of a properly formed mind and a soundly oriented will.[11]

Apathy, as we have noted, is a powerful enemy of personal development. But the remedy to an apathetic approach—say, to a person's marriage, family or job—does not lie in seeking an accession of feeling or sympathy or enthusiasm—which in all likelihood will not come. An effective remedy will depend on a decision of the will based on the conscious discovery of new motives. A person is at the end of his tether not if he lacks enthusiasm for life, but if he can find no motive for living.

It is nevertheless true that, in many cases today, affectivity may prove decisive for the rediscovery of the way of fulfillment. When a person has set out on a wrong road, the sense of being blind and the feeling of being lost increase as the road is pursued, also because it leads into darkness and isolation. Then it is most probably the dissatisfaction of the heart which can turn a person back in search of light and the warm companionship of shared values.

No proof that a person is lost is likely to be of any effect so long as he is happy to be so. But such happiness is too strange a thing to last. One's own life is too serious and immediate a matter for anyone to remain indefinitely unaware of or unconcerned about being lost in it.

---

11. "Emotional intelligence," as often used today, can be a misleading term. One thing is to advocate a proper understanding of emotions; another is to hold that a person "thinks" with the emotions, or that feelings are an alternative to (and perhaps more important than) intelligence.

6

CONSCIENCE

We have just expressed the opinion that the status of a "third faculty"—on a par with intellect and will—is not due to affectivity or feelings. An exaggerated predominance of mind and will can indeed spoil a person's affective development. But it is equally certain that one's affectivity cannot safely be allowed to dominate psychic or interior development. The person dominated by feelings is notably immature; to be unable to control one's feelings betrays a seriously undermined freedom and can turn a person into a slave of impulse. Feelings are necessary; but they can only achieve their full development and irreplaceable role when regulated by a properly formed mind and will.

However, the human person carries within another spiritual or psychic power, of such unique importance and of such independent status that a case might well be made for classifing it as a "third faculty." This is conscience.

Faculty, Feeling, Judgment?

Conscience is variously described. For some it is a sort of intuitive moral sense that operates through *feelings* of right and wrong. Others see it in intellectual terms, as a specific capacity for moral judgment. To describe it in terms of "feeling" may do justice to conscience's uncanny way of raising its voice spontaneously, and at times quite unwantedly; but it does not explain its peculiarity of speaking directly to the head, without any hint that it has come from the heart. The child that tells his first lie knows in his mind that he has done something "wrong," at the same time as he may be tempted in his heart not to own up to it.

Even though a person may be nagged by the thought, "I don't *feel* happy about what I've done," what he is expressing is not so much a feeling as a doubt or suspicion about an action. It is really a call to grow in self-awareness, to reflect more deeply on the true value and effect of his actions.

All in all, conscience does seem rather in the nature of an intellectual judgment: a "judgment of the [practical] intellect," as scholastic moralists are used to describe it. Yet this description could have its own inadequacy if taken to imply that the origins and workings of conscience are to be attributed just to the intellect. Conscience should be related not primarily to the mind, over which we can always exercise a certain control, but to truth, which stands above us and which we can accept or reject but not control. More than the voice of our intellect, conscience is an echo of a prior voice of truth. It stands behind and higher than our intellect. Its presence is something to wonder at. Anyone who takes conscience seriously must be seized by a sense of *awe*. "These are not just my thoughts; there is something higher, deeper, behind it all: *in* me—and yet *above* me."

To describe conscience as a judgment of the intellect could favor the conclusion that it derives its operation and authority simply from the inner workings of *my* mind. This conclusion is not adequate. Conscience is an interior voice; but it is not just the voice of my intellect. It speaks to my mind; but it does not come just from my mind. It is a voice that seems to echo thoughts or judgments that are not originally *mine*, for, though they come from within, they also come from above. Conscience is not just "what I think," and less still "what I want to think." In this sense, conscience claims an origin prior to both intellect and will. A person has only grasped the real dimension of his conscience and the respect due to it when he realizes that it is a reflection or resonance of truth coming from a higher, more aboriginal, source than his own mind.

Conscience does not present itself as a gradually elaborated intellectual judgment, the consequence of a previous study of an issue. It initially appears rather as a voice—from within and, we repeat, in some way from above— which questions an intention, an inclination, an action; and often urges us to examine the matter more deeply. It is not necessarily a clear light on the matter itself; but it does tend to be a clear admonition: take it easy—this needs looking into.

Conscience is not for times of clarity, but rather for moments of darkness or doubt. It appears as a ray or glimmer of light at the end of a tunnel. A person aware of the dark and looking for light can be drawn in that direction.

Perhaps the ray indicates new directions as he goes. The sincerity with which he is prepared to change his course may in the end be the key giving access to fuller light.

Conscience then has its uniqueness in relation to both mind and will. It influences and is influenced by them; but it has its "a se" existence, and cannot be reduced to a merely intellectual or merely volitive category. It must necessarily be assigned a rightful "independence" from mind and will, which affectivity can never properly claim.

Conscience appears as a guardian of personal intimacy and integrity in the deepest aspect of their sincerity and authenticity. It is like an alarm system that enters into spontaneous action or reaction, whenever our way of acting can influence the type of person we are becoming. It is a sort of self-monitor that knows us from within, with a unique interior perspective on the value of our actions: informing on how they help us progress towards genuine human happiness—or lead us away from it. It is a monitor therefore of the process of our fulfillment (or frustration).[1]

Only a superficial and thoughtless person would not want to know himself. Socrates held that "the unexamined life is not worth living." Whoever does not try to be deeply sincere with himself may gain the respect of others who see him from the outside; but he can never know what actual respect he can justifiedly have with regard to himself.

In What Way Is "My" Conscience Mine?

Conscience is always singular; we cannot properly speak of a "collective" or "social" conscience. Conscience is always personal and individual to each one of us. Yet "my" conscience is not always mine as I might wish. It is not mine to do what I like with. It possesses its own integrity. Conscience is not a rump parliament, sitting just to ratify the decisions or preferences of its "master," i.e. the person as whose faculty it appears, and who, we might think, stands higher than it. It maintains a constitutional independence from the "ego" or self. It passes its own judgments, commanding and forbidding, and will not let itself be reduced to a rubber stamp level without some form of internal struggle that in itself suggests a constitutional violation.

A conscience that never enjoins or forbids—you have to do that; you ought not to do this—does not merit the name of conscience.

Conscience commands or forbids with mysterious authority; and so—we insist—it appears as a faculty that in some way stands above a person. If it can be said to be at his service, it is with what appears to be an independent

---

1. As monitor of our every action, conscience is a checkpoint at which our thoughts and impulses and projects should stop, so as to see if they can be let pass or not.

mandate proceeding from some higher jurisdiction. However we describe conscience, what is most striking about it is this status of an internal *independent* court of judgment.

Conscience judges; its function, moreover, is to judge not the actions of other people, but one's *own* actions. Judging other people's deeds is a frequent tendency, and more often than not a bad habit. In any case, it remains a purely voluntary act; a person judges because he wants to and chooses to. The person who chooses not to judge others can learn not to do so without extraordinary difficulty. Dealing with conscience is not so easy. Conscience has its own power and autonomy. It functions: judging us, at times despite ourselves. We can want not to judge ourselves, we can gradually bring ourselves not to listen to our conscience; but conscience speaks with a voice that is not easily silenced. Deep down inside the person, it still makes itself audible. Prolonged effort is needed to muzzle it. Conscience "kicks" to survive; because its survival is necessary for us. Conscience cannot be shaken around like a stuffed marionette, or punched into shape like a pillow. It is conscience that does the shaking, and it is we whom it tries to punch into shape.

It has been said that the best way to keep one's conscience clean is not to use it. . . . The principle doesn't work, for conscience itself will not go along with such cynicism. The less conscience is "used," the more dirt and disquiet grow inside—despite the pretense that they are not there.

It is not possible for someone to tell a lie unconsciously. A person lies, perhaps on the spur of the moment, and immediately the awareness is there: that was a lie. It may be that nobody else knows; we ourselves may not want to know, but we know. There remains an accusing voice inside—which is nothing but the self-judgment of conscience—that is very hard to ignore. This, as we have said, is true of the youngest child possessed of a minimal power of reflection; the child who lies to his parents knows he has done something "wrong." His sense of guilt is the natural reaction to a closing in on self. Conscience protests against any shrinkage of self through a rejection of values.

It is inadequate, therefore, to try to explain conscience as a monitor implanted as a result of education or indoctrination. It is naturally present in every person from the outset of his conscious life. It may indeed be neglected or ignored by its possessor. The more it is neglected or unheeded, the more easily can it be manipulated or deformed by others. In any case, this can only be a gradual process. A serious deformation of conscience seems inconceivable without personal acquiescence.

The mind needs to listen to the voice of conscience in order, if possible, to achieve a clear grasp of what it forbids or commands. It is not always easy to know if what I call my conscience ("my conscience tells me") is really such, or is simply the voice of my preferences which a self-indulgent will is trying to get my mind to rationalize.

One sign of not wanting to reduce conscience to the level of an acquiescent "yes-man" to personal whims is that I listen sincerely to its reproaches for what I have done or omitted, and am prepared to follow its positive or negative commands regarding my conduct.

A "person with a conscience" is a person subject to a factor of self-restraint—arising within himself. Therefore, according to one's evaluation of the concept of self-restraint, conscience can be seen as a nuisance or an advantage. We could recall here what was mentioned about the "selfishness of the will." The will that lets itself be captivated by a pleasant option may be strongly tempted not to heed a possible negative moral valuation presented by conscience.

Rights of Conscience

This is a topic which is invoked and discussed today, as never before. Yet the discussion is not always carried on with sufficient depth. For instance, there is little or no reflection on the fact that the very "quasi-independence" of conscience—its position as a sort of higher tribunal judging the person from within—suggests that "rights of the person" and "rights of conscience" are not to be simply identified. Insofar as conscience can be considered a faculty, then one might say that rights of conscience are rights *of the faculty*, more than powers of the person. Conscience has the right to command the person, whereas the person does not have the right to control conscience.

Everyone has the right to listen to and follow his conscience; however he has no right over his conscience. His right to follow his conscience, as we will see in a moment, becomes in some cases a *duty*. An appeal to "conscience" (as conferring a right) is generally no defense for an action that needs to be justified, unless the person can show that his conscience not merely spoke to him of a right of action, but imposed on him a strict duty to act.

The first right of conscience is in fact the right to *be respected and obeyed by the person himself.* If a person does not see and observe this, then he is speaking without true understanding when he invokes the rights of conscience.

Only a sophist would argue that it is all right to proceed in an action which is the object of his own interior disapproval. Therefore, while there can be violations of conscientious rights from outside, the worst violation of conscience is interior and is committed by the person who refuses to obey it. If he perseveres in such a violation and tries to justify it, his whole system of moral defense can collapse. Raskolnikov, in Dostoyevsky's *Crime and Punishment*, commits murder. His whole drama (which ends positively and leads to his "salvation") derives from the fact that he cannot escape from the interior judgment of his conscience. If he had done so—if he had managed to do so—he might well have gone on to further crimes. Facing his conscience, without dodging or denying it, he is salvaged from the wreckage of a life and led to a new self-realization.

"Rights of conscience" cannot mean that each one has the right to do whatever he likes or claims to consider justified. His thoughts are his own; he may think what he freely chooses to think (whether his thoughts are "right" or "wrong," whether they make him "better" or "worse," freer or less free). But his actions often impinge on others; and may affect their freedom. Then his rights must in some way be conditioned by theirs.

Duties toward Conscience

We hear almost exclusively about "rights of" conscience. But it is just as important to examine *duties towards* conscience that we are all bound by. These duties can be enunciated in two main principles:

- One must *follow* one's conscience—because it offers the first and most intimate and accessible norm of action for each one. There is, however, a clear and fundamental qualification that needs to be added immediately. One must follow one's conscience when it commands or prohibits a course of action. One cannot however speak of a duty to follow a conscience that merely "permits" (i.e. that sees nothing to the contrary), offering a neutral judgment—or no judgment—on a possible action. In such a case, the exercise of one's right (*not* one's duty) to follow one's conscience must be tempered by respect for the rights of others.

- One must *form* one's conscience, because its judgments are not infallible; they can be wrong. Conscience, in the case of the person who is not constantly concerned with its formation, can become an organ of self-deception.[2] There is little depth or self-awareness in the person who lacks this concern to form his conscience and to correct its possible errors.

Since conscience is frequently a nuisance, we can be tempted to change its nature, or to silence it. The nervous system of the body at times also appears as a nuisance. It can be neutralized or anaesthetized; this, as a temporary measure, may be a necessary aid to health. But a permanently anaesthetized nervous system would leave us defenseless against serious and perhaps mortal harm to our body. So an anaesthetized conscience, with regard to a person's psychic and moral health.

Conscience can be warped; then it needs to be straightened and put right. What it cannot be is ignored. No one can ignore the voice of conscience and still claim to take himself seriously.

---

2. "That strange thing, the conscience, can be trained to approve any wild thing you *want* it to approve, if you begin its education early enough and stick to it": Mark Twain: *Huckleberry Finn*, x.

Freedom of Conscience

Mark Twain, as so often, had his tongue in his cheek when he remarked: "It is by the goodness of God that in our country we have those three unspeakably precious things: freedom of speech, freedom of conscience, and the prudence never to practice either of them." What freedom of speech means is fairly clear. But what does freedom of conscience mean? Freedom to tell ourselves that we can do whatever we *want* to?—or freedom to shape our principles or actions according to our own sincere interior weighing of what we consider right or wrong? The latter is freedom of conscience properly so called.

It follows, as part of the inviolable dignity of each person, that no one can be obliged by any authority to do things which violate the moral imperatives of his conscience. This, as we shall see in a moment, does not confer a right to carry out externally any action a person holds to be licit. But it does mean that no one can be forced to perform an action or embrace a belief which he sincerely holds to be wrong.

It is important here not to confuse freedom of conscience with "freedom of action," for they are quite different concepts. All of us have a certain freedom of action, although within definite limits imposed upon us by our condition as finite beings. Each one is physically free to do what he wants and is capable of, and to incur the unavoidable consequences: free to throw himself out of a twentieth-floor window, and to suffer the physical consequence of bashing his brains out on the pavement below; free to defraud the tax collector or rob a bank and—if discovered—to suffer the penal consequences. All this is freedom of action, not of conscience.

The swindler or robber can be fully aware not only that his action is illegal (it breaks the laws of the State), but also that it is immoral (it goes against some norm which his conscience presents to him as just and binding, over and above the positive law, and which he himself recognizes as such). If in such a situation he asserts his freedom of action, in order to rob, he is violating and perhaps enchaining his conscience, thus trampling on a part of himself that is a key to his freedom and fulfillment.

While freedom of thought and freedom of conscience do not imply quite the same thing, a brief comment on freedom of thought could be useful here. We need to bear in mind that thinking is for concluding; otherwise a person would never decide anything, never choose, never move or progress. "Freedom of thought" therefore means freedom to reach—or at least to want to reach— a conclusion. Freedom of thought that cannot or does not want to come to any conclusion is a frustrated and useless freedom.

In any event freedom of thought has a wider scope than freedom of action; but not without any limit. If the concept of freedom of thought is to retain any human meaning, it is that a person has the right to follow any line of thought which appears to him to be true. One has the *power*—not the right—to pursue a line of thinking which one realizes is leading to false conclusions; but that is an indication of human fallibility or weakness, not the reflection or expression of any human right or dignity.

With regard to external action, however, it is not possible to sustain the idea that freedom has no limit. Any society approving such a principle could not survive for long in a civilized way. If someone claims the right to hold personally that racial discrimination or the elimination of the unfit or the commercial traffic of drugs to adolescents are good things, society may feel no call, and indeed have no way, to restrain his private thoughts. It would be different, however, if he wished to go further, claiming that his right to think these views gives him the right to propagate them or to act externally in accordance with them. Then the rights of others are affected, and public authority has to face up to its mission of seeing how conflicting rights—or claims of "rights"—are to be harmonized according to some valid principle of the common good.

Some people, it is true, use "freedom of conscience" or "freedom of thought" as slogans under which to claim freedom of another kind: that of doing whatever they want and judging it interiorly as an act of a positive ethical nature, even though some external authority—the civil law, religious moral teaching, etc.—declares it wrong. What is being claimed here in the last analysis is the freedom to set up each individual conscience as the ultimate determining standard of right and wrong, also in a person's external behavior.

The question of the possible sincerity or otherwise of such consciences can be raised; but it does not have to be solved in order to realize how dangerous this approach would be if it gained any general acceptance. If "freedom of conscience" in this sense leads people to hold (sincerely, so they assert) that childabuse is legitimate, are they not to be bound by civil laws which seek to control, even with penal threats, their freedom of external action in such an area?[3]

Self-awareness, Self-acceptance, Self-esteem, Self-fulfillment

The consciousness of never having done wrong may appear as a marvelous gift; but who has it? Which, then, is better: to have done wrong things and never to admit (not even to self) that they are wrong? Or to have done wrong things and to admit it, at least to self, and try to set them right or at least to wish you had never done them? There is more *self*-respect in the latter attitude.

In 19th-century society, the Christian framework of morality was by and large still accepted. What was sinful and wrong in the past was generally still

---

3. So we cannot always underwrite the principle so well put by Atticus Finch: "The one thing that doesn't abide by majority rule is a person's conscience" (Harper Lee: *To Kill a Mockingbird*, Pt. 1, ch. 11).

considered sinful. For Victorian sensitivity, however, sin was to be avoided more because it offended society ("Establishment morality") than because it offended any higher order. According to a more interior criterion it was to be condemned particularly because *it takes away self-esteem* and "tranquillity of conscience." A dominant principle of conduct for Charlotte Brontë's Jane Eyre was to do only what "conscience and self-respect will permit."[4] She admired the (rather Calvinist) zeal and virtue of St. John Rivers, "yet he did not appear [to her] to enjoy that mental serenity, that inward content, which should be the reward of every sincere Christian and practical philanthropist."[5]

Charlotte Brontë is here echoing one of Dr. Samuel Johnson's axioms: "All that virtue can afford is quietness of conscience." One recalls, without necessarily agreeing with its caustic character, Hilaire Belloc's comment: "I would argue with the Doctor—if he were alive and before me now, and promised not to roar too loud [Samuel Johnson did roar a bit, but had died a hundred years before Belloc's time]—upon that matter of a quiet conscience. I do not believe that good men have quiet consciences. I hold that an uneasy conscience—at any rate nowadays—is the first requisite for Heaven, and that an inflamed, red, feverish, angry conscience is a true mark of increasing virtue. I have met many men with quiet consciences, not all of them wholly unintelligent, but nearly all of them scoundrels."[6]

A quiet conscience, then, is not always a good sign, especially if it lasts too long. Just as a person who never feels any physical pain may have the questionable advantage of possessing very thick skin.

We wonder if what a modern author writes is altogether valid, at least if it is applied to our context: "The happy man is at peace with himself. . . . Being at peace means to live in a calm and serene tranquillity. . . . The balanced personality is at peace with himself, being at the same time inserted into reality; this means that he is master of himself within his cultural context."[7]

If conscience becomes the monitor of self-respect, and self-respect the measure of conscience, then conduct can be quite elastic. Certainly the contemporary turn-of-millennium approach allows very considerable latitude of action compatible with the preservation of self-respect.

What has become particularly important today is that if a person has happened to do something wrong (or, to put it more impersonally, as some prefer to do, if "something wrong has happened" in a person's life), a process of *healing* is needed, which seems to mean the gradual recovery of self-esteem over a period of time sufficient to allow the *faux pas* to slip into simple oblivion.

---

4. *Jane Eyre*, Ch. 29, and elsewhere.
5. ib. Ch. 30.
6. On *"Rasselas."*
7. E. Rojas, *Una Teoria della Felicità*, pp. 358; 364.

Not just the offense against any higher order, but the very concept of repentance, has disappeared from the moral horizon. It is interesting, although perhaps not politically correct, to dig to the Victorian roots of this mindset.

Today the concern for a "good image" (or "self-image") has intensified—and been interiorized—to a quasi-pathological degree. Political figures, cinema stars, big commercial firms have always had their Public Relations agents, whose efforts have in part impressed the public at large, and in part left it skeptical, knowing that the image tends to be different from the truth. But now each individual has become his own public relations agent; and it is not only the exterior audience—the public of the street—he would like to please, but also and especially his *inner* audience: that is, himself. Each one wants to be able to hold a pleasing personal image before the mirror of his own eyes; and to be convinced or have others persuade him that this image corresponds to the truth: that he really is a person above reproach.

Self-esteem is to be achieved and maintained at all costs—even at that of unlimited self-deception. These are, of course, ideal dispositions for developing what psychiatrists designate as Narcissistic Personality Disorder, nor can it be a matter of surprise that the American Psychiatric Association says that this disorder "appears to be more common recently than in the past."[8]

Probably nothing could be more alien to this way of thinking than Santayana's suggestion that "the only true dignity of man is his capacity to despise himself."[9] Bernard Nathanson, having come to a crisis point in his autobiography, quotes this dictum of the Spanish-American philosopher and, looking back in judgment at his own troubled life, condenses his self-estimation into one flat statement: "I despised myself."[10] Much of contemporary psychology would regard such an admission as destructive of all psychological health and of any sense of personal dignity.[11] For Nathanson it marked a decisive beginning in the recovery of both.

Nathanson here places himself at the opposite pole to the "new people of the future," whom Charles Reich so fervently depicted in his 1970 best-selling *The Greening of America*. A major characteristic of that lucky and complacent generation is the total acceptance of self and the rejection of any notion of self-dissatisfaction. "The new generation says, 'Whatever I am, I am.' He may have hang-ups of all sorts, insecurities, inadequacies, but he does not reject himself on that account. There may be as many difficulties about work, abil-

---

8. *DSM-III-R*, p. 350.
9. George Santayana, *Spinoza's Ethics*, Introduction.
10. Bernard N. Nathanson, *The Hand of God*, p. 190.
11. The proponents of modern self-sufficiency have always found it necessary—and difficult—to counter all awareness of self-deficiency. "As chief apostle of the emerging cult of self-confidence, [Ralph Waldo] Emerson would spend his life in a complex effort to shut out the voices of self-contempt": Ann Douglas, *The Feminization of American Culture*, p. 20.

ity, relationships, and sex as in any other generation, but there is less guilt, less anxiety, less self-hatred. [He] says, 'I'm glad I'm me.' . . ."[12]

"I'm glad I'm me!" Why, yes: that would seem to be a good mood as a point of departure. But if it really means, "I'm glad no one is asking me—nor will I let anyone ask me—to be better than I find myself right now," then it is a formula for self-imposed mediocrity. It places the person not at a point of departure but settles him in a dead end. It is the antithesis of the attitude of G. K. Chesterton on taking up the unfinished work of his brother, who had been killed in the First World War and towards whom he entertained unlimited admiration: "Even though I can never be as good as my brother, I can be better than myself."

The self-regarding, self-justifying person is both very vulnerable and very incurable. In dealing with narcissism as a mental disorder, the American Psychiatric Association notes this vulnerability: "Vulnerability in self-esteem makes individuals with Narcissistic Personality Disorder very sensitive to "injury" from criticism or defeat."[13] A number of ironies could emerge here. The APA comment might be taken to suggest that the ideal, for mental health, is *invulnerable* self-esteem. . . . While this indeed renders a person totally impervious to criticism or defeat, one may ask whether such a disposition is an advantage, or not rather a considerable disadvantage, for the acquisition of true personal worth. Further, if unqualified self-esteem is a virtue,[14] it is hard to see on what grounds, or in what measure, narcissism is to be considered a defect.

The more narcissistic society becomes, the less will it tolerate being told that narcissism is a disorder. Sooner or later the APA may have to decide whether it will bow to what it perceives as the dominant cultural outlook and remove narcissism from its official listing of mental disorders, as it has already done with homosexuality.[15]

While psychiatrists are sorting this out, the fact remains that the right to placid and unimpeachable self-esteem is fast becoming the most inviolable of personal rights. Insofar as it implies the determination to "accept" oneself and to be accepted—absolutely and unconditionally, as one is at any given moment—it is, anthropologically speaking, a paralyzing attitude. It canonizes the "static me," turns self-satisfaction (which is often no more than empty conceit) into the equivalent of self-fulfillment, and puts a halt to any real and dynamic personal progress or growth.

---

12. *Greening* . . . , p. 235.

13. *DSM-IV*, p. 659.

14. We do not intend to imply that balanced self-esteem is a defect. On the contrary, it is necessary for personal growth: always provided it consists in true self-estimation, i.e. an awareness of both the positive and the negative aspects of one's personal character and life.

15. cf. C. Burke: "Psychiatry: A "Value-Free" Science?": *The Linacre Quarterly*, vol. 67 (2000), pp. 59–88.

PART 2

PERSONAL FULFILLMENT
AND OTHERS

✸ ✸

7

PERSONAL AND
INTERPERSONAL
FULFILLMENT

The first part of our study has spoken in general of appreciation of values and of response to them, as main determining factors in the human fulfillment of each one. If our discourse tended to be somewhat abstract, it must now become more particular, for it is to values as they are presented (or can be discovered) in the concreteness of life that we need to respond. And life in the concrete is never more humanizing or dehumanizing than in its interpersonal aspects, that is, in the various ways in which we relate to others.

This would no doubt be questioned by the extreme individualist for whom self-sufficiency is the norm and goal of fulfillment. In the individualistic view, other people, like the rest of the surrounding world, are simply raw material to be instrumentalized for a person's own self-centered development. But is the totally self-sufficient person capable of true human fulfillment or real happiness?

Is it possible to achieve happiness without any commitment to or appreciation of others? It would seem not, at least if we accept that there can be no genuine happiness without love; for love requires the existence of others. Thus, Julián Marías holds that happiness "finds its principal source in other persons . . . personal being is intrinsically pluripersonal. Unamuno was one of the first thinkers to give clear expression to this concept: 'An isolated person would no longer be a person: for whom would he love?'"[1] Most people are

1. *La Felicità Umana: un impossibile necessario*, p. 302.

made unhappy by isolation or loneliness (which is why solitary confinement is generally regarded as an intensified form of punishment).[2]

We have a radical need of others, not only to love or to be loved by them, but to *learn* from them. We are put to a particular test by values—accepting or rejecting them—when we meet them present in others, by whom they are both incarnated and personalized. "Incarnated" values: with the advantage of the concrete form this takes, and with the limitations that any particular human presentation of a value inevitably offers.

Responding to Values in Other People

In chapter three, we referred to the question of the *adequate* response to values, noticing that to know how to respond properly to each individual value is proof of criterion, maturity, and depth. We also noted the phenomenon of a frankly reduced or negative response to great and evident values even, and at times specially, in the case of a person well placed to appreciate all the wealth of that value. The phenomenon is curiously interesting and important enough to examine further.

Let us consider a work of art or a piece of music, with such clear and tangible beauty that it would seem impossible not to feel moved and elevated on seeing or hearing it. Nevertheless, in such a situation we at times meet intelligent and cultivated people with the tendency not to acknowledge the value: underestimating or ignoring it, and perhaps even completely rejecting it. We can go farther in these reflections.

First we note that such phenomena—of reduced or frankly negative responses to great and evident values—rarely occur when a work of Nature is involved. We find everyone more or less in agreement about the beauty not only of Niagara Falls, but also of an autumn landscape or of a flower as simple as a violet.[3] This leads to a point which seems valid and worth noticing: the element of partialness or imperfection almost inevitably present in every concrete value seldom gives rise to difficulty in its appreciation—except when the value itself has to be credited *to a person.*

Let us join the group of tourists enraptured before Niagara Falls. Curiously enough, the judgment about Niagara could become an object of controversy if

---

2. Jean-Paul Sartre pushed the contrary thesis to the limit, seeing the presence of others and the futile endeavor to "communicate" with them as the essence of unhappiness and frustration. Hence his well-known phrase, "L'enfer, c'est les autres": "hell is other people" (*Huis Clos*, Sc. 5). The person who sees others so—unable to stand them, finding nothing good in them, nothing to appreciate or to rejoice at—indeed lives in a sort of hell.

3. A quibbler might object: but a violet cannot compare with a rose; a rose is much more beautiful. Agreed: but the contrast does not take from the fact that *both are* beautiful! Would we be richer if we only had roses?

someone looking at the falls were to remark: how beautiful are the works of God; praised be the Lord! To so trace Nature back to God can certainly be annoying to the professed atheist, but that is not the point which interests us here. Atheism apart, it is peculiar to find that the attribution of a work to a person seems to act as a factor modifying the judgment passed on the work itself, at times provoking an uncalled-for negative reaction.

This is odder still if we consider that a great part of man's dignity consists precisely in his capacity not only to shape values in works of his intelligence or his hands, so (as we have seen) incarnating them, but also to *personalize them*, so that they come alive according to his own peculiar way of being. This human capacity to embody and personalize values creates the climate and basis for interpersonal, social and cultural life. When a person finds in another some value "incarnated" with particular effectiveness, a favorable situation for dialogue is produced. If a person has the capacity to appreciate values in others (and if no other factor exists that can or should prevent a response), this fosters a situation of intellectual and spiritual participation or communion which easily becomes a communion of wills; thus mutual appreciation, friendship, solidarity, or love are born.[4]

The logical reaction before any value, either in a work or in a person, should be one of admiration. As we are seeing, however, it is not infrequently easier for us to admire a value when we can prescind from the person. It often happens that, although rather easily satisfied at the great or small beauties of nature, we adopt a more severe and demanding judgment when the activities of people are concerned (an artistic work, a professional success, an athletic triumph, etc.); and it even seems that our judgment becomes more critical precisely because it is the action of *another person* that is in question. When admiration involves a tribute to a person, *envy* seems to enter, threatening to upset the judgment.

In the same line of curious things, and as a phenomenon not difficult to verify, a critical reaction is likely to be more intense if the person is living rather than dead, if he or she belongs to our own generation rather than to one past; and more so still if he or she is an acquaintance, someone we know personally, rather than a stranger.

Envy or Admiration

Envy is connected with admiration. In fact, it seems unlikely that someone not capable of envy would be capable of admiration. There is a positive envy which,

---

4. Karol Wojtyla writes: "The distinctive characteristic of the personalistic approach is the conviction that to be a person means to be capable of participation" (*The Acting Person*, p. 275); "I conceive participation in *The Acting Person* as a positive relation to the humanity of others . . ." (*Person and Community: Selected Essays*, p. 237).

properly channelled, can be a stimulant to a person's development. And there is a negative envy which rather marks the *degeneration* of admiration, and shuts a person within his own limits. Envy accompanied by admiration can provoke emulation, i.e. the desire to acquire some good quality possessed by another or to measure up to his actions. It opens new horizons of personal challenge and becomes a source of purpose and joy, as long as the person is prepared to rise to the challenge and seek that higher level of competence or performance.

When we *admire* someone for a quality, the quality attracts us *to* the person; our mind is centered on both the quality and the person. When we (negatively) *envy* someone for a quality, the quality is appreciated but not the person; the quality serves rather to separate us *from* him. Over-concerned at our own lack, we are tempted to reject or dislike the person, as if his possession of the quality drew attention to our deficiency. Sensing that we cannot be better than we are, we would be happier if he was not as good as he is; happier to live in a poorer world so that we could feel less humbled.

Envy without admiration can stifle emulation and paralyze personal growth. It is a mean disposition which finds a cause of sadness in the talents of others and would happily be convinced that they are not so talented, so as to be able to rest in self-satisfaction without challenge or disturbance. There should be little difficulty—so one feels—in extending (even in increased measure) the appreciation, surprise, or enthusiasm provoked by a work of value to the person responsible for the work; a reaction that, as we have mentioned, can begin or strengthen a well-grounded interpersonal relationship and perhaps a close friendship. "I want to know not just the work of art but also the artist; so as to offer my congratulations." However it is not always so; the personalized aspect of the value, instead of generating an enthusiastic rapprochement of people, can provoke disturbance, separation, and distance.

Of course, this negative reaction does not always take place. Yet it happens so frequently as to suggest a certain law of appreciation: "To admire, without paying attention to the artist or creator, is not difficult; but to recognize a creator often poses a challenge." The difficulty in responding to a value when this involves the acknowledgment of a creator or author is indeed curious. Why should the presence of the artist produce a negative effect? His presence seems even to *lessen* the appreciation to be made, and so is a disturbing factor that upsets the discernment of the value itself.[5] Why? Is it that we all would like to be unique as creators? Whatever the reason, the fact is when the "I" finds itself faced with a "you," admiration—even when it is fully merited—is not always easily given. The positive and enriching reaction of

---

5. On the level of intellectual discourse, perhaps we can perceive something of this in Pascal's remark: "One is normally more convinced by arguments one has thought out for oneself, than by those coming from the minds of other people."

admiration does not always prove stronger than the negative and impoverishing reaction of envy.

To judge others is dangerous, though at times necessary. When it is necessary, then one must judge *humbly*, with the conviction that there is much in each one that escapes my personal and limited appreciation. One must judge *positively*, seeking to learn without dwelling unnecessarily on what seems negative. One must judge *actions and not intentions*, for we can seldom grasp intentions. An action may be good, although the intention is bad; an action may be bad, despite a good intention. And one must judge with *discernment*, distinguishing in my contact with another what is good for him and/or for me, from what may be bad for him, or for me.

Appreciating Others

We would all like to be unique, and to be appreciated and admired by others for our uniqueness. But if we are not capable of admiring the uniqueness of others, such an aspiration is not reasonable. It is not by striving to be unique that we will be unique, it is by striving to be ourselves. And—revealing paradox—it is by striving to appreciate the uniqueness of others and forgetting ourselves, that we realize our own unique potential and become ourselves.

To be capable of appreciating our own talents and experiences but not those of others, reveals a narcissistic trait that has an immensely reducing effect on life. "To be able to enjoy life in a process involving a growing identification with other people's happiness and achievements is tragically beyond the capacity of narcissistic personalities."[6]

In any case, if the only good things I am able to rejoice in are those I can credit to myself, it should be obvious that the number of good things I'll meet in life is going to be woefully reduced.

So, to achieve greater self-esteem—to esteem oneself more—is dubious evidence of real personal development. To be esteemed more by others might seem to offer greater confirmation, but remains ambiguous. To grow in esteem *for* others is the more genuine test.

There have been in the course of history, and there are today, people of quite extraordinary human calibre, with rare gifts of mind and heart, of understanding and openness, of courage and nobility, inspired by the highest ideals and living up to them through their lives. Among those who have known such exceptional personalities, probably not all possessed the capacity to recognize their calibre fully, and fewer still the receptive openness to draw full enrichment from the acquaintanceship.

---

6. Christopher Lasch: *The Culture of Narcissism: American Life in an Age of Diminishing Expectations*, p. 41.

To come to know and to be able to benefit from one single person in whom practically all human qualities are embodied, remains an unlikely eventuality for most of us. The challenge is rather to discover and appreciate the whole range of human qualities and values, as they are spread out in partial embodiments in the many different people we do meet.

It is therefore a serious limitation if a person is so unresponsive, so closed on self, as not to be able to appreciate and be enriched by a value not only in nature or in art, but particularly in the people around him. It is a limitation of a different order if a person is in fact capable of appreciating a value, but refuses to do so because he would then be led on to the acknowledgment of the special merit or power of someone else, the artist or creator behind it. How many people live next to inspiration and yet are not inspired!

Therefore the contemplation-acceptance of "ideal" values, of values "in the abstract," is not sufficient in order to develop as a person. We could withdraw into a life of pure contemplation of Being; but it is not the normal or adequate way for the majority. Man is not only spirit—mind and will—he is also body. It is not, we repeat, in a world of abstractions that we develop our life, but rather in the concrete world of animate and inanimate objects and beings. Exceptional values, present in a very pure form, exist in some of these, and to discover or respond to them should not be difficult. In others, values are diminished or hidden; and nevertheless it is important to learn to discover and appreciate them. In others still values are disfigured or perverted. In this case there is special need for a reaction of deep discernment, so as to reach the healthy nucleus which is probably still there, a prior stage for any possible attempt at redeeming or rehabilitating the value itself and the person who exhibits it, both of which are in a process of dissolution.

The discovery of values—openness and receptivity toward them—takes place in the surrounding world: values in material things, in (good or bad) events, in art, and especially in interpersonal relations with other people.[7] To a large extent, it is a capacity of admiration for others which most makes a person develop. There is a real potential for development in the person who feels "small" beside someone "great," but does so without jealousy or a sense of frustration or self-pity, being rather inspired to grow himself. There is truth in the statement that "no sadder proof can be given by a man of his own littleness than disbelief in great men."[8] Admiration offers a way of escape from that dungeon of self-induced conceit which we all tend to build for ourselves, and from which moments of truer self-awareness make us turn in abhorrence.

---

7. The process intensifies in regard to the daily actions of people around us: employees, superiors, rivals. Very often, the closer the relationship, the more critical the reactions. Moreover, the *positive* appreciation of what is good seldom keeps abreast of a negative reaction to what is, or seems to us to be, defective.

8. Thomas Carlyle: *On Heroes and Hero Worship*.

"No one can live without admiration. A spirit dwells within us that feels horror at ourselves."[9]

This of course lies in direct contradiction with the central tenet of modern popular psychology, a tenet that is gospel to the "me-generation": self-realization means self-contentment. Self-esteem or self-confidence may have a legitimate basis; but that does not take from the fact that they are characteristics which easily lead people astray in both judgment and action. The importance psychologists attache to them may indeed encourage the shortcut to "maturity" parodied in one of Virginia Woolf's works: the quickest way to acquire "the invaluable quality of self-confidence" is to think that "other people are inferior to oneself."[10] In the *Forsyte Saga* series, John Galsworthy only slightly attenuates this cynicism as his "modern young things" express their contempt for Victorian class snobbery: "No one nowadays takes anyone else as better than themselves."[11] Is it not the eternal return of what T. S. Eliot describes:[12] "people who want to feel important. . . . Absorbed in the endless struggle to think well of themselves?"[13]

Without the capacity for admiration of others in their worth or merit there can be no real personal growth and little true social bonding. Yet one not infrequently comes across calls for a "new consciousness" that "rejects the whole concept of excellence and comparative merit. . . . [It] refuses to evaluate people by general standards, it refuses to classify people, or analyze them. Each person has his own individuality, not to be compared to that of anyone else. Someone may be a brilliant thinker, but he is not "better" at thinking than anyone else, he simply possesses his own excellence. A person who thinks very poorly is still excellent in his own way. Therefore people are in no hurry to find out another person's background, schools, achievements, as a means of knowing him; they regard all of that as secondary, preferring to know him unadorned. Because there are no governing standards, no one is rejected. Everyone is entitled to pride in himself, and no one should act in a way that is servile, or feel inferior, or allow himself to be treated as if he were inferior."[14]

Is individual "pride in self" which is not based on some objective worth likely to make a person more "accepted" by others? Should I never feel or admit that someone else is "superior" to me in this or that quality? Does the acknowledgment of another's superiority necessarily prove that I have a "servile" outlook,

9. Paul Claudel: *Le Soulier de Satin*, I, Sc. 7.
10. *A Room of One's Own*, ch. 2.
11. *The Silver Spoon*, Part III, ch. 10.
12. *The Cocktail Party*, Act 2.
13. The power struggle of politics is especially intense. Perhaps that is why vindictiveness seems so strong at times among politicians. Along with Thomas More, Abraham Lincoln is a notable exception: cf. William L. Miller: *Lincoln's Virtues: an Ethical Biography*, pp. 406–426.
14. *The Greening of America*, p. 243.

or could it not show that I am enthused at discovering someone to admire and find myself personally motivated by having a higher model to emulate?[15]

We hold by the point made in the last chapter: unqualified self-esteem—the happy self-contentment of the modern age—paralyzes personal growth. Moreover it is an attitude which may indeed impede conscious admiration of others, but can seldom stave off eventual self-disgust.

For each one's genuine development, therefore, a response to impersonal values is not enough. It is necessary (and indeed critical and definitive) to recognize, discover, and respond to personalized values, also as they are found in others. Indeed, the very fact that values connected with people are so often more difficult to recognize or admire than those which prescind from people, suggests that the acknowledgment of person-related values indicates or induces greater self-realization.

Let us look further into these peculiar difficulties which tend to appear whenever the response to values is placed in an interpersonal context.

Learning from Imperfect Persons

Perfect people do not exist. I am an imperfect person, and I am surrounded by imperfect people. Each of us finds it hard not to play down our personal imperfections and limitations, and just as hard not to exaggerate the imperfections of others. Yet people will manage to get along only if they establish their relations on objectivity and truth. Indeed, it seems no exaggeration to say that the greatest obstacle to harmonious social or interpersonal life—and to each one's personal enrichment through social life—is a critical spirit which is over-ready to recognize the defects of others and to remain closed to the values they possess (even, I repeat, if these values are present in a defective form). This interpersonal relationship—with other people endowed with values but also with limitations or defects—is necessary so that social communion can lead to the person's development, openness, and fulfillment. And in this process an effort of discernment or understanding is necessary; as is a struggle against the self-centeredness of envy, ultimately rooted in pride.

We said earlier that man cannot grow and come to be truly great except in the conscious presence of what is greater than him. Hence the difficulty in growing humanly which is experienced by a person whose attitude is that he

---

15. Individualism does not take kindly to the notion of having or needing a "model" to emulate. The *Encyclopaedia Britannica*, in an article on "Self-analysis" [in art], thus describes the canons proposed by the 19th-century Romantics: "Forget the 'model,' for there is no such thing; avoid conformity; discover your true self, the buried child; be authentic and sincere." Since then, it notes, there has been no lessening of the tendency to seek our "originality" from within, and adds a comment worth pondering: "Introspection naturally implies an inner life worth looking into."

will not admire anything, or—worse—will not admire anybody. Such "self-protective" jealousy blocks growth and diminishes the person.

There is a view among economists that "wars and economic depressions or recessions have historically resulted in increases in protectionism, while peace and prosperity have tended to encourage free trade."[16] Be this as it may, social and personal peace are certainly favored by free trade in values, something which naturally develops when the protective barriers of jealousy are lowered. This is not a matter for governments, but for the free response of individuals. Each one who makes this response raises the standards of civilized living.

The possibility that the enrichment we can receive from others may be nullified by a pathetic envy points of course to what is the ultimate hindrance to personal development: the pride of wanting to be not just a unique self, an unrepeatable self, but a *higher* self: the absolute Number One.[17] It is the pride of not being prepared to *rise* to values, to be enriched by them and appropriate them at *their level*, but wanting to situate ourselves "above" them, by considering them "below" or "beneath" us.

If jealous envy is let grow, it develops into hatred; and while hatred may seldom go so far as to actually kill the other, it will only cease with his death.[18] Jealousy at the higher way another person incarnates a value reflects an implicit desire to be rid of the other whose existence, as a constant reminder of my deficiency, is an irritant and a source of unhappiness to me. Even if I possess that value in part, the discovery that someone else possesses it more fully can make my own possession or expression of the value seem hollow in the presence of his or hers, and destroy the satisfaction I hitherto drew from it.

Peculiarly, nothing would be solved even if the other disappeared from the scene, for once I have met him, it is already too late. The experience has driven home my limits and dispelled my illusions about my own value. Even the elimination of the other would not make me grow, nor raise me one inch towards the new level of possibilities he has opened up to me but which remain beyond my reach. The negative reaction towards the other, as if he had in some way offended me by his possession of the value, is in effect a rejection of the very value he expresses.[19]

---

16. *Encyclopaedia Britannica*: under "Protectionism."

17. In pathological terms this is classified by the American Psychiatric Association as "Narcissistic Personality Disorder." Narcissistic persons, it notes, "are preoccupied with fantasies of unlimited success, power, brilliance . . . and with chronic feelings of envy for those whom they perceive as being more successful than they are" (*DSM-III-R*, p. 350).

18. Self-centeredness and ambition combine here. The more self-centered ambition is, the more calculating and meaner it becomes. If one cannot beat one's rivals, the temptation is to see how to incapacitate or eliminate them.

19. Cf. J. de Finance: *L'Affrontement de l'autre*, p. 164.

To want to give without receiving is generally a sign of lack of self-knowledge and perhaps of self-deception, both rooted in pride. For we need others. We need to give to them and to receive what they have to give: to give to them disinterestedly and to receive from them gratefully. Some persons constantly seek the esteem and admiration of others: a sad vanity which creates an artificial dependence and limits true interior growth. At the opposite extreme, some cultivate an absolute indifference towards others; neither wanting their esteem nor esteeming them, as if either disposition showed an immature personality. Nevertheless, we all stand in need in relation to others, though perhaps this should be considered from a different angle. It may not matter if one enjoys little or no popular esteem, for one can be a mature and fulfilled person without being liked by others. But one cannot achieve any true human fullness without liking them; i.e. without the capacity to appreciate the values they embody, however imperfectly.

There are very few people in life from whom we have nothing to learn. Pride often makes us look down on someone who appears inferior to our superficial eyes, yet carries inside a value, a point of knowledge or experience, that would enrich us if only we were prepared to receive it. In short, it is necessary to open one's channels of communication, to learn to appreciate, to admire, to listen; to learn to converse.

Children at school are often too lazy, but seldom too proud, to learn. They naturally look up to their teacher, and have no trouble in realizing that he or she has much to teach them. No doubt the same can be said of university students, always allowing for the presence in them of a more developed critical capacity.

It can be very different with people who are in what should be the full maturity of life. So often there is a resistance to learning from our equals (and even more so from those we perhaps consider our inferiors) which would seem to have nothing to do with true critical discernment. We admire—or envy—the tennis technique of a colleague. But instead of asking him or her for tips about how to acquire the same technique, we prefer going to a coach or to a teach-yourself manual. Life offers a lot for the asking; but not to those who are too proud or complicated to ask.

Our grasp of values is enriched through our contact with others. We appreciate a work of art, we discuss it with another, and perhaps we discover in his appreciation aspects which ours had missed; and vice versa.[20]

To "respond" to a value in the work or life of another is to *communicate* with that other. This "communion in values" unites people over the ages. We

---

20. Some film actors, it is said, spend their old age viewing *their* great films of times past; but are no longer capable of admiring good acting—better acting—in someone else. If so, it is a sterile feeding off what they have been. Their vanity may be thereby sustained or grow; they will not grow.

can see it, for instance, in how enthusiasts of a particular composer or a musical group feel at one in a concert. Why, then, must I see others as rival possessors, and not as "co-communicators," of values?

It is important therefore to recognize and resist the over-critical attitude we so easily adopt towards others and which in the end isolates us. There is a whole social trend today not to believe in others, to regard them in a negative light, without finding any real aspect of value in them. This lack of positive appreciation produces increasing unhappiness. As La Rochefoucauld remarked, "A person whom nobody pleases is much more unhappy than one who pleases nobody."[21] It is difficult for such a person not to become "a gossip," that is, a social propagator of small-mindedness.

Interpersonality thus begins to appear as an essential factor in human development. Society must be built on some sense of common values which are necessary to sustain people in the efforts to live and work together, and to appreciate and learn from each other. Without these efforts there will be neither cohesion to society nor growth in individuals. Few people can develop adequately in a life of isolation. Social living, with its interactions and challenges, is the normal setting for personal growth.

In a brief study it is not possible to consider all of the areas of interpersonal and social relationships, or to do more than touch on the main issues they involve. In the next chapter we will briefly consider some major topics connected with social life: education, work, politics, justice and law, the common good, human rights. Sexuality, marriage, and the family play such an important role in the relationship between people that separate chapters are devoted to them.

---

21. "Un homme à qui personne ne plaît est bien plus malheureux que celui qui ne plaît à personne": *Maximes*.

8

SOCIAL LIFE

Man is not fulfilled on his own; he is a social being. His development as a person has an essentially interpersonal aspect. By nature, he is not isolationist, being neither materially nor psychologically self-sufficient. He satisfies his material needs more easily in collaboration with others, in a situation which ideally allows each one to contribute his particular talents to a cohesive social life, and to benefit from the contributions of others.

Man's spiritual needs are also more easily satisfied in association with others. Our human capacity to discover and even to "create" values leads naturally to the desire to communicate them, in a relationship of dialogue. Adequate enrichment of the mind can scarcely ever be achieved without contact and contrast with other minds; the same holds for the experience of goodness. The life of almost everyone is marked—usually in a very positive way—by the interpersonal experiences of family, friendship and marriage.

Friendship is a special interpersonal relationship which links two or more people in particular awareness of shared values. Communion between friends, usually supported by a strong factor of liking, can flow and grow even without vocal dialogue. The urge to share, to accept and be accepted, the need to come out of ourselves so as to be happy, the sadness at a friend's absence, the joy at his or her presence, the impact of the personal uniqueness of our friend (considered to be as valuable as, or even more valuable than, our own uniqueness), the sense of personal incompleteness without our friend, the readiness to receive him into one's innermost life in such a way that he now seems an integral part of ourselves. . . . Any philosophy of self-sufficiency must face these and other challenges posed by the human phenomenon of friendship.

On a broader interpersonal level, the stronger the sense of shared values among people in general or among those who make up a particular group, the deeper the dialogue and the better the basis for social cohesion. A relationship of trust in social life becomes practically impossible without an awareness of values held in common.

When the overriding concern in a society is the economic sharing of material goods, it is hard to avoid seeing others as rivals. A more truly human society can emerge when others are seen as a source of values—to be discovered, admired, protected; and as collaborators in a team venture.

Without this challenge of social life—in communion, collaboration and appreciation towards others—people do not achieve fulfillment. Society does finds its justification not only in a logical distribution of work and roles, or in the need for a minimum of civic order. It must also be ordered to the personal fulfillment of each citizen.

The Structure of the Human Community

Any truly human society must be made up of free and responsible people, who work and live together, collaborating in justice under a legitimate authority, and inspired by love or at least by respect and mutual appreciation.

Freedom and Responsibility. Freedom is understood in its true nature as a value, and can be adequately exercised in a way worthy of man, only when it is accompanied by responsibility. A sense of responsibility should guide every free action, being a proof of respect toward the same value of freedom present in the life of others. In fact, freedom without the corresponding responsibility is always a *pathological* freedom. Whoever claims a freedom free from responsibility shows that he neither understands nor really loves freedom.

It is interesting to recall the title of one of the best known works of Karol Wojytla: *Love and Responsibility*. "Freedom" and "responsibility" are necessarily connected. The title of Wojtyla's book suggests that responsibility is not to be measured in terms of freedom only, but that in interpersonal relations— relationships which are authentically human—it must equally and perhaps preferentially be measured according to love.

Education. Individualism can only find an artificial and external harmony between personal and social education. Social education for the individualist means learning how to *advance oneself* in life, as cleverly and effectively as possible, weaving one's intricate way among rivals.

A properly assimilated personalist philosophy[1] finds natural and internal harmony between the development and fulfillment of the individual, and his role and responsibilities in society. Growing appreciation of others and concern for them is a standard of personal development. Work is a means not only of personal advancement but also a contribution to the common good. Social duties are not just obligations, but also values (truthfulness, honesty, justice, service . . .) to be responded to.

"If there is an essential equality between men that challenges all empiric inequalities, it is equality of vocation, not of leveling; it must open the possibility to everyone of an equivalent destiny, on the condition of a similar effort by all."[2] This is a fundamental principle that should underlie all education.

It is logical that education for social life be aimed at preparing each individual to be able to perform work that is useful for the overall whole. This aim, however, does not reach far enough. From the anthropological-personalist perspective we have adopted, readying people for service is an important function of education, but it does not suffice. It would not even be enough to provide young people with cultural formation apt to broaden each one's personal horizons, offering a certain knowledge of the values of literature, art, etc. The fundamental capacity that human education must communicate is that of *appreciating* values in others. Without this capacity it is not possible to develop the basic virtues that turn life together into communion and make a society truly human and humanizing:[3] respect, understanding, admiration (without either envy or jealousy), emulation, gratitude, generosity, friendship, team-spirit, collaboration, sense of complementary roles . . .

From a personalist point of view, life and commitment in society must indeed be marked by service, which could well be taken as a personalist "motto." However, service itself will not be really personalist if it is not accompanied by appreciation of others.

When education in the awareness of just responsibility has a personalist base, it fosters a desire to give to others what properly belongs to each one, also because it would be contrary to our own growth to keep it. True civic education should help people understand and assimilate a sense of interdependence: their shared duty towards the common good.

---

1. For the difference between individualism and personalism, see Appendix II.

2. Emmanuel Mounier: *Oeuvres*, II, p. 509.

3. We could draw a distinction between society, when people simply coexist in a state perhaps of mere mutual tolerance; and "community," when they really live together, where each one, a defective person, grows by learning to appreciate others, who are also defective people. Community involves giving *and accepting*; it calls therefore for mutual openness, and a readiness to combat the human tendency to envy which we have already noticed and to seek mutual and full enrichment and development.

Work. Ecologists rightly criticize the destructive effect that men's work has so often had on the environment; and they lobby for working conditions that will protect our surrounding heritage. Their criticism does not go far enough. What needs to be remedied is the destructive effect of many forms of work not just on the environment, but on people themselves. To say that our work should tend to "humanize" our environment is a mode of speaking. The positive aim it expresses will only be achieved if work tends to humanize *us*; which means to fulfill us as people, along the lines of fulfillment we have been delineating.

What is the intrinsic justification or aim of work? To earn our living? Fair enough. To make a lot of money? If that becomes the goal, a person may turn from a type of work he enjoys to one he doesn't but which pays more; then it is not clear that his choice is really fulfilling.[4] As a means to prestige? If all a man looks for in his work is prestige (or, in less elegant terms, vanity and self-importance), then his work has no real value in itself; and so, if there was no one around whose admiration seemed worth working for, then his work would be valueless and inherently boring.

In Robert Bolt's "A Man for All Seasons," there is an episode where Thomas More is trying to convince the ambitious young Richard Rich to keep out of politics: "A man should go where he won't be tempted. . . ." He suggests that Rich become a teacher instead. More insists: "Why not be a teacher? You'd be a fine teacher. Perhaps a great one."—RICH: "And if I was, who would know it?"—MORE: "You, your pupils, your friends, God. Not a bad public, that . . ." Rich was not convinced.[5]

In fact some people might be prepared to reduce their public still further, being content to play for their own applause, with themselves as the audience to please. If a person in such a case is hard to please, he will probably be a perfectionist.[6] If he is easy to please, he is likely to be lazy as well as conceited.

---

4. From the subjective viewpoint, "job satisfaction" is certainly a major measure for gauging the intrinsic value of work. Money, for instance, is a value extrinsic to work itself. No matter how much money a person makes, if his work does not possess any intrinsic value to his eyes, he may esteem the salary it brings him—but will be bored and perhaps disgusted at the work itself. He may have "salary satisfaction," but not *job* satisfaction. Nevertheless it remains difficult to convince people today that salary or "power" are not the decisive measures in evaluating a job. And yet a bartender or barber who is interested in people and enjoys talking with them, in all probability gets much more satisfaction out of his job in its everyday details than a business executive who only enjoys himself and perhaps his power to command people and situations.

5. Among other defects, Rich was vain. Vanity tends to make a person measure his worth by the esteem other people have for him. The proud man is content to admire himself, with or without good reason. The vain man is content only if he enjoys (so at least he thinks) the admiration of others.

6. Having fallen victim to that perfectionism which sees duty more as a challenge to one's own capacity (and its fulfillment as a condition for increasing self-esteem) than as a truly human response to values.

In any case, there will be no enrichment from outside. Interiorly he may feel his Ego grow, without ever asking himself is *he* is growing.

"The artist works to *express* himself, the worker works to *maintain* himself," can be an irritating statement to all who are not artists. It offers a clue, however. Every job is potentially a work of art, a means by which a person can express himself. We are all artists. Every worker can be an artist, once he becomes aware of a *value* potentially present in his work—which can be extracted from it by his own intention and effort.

To be of real worth, work—whatever its human standing—must have some value and purpose, proper and intrinsic to itself.[7] Thoroughness, order, method, attention to details, "doing a good day's job," are all qualities that a person can put into his work (he must put them; otherwise he won't find them there). Earning his living, developing his character, maintaining his family, are also values that should be present and that a person needs to keep before him; otherwise he may be overcome by the monotony of repetition. Repetition of values does not decrease the values (rather the opposite); but it can blunt the sense of value possessed by a superficial person.

It is hard to discover the full value of your work, if you lack a sense of community or solidarity with others. The intrinsic value of work after all does not stop with enrichment just to the worker, but extends also to the building of the community. Work too needs broader horizons. True self-realization through work can only come if the personalist spirit that motivates it manages to overcome the confining limits of self-concern and self-satisfaction, substituting the nobler satisfaction of contributing to the social whole, to others.

In other words, a fuller sense of value in work calls for "a reappropriation of the idea of work as a contribution to the good of all and not merely as a means to one's own advancement. If the extrinsic rewards and punishments associated with work were reduced, it would be possible to make vocational choices more in terms of intrinsic satisfactions. Work that is intrinsically interesting and valuable is one of the central requirements for a revitalized social ecology. For professionals, this would mean a clearer sense that the large institutions most of them work for really contribute to the public good. A bright young lawyer (or a bright old lawyer, for that matter) whose work consists in helping one corporation outwit another is intelligent enough to doubt the social utility of what he or she is doing. The work may be interesting—even challenging and exciting—yet its intrinsic meaninglessness in any larger moral or social context necessarily produces an alienation that is only partly assuaged by the relatively large income of corporate lawyers. Those whose work is not only poorly rewarded but boring, repetitive, and unchallenging are in an even

---

7. "Perhaps work that is intrinsically rewarding is better for human beings than work that is only extrinsically rewarded": Robert N. Bellah et al.: *Habits of the Heart*, p. 295.

worse situation. Automation that turns millions of our citizens into mere servants or robots is already a form of despotism, for which the pleasures of private life—modest enough for those of minimum skill and minimum wage—cannot compensate."[8]

It is not a question of fostering an exaggerated altruism; and less still of trying to impose an adequate distribution of roles, assigning to each person the work for which he is considered to be best fitted. Professional work of whatever type is a means of self-fulfillment and, as such, must be the object of a free personal choice. Ideally each person should have the freedom to choose the type of work to which he will devote himself. But it is important that in the initial formation received—at school, in university, etc.—he is helped to consider his future work not only as a legitimate means of self-fulfillment, but at the same time as a way of promoting the fulfillment of others.

Work conceived and lived this way certainly implies reaching beyond ourselves and so achieving truer personal growth. Can we reach farther still in our work? Can we broaden out our working horizons to discover even greater values? Thomas More spoke of having God as an appreciative "audience" to one's work. If what he said can be taken seriously, then any work could be imbued with an unlimited sense of meaning and value. Most of us would like to find some real "greatness" in our life and work. Modern psychologism tries to convince us we are wrong, offering us contentedness but not greatness. "To try to relate 'ultimate concern' to everyday behavior would be exhausting and nerve-shattering work: indeed, it could effectively inhibit less grandiose kinds of work. . . . In the workaday world, there are no ultimate concerns, only present ones."[9] But surely it is the absence of greatness which drains everyday behavior of real vitality and leaves us exhausted? And how can present concerns appear as "great" unless they can be related to an even greater ultimate concern? Indeed, can any thinking person be really content without possessing some sense of ultimate concern or greatness? Yes, ultimate concerns, ultimate values, do keep floating somewhere on our horizons or in the back of our mind. However it is not yet time to consider them in our study, or to broach the question whether anthropology can legitimately consider the possibility of a transcendent dimension to life.

Politics. Politics in the true sense of "the art of government" is already debased in meaning if it is understood just as a power-struggle; or, more abstractly, as a system of procedural rules which allows individuals to enter into fair competition for posts of power, at the same time as it enables the electorate in a democracy to have a say in who will hold these posts.

---

8. *Habits . . .* , op. cit, pp. 287-288.
9. Philip Rieff: *The Triumph of the Therapeutic*, p. 54.

Politics, as a career, is in the line of medicine or teaching. It is—it should be—a *service* profession. The politician's calling is one of special public trust. He is chosen or appointed to direct government to the service of the good of the people, the "common good." If his dominant aim in entering politics is to enhance his ego with a sense of power, he may or may not come to be considered by others a successful politician, but he will remain a reduced man.

This does not have to happen. The person who follows a political career is certainly seeking to exercise part of that authority with which government must be endowed. But authority can be understood and sought not principally as an embodiment of power, but as a means to advance the rightful good of one's country and its people. A person who understands this as the true nature of authority can approach politics in an authentically vocational sense.

Dedication to politics offers a pitfall not unlike that which can accompany the pursuit of material wealth. Power can no doubt be regarded as a "value." Yet, unless accompanied by those interior qualities which by themselves confer moral authority, it has no place among values of the spirit. Power is real enough; but, like material values and perhaps more than any of them, it tends to foster illusions. To have power and be able to make it felt can create a sensation of being superior to others, more "fulfilled" than they are. It remains an illusion, however, just as much as the illusion that being richer makes one better as a person.

Only whoever accepts the responsibility—towards others—of authority, can see its possession and exercise as a service of something higher than self. This makes it possible to follow an outward and upward path, no longer simply of self-assertion but of true self-realization, a large part of which is effected by the desire to contribute to the good of others.

There will never be an end to the debate about modes of government or about the political or economic system that works best. Men find it hard to shake off the utopian dream of "systems so perfect that no one will need to be good";[10] yet no system is likely to work justly and well unless it is managed by people who are not only competent but also honest. The founding fathers of the American republic commonly held, in the expression of James Madison, that "to suppose that any form of government will secure liberty or happiness without any virtue in the people is a chimerical idea."[11] Many centuries earlier Thomas Aquinas pinpointed the issue more precisely, making the good order of society depend indeed on the people at large, but above all on those governing: "the common good of the state cannot flourish unless the citizens be virtuous, *at least* those whose business it is to govern."[12]

---

10. T. S. Eliot: *Choruses from the Rock.*
11. Quoted in *Habits . . .* , op. cit., p. 254.
12. *Summa Theologica*, I–II, q. 92.

Honesty—in politics, business, professional activity, and indeed in all human dealings—understood as an aspiration toward fulfillment, badly needs to be fostered in our contemporary world. Honesty may not be the best policy if one's overriding value is material advantage, but dishonesty is the surest way to lose self-esteem. Whatever its value for external success, honesty remains an absolute requirement of personal worth.

The dishonest man knows in his heart, if he can still reach and read it, that he is not worthy of real esteem. He should realize that those closest to him (spouse, children, real friends) also know this, and that if he is envied (for he will not be admired) by some around him, such envy comes from people whose esteem is not worth having.

Some people are too proud to be cheats, simply because it would wreck their self-esteem. There may be a certain pharisaical ego-centrism in this motive, but it at least keeps a person open towards a value which is fundamental for both personal and social life. Hence it is no exaggeration to say that all open-ness toward real values has collapsed in the dishonest man who prides himself on his dishonesty.

Justice and Law. "If there is justice, and if law is based on a discernment of what is just, dialogue can begin and benevolence can appear; so we come to what is ours in common. The first form of culture is law. Its effectiveness means that barbarism has been overcome: men have always been civilized this way."[13]

No society can be healthy unless it is inspired by a sound concept of jus-tice embodied in an adequate political and legal system which can effectively protect rights and equitably resolve conflicting claims. The more the mass of citizens esteem and love the values of justice (without remaining at a level of simple acceptance and obedience to its demands), the healthier the society. A sense of the dignity and the rights of others engenders a basic love for justice. At one extreme this can favor a readiness to acknowledge when you are wrong, to apologize, to make up and give back. At the other extreme, when, despite everything, claims have been taken to a court of law, this sense can facilitate the acceptance of hard but just judicial decisions.

If the efficacy of the law depends totally on law-enforcement agents, then something is wrong either with the law or with those who are obliged to accept or fulfill it.

The norm of justice is "to each his due." This is a principle very different from that of egalitarianism: "to each the same."[14] Egalitarianism would appear to have gone from a period of considerable strength as a political-economic

---

13. R. Yepes: *Fundamentos de Antropología*, p. 312; cf. ibid. 297ss.
14. Or in its communist expression: "from each according to his capacity; to each according to his need."

program into sudden decline. Yet it still dominates much of modern education. Practical reasons (the need for trained teachers, equipment, examinations) will certainly oblige many educational systems to offer the same basic curriculum. From the personalist point of view, however, education must aim at eliciting or bringing out the distinctive personal qualities of each student, at the same time as it teaches each to appreciate the different qualities of others. Education is not defective if it promotes differences—which it must inevitably do. It is defective if it does not seek to foster a positive appreciation of these differences on the part of those being educated.

The Common Good. A society cannot survive without some sense of common values. But values can no longer be common when each individual claims the right to define them as he wishes[15] or when they are simply understood by each as "whatever makes me feel good." Then they cease to constitute a common language of communication, or to form reference points and sources of unity. The individualist, whose ideal society is totally at the service of his own advancement, has little notion of a "common good" and little interest in it. With the personalist it is different. The sense of values, the concern to respond to them and see them grow, the awareness of how they can be incarnated in others—all of these are factors which help him understand that social life itself can evolve in a way that facilitates (or hinders) the presence, discovery, and communication of values; and therefore the enrichment (or frustration) of each and every one, including himself.

To the personalist who possesses this awareness, the "common good" appears as an exceptional value in itself. It represents the order within which the rights, interests, and development of each one are best harmonized and favored. When this order can only be achieved (as at times is inevitably the case) through individual interest yielding to the higher common good, then this yielding not only seems reasonable in terms of the common interest, but takes on the character of a personalist value in itself, through response to which the individual's good is even more powerfully realized. Besides, there is no possibility of any deep or enduring self-respect without a sense that one's own life is beneficial also to others.

Human Rights. Human rights is one of the anthropological issues most frequently invoked and debated today. A person deprived of his human rights is a slave. A person who is unaware of his human rights is easily exploited. A person who invokes human "rights" which are really human *wrongs* may harm himself (the "right" to take heroin, for instance), or harm others (the "right" to corrupt minors).

---

15. something characteristic of modern "liberation" movements. "The meaning of liberation is that the individual is free to build his own philosophy and values, his own life-style, and his own culture from a new beginning": *The Greening . . .* , p. 241.

To have the power to do something is not the same as to be *entitled* to do it. More than two thousand years ago, Socrates already combatted the Sophists who held that "Might makes right." The human quality of society ever since has grown—or been undermined—according to the respect, or to the practical contempt, shown for the principle that right cannot be equated with power, or power with right.

Two major questions arise in the matter of human rights: their definition or specification, and their justification or basis. The issue of their definition concerns both *what* they are and *who* can define or detail them. As regards what or which are the basic human rights, one can quickly list a number about which there is no great likelihood of disagreement: the rights to life, to liberty, and to the pursuit of happiness; the rights to free choice (of state of life or religious faith), to free expression of political or other opinion, to due process before the law . . .

As an initial list, it appears fairly simple. Yet we can already discern the underlying complexity. For instance, while we all have equal claim to these rights—precisely because they are human rights—we cannot claim to exercise all of them in an absolute or unlimited way. My freedom of action, after all, can very quickly cut across the freedom of action of others. Then either I voluntarily curtail my own freedom, or reach an agreement with others for an acceptable mutual curtailment, or else the law steps in and imposes some sort of workable arrangement on all of us. Otherwise social life is not possible, and freedom can defeat freedom. I am free to drive on either side of the road, or never to stop at an intersection; but if I claim a "right" to that freedom and begin to exercise it. . . !

Who is going to define and specify human rights? Does anybody have the *right* to do so? Yet a free and democratic society can scarcely be maintained unless young people growing up are informed about the nature and extent of their basic human rights. For this reason at least, some definition must be offered. Is everyone to define his own personal rights—as would be the logical opinion of those who hold that each person is a self-defining subject (with the basic *right* of self-definition) regarding the whole of his life? Whatever about the survival of human society on such a basis,[16] it is surely evident that with such an approach one is no longer talking about *human* rights, in any real sense, but simply about my rights? This is the temptation of the individualist, who finds it hard to be in favor of human rights at all.

---

16. John Paul II wrote: "When freedom is detached from objective truth it becomes impossible to establish personal rights on a firm rational basis, and the ground is laid for society to be at the mercy of the unrestrained will of individuals or the oppressive totalitarianism of public authority" (*Evangelium Vitae*, no. 96). "If there is no ultimate truth to guide and direct political activity, then ideas and convictions can easily be manipulated for reasons of power. As history demonstrates, a democracy without values easily turns into open or thinly disguised totalitarianism" (*Centesimus Annus*, no. 46).

We leave the reader to supply his answers to the many important questions that can arise here, and turn to the other major issue concerning human rights, that of their justification or basis. There is little to say. What can warrant the attribution of the term "human" to a particular right? After all, human rights are not the same as legal rights or moral rights or acquired rights. . . . A person's entitlement to a human right does not derive from some positive legal instrument, such as a will or a contract, nor does it depend on other formal proof. His claim to the right rests on a very simple fact—that he *is*, and that he is *human*.[17] This establishes his right and makes it inviolate. Human rights are not conferred (although their exercise may be protected or restored) by civil law, or act of Congress, or declaration of the United Nations. Legislative bodies or parliamentary majorities can recognize or deny the existence of human rights, but they do not and cannot create them. They can refuse to acknowledge them, prohibit their exercise, expunge them from constitutions. They cannot really abolish them, for they exist prior to all legislatures and constitutions.

Democracy implies the free interplay of individuals, groups and parties, seeking a public mandate from the electorate to pursue specific policies in governing a country within the established constitution or order. A new group or party can obtain a majority, and with it the mandate to govern. But nothing in their mandate authorizes them to deprive any minority of their human rights, or indeed to change the definition or nature of human rights. Human rights are not a product of democracy. They antecede it, and are in fact its only lasting guarantee. To accept the principle that human rights are to be subordinated to democratic processes, which could therefore change or abolish them, is to negate the very idea of *human* rights which by definition are prior to and independent of any positive law; it is to dehumanize and decivilize both democracy and society, and to leave the individual citizen without any inherent protection against eventual abuses of the law.

It is not in the personality but in the humanity of each individual that human rights are grounded. Each human being, independently of age, health, mental condition, etc., is an inviolate subject of human rights. To exclude any human being from the attribution of human rights is not only to "dehumanize" him, but is a step toward the dehumanizing of the very world we live in.

---

17. A human right "is quintessentially general or universal in character, in some sense equally possessed by all human beings everywhere, including in certain instances even the unborn": *Encyclopaedia Britannica*.

9

THE HUMANIZING ROLE
OF SEXUALITY

Human sexuality is a remarkable and multifaceted phenomenon. In this chapter and the two following we will consider it under three aspects: sexuality in general, marriage, the family. The three can be said to correspond to sexual identity and appreciation, sexual love, and sexual fruitfulness.

❍❍❍

In the anthropological view presented up to now, our point of departure has been man as an incomplete or "unfinished" being. Each individual must seek fulfillment, not however in an immanent fashion—not just inside himself. Within himself he does not find the necessary means to fulfill himself: he is not self-sufficient. He must transcend and go beyond himself; it is by opening to values and responding to them that he is fulfilled.

We have also considered that this process of opening meets resistance: on the one hand, when we are faced with "difficult" values whose acceptance can threaten our easy self-centeredness; and on the other, when we are tempted to react with jealousy, rather than admiration, to values incarnated in other people. The desire to be or feel ourselves "self-sufficient," thinking we can make it by ourselves, is present in both these situations. This desire renders it particularly opportune to look here at what in a certain way appears as a protective factor against individualistic self-sufficiency: the division of mankind as a whole into two halves, each of which is seen (although not always adequately) as a complement to the other: in other words, the factor of human sexuality.

The Two Modalities of the Human Person

In the fact that human beings exist in two modalities—masculine and feminine—we can (to my mind we should) find a clear and original confirmation of the thesis that man has need of others in order to perfect himself. Any genuine fulfillment or development of the human person can not be achieved without adequate sexual interaction.

The sexual instinct in the case of man is—ought to be—broader than mere physical-corporal attraction. We cannot reduce the understanding of human sexuality to its obvious procreative orientation. The *distinctive* dimension of human sexuality is not exhausted (and would not even seem to consist) in procreativity alone, where animal sexuality in contrast finds its whole purpose and meaning.[1]

The bodily aspect of human sexuality is certainly fundamental. However, it could be regarded not only as its most obvious aspect but also, in a way, as its most superficial. When a mainly physical and bodily perception of human sexuality predominates, there is a grave risk of its being reduced to a merely animal dimension.

From the anthropological point of view we can distinguish three aspects to the phenomenon of human sexuality:

1) a first aspect which affects the understanding and development of the personal life of everyone, proposing different characteristics or human ways of being which—if one is capable of perceiving them—tend to disclose the wealth and potentiality of each person's own human nature. It is always in this sense that sexuality should be first considered and studied. It is this aspect which reveals sexuality as an anthropological phenomenon of the very first importance. Its dynamism points not primarily to attraction and love between one man and one woman in particular, but to *appreciation between men and women in general.*

Sexual appreciation is peculiarly human, and is necessary for truly human growth.[2] It is necessary, moreover, if sexual desire, which we share with animals, is not to remain simply animal but also is to become

---

1. In animals, sex has an exclusively reproductive function. In humans, sex has a reproductive function; but it also has a perfective function.

2. This applies to everyone, including those—especially Christians—who choose a celibate life. Christ is the perfect exemplar of manhood, Mary that of womanhood. In each a perfect integration of all the human virtues (whether "masculine" or "feminine") is found. In each, the Christian who freely chooses celibacy out of love finds an unsurpassed model for his or her growth in sexual identity.

genuinely human. In the absence of any true human sexual appreciation, there will be little ability to humanize sexual desire. Sexual desire without sexual appreciation is the growing result not only of pornography, but of transient sexual affairs, and of the failure to achieve—or the loss of—sexual identity.

2) a second aspect which, on a more specific level, offers a singular form of communion with a particular "You," committing one's own person in an unparalleled relationship of donation of self and acceptance of the other: i.e. the conjugal relationship of *marriage*. Since marriage, for the great majority of humanity, constitutes the closest and most intimate interpersonal human relationship, its role in genuine development must necessarily be unique.

3) a third aspect which is the natural result of the second: the formation of a broader communion—*the family*—where human life is perpetuated and developed, and where each new person becomes from the beginning not only the fruit but also the disciple of love. In the educative and humanizing function of the family, the role of sexuality also appears under different aspects.

Before proceeding to a more detailed consideration of these individual points, it could be useful to dwell briefly on a phenomenon that concerns all three: the feminist movements of modern times. Seriously initiated more than one hundred years ago, feminism (we really should speak of "feminisms") has strongly marked the twentieth century. It continues to take many forms, without having arrived yet at any definitive expression that might be fully coherent in itself as well as consistent with the deeper insights of anthropology.

For years, in an endeavor to correct the many abuses of preceding centuries, feminist claims have accentuated equality of rights and dignity between man and woman. Wholehearted support is due to these efforts to achieve a genuine recognition in practice of woman's equal dignity with man, along with her equality of opportunity to participate fully in public life: in the political, professional, social spheres, etc. Nevertheless it must be added that a large part of the feminist movements, in centering almost entirely on issues of equality and dignity, has neglected and even obscured other aspects to human sexuality which are anthropologically fundamental and which cannot be disregarded without grave loss to both men and women. These are above all: a) the *complementarity* of the sexes, which harmonizes their equality with their differences; and, more fundamentally still, b) the sexual identity proper to each: an identity understood also as a goal to be attained by each individual so as to "realize" his or her own life. These two aspects are interdependent, for without well-defined sexual identity on the part of those who compose each sex, there cannot be genuine complementarity between the two.

The Response To Sexual Values

Let us now consider the first aspect of the sexual phenomenon. To deal with the subject adequately requires limiting—or, as the case may be, broadening—our view of sexuality in order to see its *humanizing* role. In some ways this is the most universal and important aspect of sexuality, where it appears as a fundamental factor in the integral human development of the individual. What is meant here is not merely the biological origin of each one from the union of masculine and feminine elements, but rather the fact that man and woman cannot fulfill themselves adequately without a clear appreciation of the two modalities or expressions of humanity: the masculine and the feminine. They need to recognize the values—of character and attitudes—of each sex and to respond to these values, so as to develop both those considered more characteristic of each person's sex, as well as those regarded as typical of the other.

The sexual condition pertains to the person, not just to the body. To develop one's personality fully, each one should be able to assume and integrate his or her own sexual condition. A major obstacle to self-fulfillment is created by the attempt to live without reference to (or, worse still, in rejection of) one's distinctive sexual character.

In other words, each person (and this applies particularly to the adolescent's situation as he or she commences the more conscious process of maturing) finds himself or herself with two images of humanity that are equally valid. Neither the masculine modality alone, nor the feminine alone, offers a full model of humanity. It follows that the genuinely human character of a society or a civilization is necessarily connected with the presence, and with the fruitful interaction in it, of authentic values which are both masculine and feminine.

"Harmony between sexes is by no means to be limited to the area of sexual life, but implies a genuine *need for communication* and understanding between the two halves of humanity. Hence the harmony of the family, of institutions, and of the whole of society is connected with it."[3] This harmony between man and woman, which is so endangered today, can only be reestablished through the recognition not just of an equality of rights (which derives not from their sexual condition but from their shared humanity and, subordinately, from their shared citizenship), but of their interdependent diversity and complementarity. Men need to be made more human—richer, that is, in humanity—through the presence of women; and vice versa.

The survival of a society depends on the maintenance of a sense of mutual help and complementary roles. More important than any awareness

---

3. R. Yepes: *Fundamentos . . .* , op. cit. p. 271.

of complementarity, let us say, between magistrates or lawyers and police, is the sense of the complementarity between man and woman. If this sense is lacking, society can become technically more developed, but will enter on a process of human decline and perhaps of disintegration.

To grow, we must learn to relate to others, discovering them in their originality and respecting them in their legitimate differences. Difference of gender gives rise to particular modes of interpersonal relationships which tend to deeply configure each person's human life. Today an impoverished (and at times warped) notion of sexuality means that the sexual development of individuals is severely limited and in some cases even completely stunted. A man whose mind fixes on the exclusively physical characteristics of woman and is blind to the character or spiritual qualities that make up femininity, is humanly underdeveloped; he lacks that true understanding of human sexuality so necessary if he is to mature. The same is true of the woman who is content to draw men's attention to her feminine body and has no interest in (and perhaps does not even understand) the nature, challenge and power of the feminine spirit or soul.[4]

Contemporary society is marked by a striking unawareness of the distinctive and humanly enriching character which should specify the different modalities of relationships between the sexes: from the most general form of that relationship simply between man and woman, to all the particular sexually characterized relationships of boy-girl, sister-brother, mother-son, father-daughter, fiancés, and specially of wife and husband. When the peculiar modes of these relationships are properly understood and lived, they powerfully help each one to grow in humanity. Conversely, few phenomena can present a greater threat to both individual development and social harmony as sexuality conceived just in terms of physical differences or, worse still, of a power struggle between the two halves of humanity.

Traditional Conception of the Masculine and Feminine Characters

Whatever way we choose to express the masculine or feminine typification of the human person, it will probably provoke the immediate critical reaction which every type of generalization tends to elicit. An "active" masculine character in contrast with a "passive" feminine one; man devoted to the public

---

4. Few women, if any, would like to grow a mustache: a masculine feature that would be a feminine defect. There are other masculine traits that render women less attractive. Yet many women today seem to be losing their ability to distinguish between qualities which perfect their distinctive feminine character, and other qualities which render them more masculine and therefore less identified as women.

forum and woman to the home; reasoning in contrast with feeling or intuition; justice in contrast with pity . . .[5]

Today such an analysis is less and less accepted. It seems to offer simple stereotypes and over-rigid portraits that assign ways of being, characteristics, and virtues exclusively to one or the other sex, as if the values or virtues to be developed and assimilated so as to attain a properly fulfilled personal humanity were fundamentally different in the case of man and woman.[6] Today it is rather held that each human person can achieve integral development only if he or she acquires all the human values or virtues. When, as not infrequently happens, someone sees that a quality is particularly lived by a member of the other sex, this should lead to the realization that he or she also needs to live that virtue, even if in a manner more corresponding to his or her own sex. For instance, woman can and should be brave, and man should be sensitive and tactful.

It is preferable to start from the basic principle that all the human virtues are to be assimilated by every man and woman. What the sexual phenomenon reveals in this field is that there are masculine or feminine ways of living each virtue (or its opposite defect), and each sex must learn—according to these different ways—from the other. This again highlights the point that woman represents humanity as much as man, but each sex does so in its own necessarily partial way.

In psychological studies significant ground is being gained by a school of thought which, basing itself on the equal dignity of man and woman, proposes distinct models for the development of the sexual identity of each. It points out that the standards hitherto generally applied in the field of psychology to gauge an individual's degree of human maturity, have corresponded almost exclusively to a model of masculine development. The result has been to define "man" by human (and not first by masculine) characteristics, and "woman" by feminine (and not also human) characteristics. This has given an *incomplete* idea not just of woman, but of man too.[7] Once such masculine standards are applied, the results logically "prove" the "inferiority" of woman, in the light of almost all the values considered as a key for a successful life.

Within the newer view, human maturity is to be measured in a different way according to whether the person is a woman or a man; feminine maturity is as valid and important—for individual and social development—as masculine;

---

5. Certain data are unquestionable: a) man is almost always physically stronger than woman; b) only woman can conceive and give birth. Are these two facts comparable? Whoever thinks so, and at the same time appreciates strength more than motherhood, will almost inevitably come to the conclusion that man is superior.

6. One can allow, nevertheless, that the hierarchy and combination of values should be different in each case.

7. Cf. Carol Gilligan: *In a Different Voice*, Harvard University Press, 1982, Blanca Castilla, *La Complementariedad Varón-Mujer*, Madrid, 1993.

and all the "values" or "virtues" which the person of one sex must try to incarnate as proper to their own sex, are values to be assimilated—perhaps with a different modulation—also by those of the opposite sex. "It needs to be underlined that masculinity and femininity are distinguished not so much by a distribution between them of qualities or virtues, but rather by the peculiar way in which each one incarnates them. Virtues after all are human, and each person should develop them all. It is not clear therefore that there are tasks or jobs specific to man and to woman."[8]

"Gender equality" can be a misleading expression. "Personal equality" might seem preferable. However, "equality of dignity and opportunity between men and women," though a cumbersome phrase, expresses greater precision. Man and woman are not "equal" in their respective sexual nature; they are quite different. They are not "equal," but *complementary*. Even the concept of "personal equality" can be improperly understood. Persons are *equal in dignity*; but there are no two "equal" (i.e. identical) persons; each person is unique.

In fact it seems correct to say that there is a masculine way of developing feminine characteristics and virtues, and likewise a feminine way of incarnating masculine virtues. The modalities or nuances of this particular process are no doubt so rich and different as to escape any classification. The way in which a man shows tenderness (a feminine virtue, and not a masculine one?), or in which a woman confronts a dangerous situation, will almost certainly not fail to express the sexual identity proper to each one. There seems no reason to maintain that a woman is necessarily less feminine because she has developed a strong sense of competitiveness (think of the different reactions—so often visible in gesture—of a man or a woman in the moment of winning an Olympic competition).

The human person cannot develop adequately—that is, become fully human—within a framework of purely masculine or purely feminine values (a society itself may be excessively masculinized or excessively feminized). Only whoever appreciates values in both the sexual modalities in which they can be found, and tries to practice them, follows an integral human way of character formation. Human personality is necessarily expressed through femininity and masculinity. Man just like woman represents humanity in its diversity and in its diversifying action.

It is pointless, therefore, to discuss which of the two sexes is superior. In each case that *person* will be "superior" who manages to develop the characteristic virtues of his or her own sex (overcoming, if he or she is able, the defects which can also be considered peculiar to the same sex), while at the same time searching no less to understand and develop (perhaps, I repeat, with a slightly

---

8. B. Castilla, op. cit., 78.

different human tonality) the "typical" virtues of the other sex. One can in effect say that to become more fully human, each sex must learn "humanity" from the other.[9] In any case, any possible superiority will depend on the adequate achievement of each person's own sexual identity. No doubt one could for instance say that "she is more a woman than he is a man," the sense being that she has been more successful in establishing her proper sexual identity.

In passing we would call attention to what is a major (and paradoxical) defect of mainstream feminism: its marked reluctance to define "feminine." The original feminist claim was mainly civic and political, a claim to the same legal rights and to equal educational and professional opportunities, for women as for men. The claim was, beyond dispute, absolutely legitimate and just. But nineteenth-century political and social feminism gave way to a twentieth-century "equalism" of a predominantly psychological nature. The main concern now became "self-realization" or "self-fulfillment." Elsewhere we question whether the self-assertive and self-centered presuppositions of most of modern psychology can lead to true fulfillment. Here we simply note how this new psychological feminism shows little or no interest in considering whether fulfillment, for a man or a woman, has any necessary relationship to sexual identity. If, as is often popularly expressed, to be fulfilled means "to be oneself," is male sexual identity of no relevance to a man in his effort to "be himself," or female sexual identity to the woman who wants to "be herself?" Or is the unisex trend of psychology right in holding that the whole concept of "being oneself" has absolutely no relationship to whether one is a man or a woman? We hope to enter more fully into this question in another work.

The Sexual Identity of Man

The psychological portrait which man offers is probably simpler than that of woman. He is physically stronger; he has a tendency to conceive fulfillment in terms of struggle, as a matter of surpassing oneself and surpassing others. He is therefore more inclined to active competition, and perhaps to exterior affairs. He easily tends to excess in physical activity, and even to violence and cruelty. He possesses a special impulse towards independence; the idea of self-sufficiency is probably a greater temptation for him. Nevertheless, he remains incomplete. He needs a complement; and in particular a humanizing influence. An authentic discovery of woman can be the condition for him to become more human.

---

9. One psychologist suggests that "optimal mental health is reflected in psychological androgyny, or the coexistence of masculine and feminine traits which are expressed in appropriate situations (e.g. tenderness with one's children and competitiveness with one's tennis opponent)": *American Journal of Psychiatry*, vol. 147 (1990), p. 910.

Julián Marías says that "the nucleus of man's condition is precisely *enthusiasm for woman*."[10] The Book of Genesis speaks of the reaction of joy in Adam when he first beheld Eve. It was the initial human response to sexuality, a response not of desire but of sexual enthusiasm, of someone who has found a new dimension to life that fills in something he now realizes was lacking. The deepest reaction to sexuality should in fact be one of joy, joy before what is designed to be complementary and therefore fulfilling and enriching. Certainly both sexes need to understand this, just as they need to try to create and maintain the conditions that facilitate this reaction—which seems less and less frequent in today's society. Man has probably the greater need for understanding in the matter; woman the more decisive role in creating the conditions which facilitate the adequate human reaction.

Among major aspects to be noted here is how the instinct of respecting or protecting woman, as well as admiration for virginity and for motherhood, is fundamental to the development of true masculine character. Modern man is not different with regard to these needs; the problem is rather that he may not be aware of how deep his needs are here. The situation is more serious inasmuch as the dominant social and cultural atmosphere in no way encourages him to take stock of these needs or of his lack of awareness of them; rather the contrary. Another question is whether women appreciate their role in this.

Fred Uhlman, in his masterly short novel *Reunion*, notes the "ingenuous" way in which, in the 1930s, two sixteen-year-old boys exchange ideas on girls: "And we talked about girls. By the blasé standards of today's adolescents our attitude was incredibly naive. To us, girls were superior beings of extraordinary purity, to be approached only as the troubadours of old approached them, with chivalrous fervor and distant adoration."[11] Teenagers today, if they have had no other model to go by, can hardly realize what a loss is involved in the contemporary disenchantment with the other sex. Is the adolescent world richer for being told that it is stupid to want to be a hero to one's heroine or a heroine to one's hero; in other words that the romantic concept of the relation between the sexes is dead and gone forever?

Romance seems absent—sadly and perhaps cynically absent—in modern presentations of man-woman relations. Contemporary sexual culture is sensual but not romantic. Attraction is becoming bereft of human charm and reduced to simple animal magnetism. The girl seems no longer to dream of her Prince Charming, nor the boy of his Princess.

The prince wants to adore his princess; the princess wants to care for her prince. Adoration and caring are shown in different ways; but both mean loving *service* of another. It is urgent that service and the different ways (including the

---

10. op. cit., p. 318.
11. *Reunion*, London, 1994, p. 41.

complementary masculine-feminine ways) in which it is manifested be understood—be rediscovered—as an expression of love.

Nowadays we seldom hear mention of learning "to be a man" (and yet it is more important than ever to grasp the message underlying the expression). We hear even less, I think, of learning "to be a woman." Properly analyzed, there is probably a greater challenge in the "be a woman," addressed to a girl, than in the "be a man," directed to a boy. Yet many girls today might not be able to say what they are being challenged to.

The type of "sexual education" that has emerged in the last few decades is reduced to the limits of exclusively physical-biological instruction. From a truly human perspective, far from meriting to be termed sexual education, such instruction is rather in the nature of a "deformation" of the human understanding of sexuality, and ends up by producing desexualized people, with the consequent impoverishment of individual life and social living.

Virginia Woolf, one of the most innovative novelists of the twentieth century,[12] claimed equality of opportunity with men; yet did not want to use her own notable literary talents in a masculine way. She realized the danger of women letting themselves become more and more like men and, far from desiring to eradicate the differences between the two sexes, wanted education to strengthen these differences. She considered that the historical bottling up of woman in the home, had in fact given her a "creative force" which she should now be free to unleash in its fullness. "But this creative power differs greatly from the creative power of men. And one must conclude that it would be a thousand pities if it were hindered or wasted, for it was won by centuries of the most drastic discipline, and there is nothing to take its place. It would be a thousand pities if women wrote like men, or lived like men, or looked like men, for if two sexes are quite inadequate, considering the vastness and variety of the world, how should we manage with one only? Ought not education to bring out and fortify the differences rather than the similarities? For we have too much likeness as it is."[13]

One is born either male or female. One *is* a woman or a man, by birth. What then is meant by "learning to be" or "to become" a woman or a man? How does a girl become a woman? What model or ideal should she follow: that of becoming "more like a man," as Henry Higgins would have had it?[14] George Bernard Shaw, as adapted by Alan Jay Lerner, was perhaps giving a man's view of mistaken feminism, as he saw it. Much more interesting and important are contemporary efforts to identify where much of feminism may have gone wrong, and to propose a sounder version.

---

12. She was a founder of the avant-garde and atheistical "Bloomsbury Group." Her *A Room of One's Own* (1929) is a classic of the feminist movement. Recurrent fits of depression led to her suicide in 1941.
13. *A Room of One's Own*, p. 132.
14. *My Fair Lady*, Act Two, Scene 4.

The Sexual Identity of Woman

The last two decades have witnessed the emergence of a new feminism. Building from suppositions not just of equal dignity and opportunity for the sexes, but of complementarity between them, it emphasizes woman's distinctiveness and points of characterological difference with regard to man. Hence it holds that woman has her own way of achieving personal maturity and human fulfillment. This neo-feminism is in direct contrast to the hitherto dominant feminist trends, which tended rather to hold that "equality" is better proposed by insisting on similarities between the sexes.

According to this "complementarity" analysis, woman is characterized in general by a special "caring for others" attitude or ability. The feminists of the former predominant school see in this an implied subordination of woman to others (especially to men), something they find not acceptable; moreover, if at times they try to connect the two major human characterological models ("autonomy" and "relatedness"), there seems little doubt that for them personal "autonomy" remains the more important factor.[15]

If it is true that to "develop" or fulfill "self" in the masculine mode means making one's self independent *from* others, while the "self" in its feminine mode develops through relating *with* others ("separation" in contrast to "connection"), then women, in appraising and creating their own identity, need to use certain parameters that are peculiar to them.[16] Some psychologists also hold that masculine identity is forged in relationship to the world, while feminine identity is actuated in relationships of intimacy with some other person.[17] If this is so, then the idea of "human maturity" as applied to each sex (and despite many factors in common) is probably to be appraised according to different although equally valid definitive norms. The major questions of sexual identification and sexual education should perhaps work from the idea that a mature woman and a mature man relate differently to the world.[18] Man is used to considering himself superior (from his point of view); notwithstanding this, the intelligent woman has always been convinced of her superiority—from her point of view, and in the human areas that naturally fall under her dominion. At the end of *My Fair Lady*, Henry Higgins, despite himself and his self-sufficiency, has learned to love Eliza and to miss her. When she

---

15. Cf. S. Berlin and C. G. Johnson, "Women and Autonomy": *Psychiatry*: vol. 52 (1989) pp. 79–94.

16. Cf. C. Gilligan: op. cit., pp. 24–39.

17. Erik H. Erikson: *Identity: Youth and Crisis*, New York, 1968, quoted in Gilligan, op. cit. p. 13.

18. cf. Gilligan, op. cit. 167–168, where she gives the opinion of another psychologist, David McClelland. "McClelland reports that while men represent powerful activity as assertion and aggression, women in contrast portray acts of nurturance as acts of strength. Insofar as his research on power deals 'in particular with the characteristics of maturity,' he suggests that mature women and men may relate to the world in a different style."

returns, he hides his joy under a gruff "Eliza, where the devil are my slippers?" And she, who had earlier fallen for him and was then so resentful at his lack of appreciation for her, now understands—and realizes that he too understands and loves. She accepts a relationship where he will continue to "boss" her, but in constant surrender to the fact that he *needs* her. Now she knows herself needed—and loved. Each has surrendered, and each has won. The "war of the sexes," in its minor or major expressions in married life (where it also occurs), can only be settled when victory is understood in terms of surrender, and surrender is seen as victory. It is the loss-gain experience of two persons each of whom gives self and accepts the other in a love-union where the two become one.

In the past perhaps more than in the present, the scope of sexual identity also extended to the idea of "sinning against one's own sex": for example, yielding to cowardice, in the case of a man or, in the case of a woman, to immodesty or unfaithfulness.

"Women are extreme; they are better or worse than men."[19] It is not a view that is easy to appraise. Nevertheless, the impression traditionally existed, and probably still exists, that woman needs to act according to a higher level of goodness (or a superior degree of morality). Nor is it easy to appraise the reasons which Julián Marías suggests for this: woman "needs to be happy with herself, to feel all right when she meets herself."[20] If this is true, and if it is true that woman has traditionally maintained a greater goodness (or a higher degree of morality), it could also follow that the immoral woman is likely to be threatened by greater self-contempt than the immoral man.

In attempting to explicate sexual identity, it would be as absurd to ignore completely the distinctive procreative roles of man and woman, as to limit this identity to these different roles. While the cooperation of both man and woman is essential in bringing children into the world, it is clear that woman has by far the greater part to play.[21] This is a fact, whether we choose to regard

---

19. La Bruyère: *Les Caractères*.
20. *La Felicità Umana . . .* , op. cit., p. 333.
21. Blanca Castilla suggests that man and woman have distinctive modes of opening and giving self: man, outwards; woman, inwards—by receiving within herself. She illustrates this in the different roles each has in procreation: "The process of procreating, although undoubtedly neither the only nor the most important way of loving, presents this in a plastic manner. Man in giving himself, comes out of himself. Coming *out of* himself, he surrenders himself to the woman and stays *in her*. The woman gives herself, but without coming out of herself. She opens herself so as to receive *within herself*. Her way of giving self is different from, and at the same time complementary to, that of the man, because it receives the man and his love. Without the woman the man would have nowhere to go. Without the man the woman would not be able to receive and welcome. The woman welcomes the fruit of the contribution of both and keeps it until it germinates and develops. While the man is also a protagonist in the whole process, it is carried on outside him. Later on the woman continues to 'open,' giving birth to a being that possesses its own life.

it as an unfair disadvantage and burden, as a simple duty or mission, or as a unique privilege.[22] Within this last view a first principle of feminine role and identity could be formulated as: Woman's most distinguishing role is "to give life to humanity and to give humanity to life."[23]

Femininity

At the same time, "femininity," considered as a value that attracts man, has little or nothing to do (at least in its first and broadest expression) with potential motherhood. As a value, it is manifested and appreciated much less through its physical or corporeal expressions than by those which are spiritual or characterological. Our generation may indeed have lost a natural understanding of this. Half a century ago, "feminine grace" was a concept filled with great meaning, to both men and women, and an attribute that girls and women sought to develop and perfect. No doubt there was in this much that was conventional; and yet there was also much that was very human. Today "feminine grace" seems to be a notion that many women do not really understand. As for men, while they probably do not consciously think of the concept, they are still enormously impressed and attracted by the reality when they encounter it. The impact of Audrey Hepburn, back in the 1950s (in contrast, say, to that of Marilyn Monroe), could serve as an illustration.

Feminine grace has certainly something to do with behavior, insofar as outward bearing suggests interior quality. Yet it is not mainly identifiable (far from it) with mere physical beauty. It is truly a form of "sex appeal," although not in the sense in which the term tends to be used and understood today. Girls who are not physically appealing can make themselves attractive to the other sex by means of feminine grace. Grace in action and look is a revelation of interior character and self-possession: qualities in a woman that appeal to any man of worth.

Through the woman and with her the man is also in the child. The man is in the woman and in the child, but as it were from outside. The woman, however, is a place of abode: *home*. The man is in the woman. The child, even when it is outside its mother, in a certain way continues in her. The woman too is in the child, but fundamentally they are in her" (*Persona y Género*, Barcelona, 1997, p. 78).

22. "A primary truth of sexuality which our modern world seems to be losing sight of: if nothing makes a man respect a woman so much as motherhood, this is because motherhood takes her out of the category of an object to be possessed, and introduces her to that of what should be revered. Sex, divorced from its reference to parenthood, is robbed of its dimensions of mystery and sacredness; a fact which applies with special force to motherhood. Nowhere else does the mystery and glory of being a woman appear as in her capacity to be a mother. Few men are not stirred by this mystery. Yet today not many women seem to glory in it": C. Burke: *Covenanted Happiness: Love and Commitment in Marriage* (Scepter, 1999), p. 11.

23. P. Urbano: *El Hombre de Villa Tevere*, Madrid, 1995, p. 62.

Our modern age puts a premium on physical looks, and thereby penalizes the girl who is not particularly endowed in that way. Worse still, the current social ethic pressures her to be "sexy"; maybe she can manage to do so, but in that case she exercises on men a totally different attraction from that of being "feminine." The nineteenth century was a period when women were certainly less socially "liberated" than today; yet its literature frequently reflects situations where a woman who is feminine, even if plain, has a greater power of attraction than one who is beautiful but lacks "femininity." *Jane Eyre* (particularly in its film version) is a case in point.

It could be argued that a woman who does not acquire genuine feminine grace (which lies within the reach of all women) suffers a greater limitation in sexual identity than a man who is weak or lacks drive.

Gentleness, tenderness, feminine tact, modesty. . . . These are among the qualities that a man, consciously or unconsciously, looks for in a woman. If he marries and does not find them in his wife, disillusionment sets in; the marriage can begin to break down. Something similar can be said for the woman who does not find in her husband a certain strength: the capacity to face job or family difficulties with optimism and initiative, and particularly the strength of taking a full share in building the family and home.

If sexual awareness centers on physical relations, the potential of sex for giving happiness becomes greatly limited. Morality apart, sexuality is impoverished and becomes impoverishing if it is reduced to tactile sensation or absorbed in physical appetite, whereas it is enriching when it is a school where one learns to appreciate complementary qualities. A man can constantly find inspiration in what is feminine, a woman in what is masculine.[24] A woman who emphasizes the merely physical aspects of her sex easily bring out the worst in man. It is when she develops true femininity and shows it that she inspires him. The same applies vice-versa, but not so powerfully. So we understand how it is that woman has such humanizing and saving power— or the opposite.

In physical strength man is superior; the compensatory qualities woman possesses do not lie in the merely physical field, but in that humanizing power of hers. Emmanuel Mounier writes of woman's inexhaustible and consuming need to give herself, and suggests a double consequence: "from this comes her weakness, for she always feels the need for support; but also her strength, for she is the main enemy of selfishness in this world."[25]

Man has more muscle; woman more heart. But if woman sets out to develop her muscle and not her heart, she will be inferior. Traditionally she has been held to have a greater capacity for self-denial than man; and this was

---

24. Cf. Julián Marías: *La Felicità Umana*, op. cit., p. 326.
25. *Oeuvres*, II, 507.

thought to constitute one of the most attractive and authoritative aspects of her womanly character. "That feminine sweetness which has its most frequent foundation in self-denial."[26] This view of a nineteenth-century author will provoke varied reactions today. Many women would probably doubt whether they want to be considered "sweet." Many more, in tune with the individualism of the age, would look on "self-denial" as an alienating defect. This is certainly the case with most modern feminists: and the model of woman that their feminism offers is certainly free of such a trait. And yet, self-denial in its personalist sense (self-gift; self-forgetfulness) is a virtue and a sign of maturity.

It is particularly difficult for a woman to overcome the inner conviction that "self-assertion" is often merely selfishness: something which stands in opposition to the gift of self that is so necessary for the attainment of feminine identity. It is not easy for a woman to find her identity through self-assertion.

The masculinization of women is often the result of badly directed feminism. So many women, unable to recognize true and distinctive feminine values, push their imitation of men to the point where they find little difficulty in assimilating men's defects. Is it overly negative to suggest that we are heading toward a society dominated by (the worst of) masculine qualities? "When women, entering professional life in a masculinized world, adopt masculine 'defects', they become *hard and violent* (instead of strong), *independent and uprooted* (instead of sociable and linked to personal values), *technical* (instead of practical and concerned with what is concrete)."[27]

Those who seek fulfillment through self-assertion, and fail, lapse at times into self-pity. This may happen more often in the case of women, since self-pity is possibly a greater trap for them than for men. Then feminine courage and fortitude need to be particularly summoned up.[28]

Radical feminism thinks that women have been treated badly and without respect throughout most of history; and it seems undeniable that this has been so in very many areas. What is surprising is that these feminists fail to appreciate *how*—and *why*—so many cultures have regarded women with such profound respect and with limitless admiration. How is it that these feminists have let "motherliness" or "sisterliness" become almost unmentionable words—at least for them? All the positive content of these feminine qualities, as well as all

---

26. A. Trollope, *The Prime Minister*, Ch. 5.

27. B. Castilla, op. cit. p. 48. Later Castilla wonders if the process of "learning the worst from the other" may not in fact be two-directional. She suggests that in consequence of the unawareness of and the failure to search for proper sex identity, "we are witnessing the spread of a type of decadent society where each sex, instead of learning from the qualities of the other, imitates it also in its defects" (ibid. p. 52).

28. The increasing anger and frustration present in certain feminist writing could suggest an underlying self-pity; the more able the writing, the more easily the self-pity can spread from writer to reader.

the challenge involved in developing them, are being ignored or deliberately sent into oblivion; as is the inexpressible gratitude on the part of the many men who venerate the presence or the memory of their mother or sisters.

Unisexism

Unisexism, with its downplaying of the differences between the sexes, tends to reduce the attraction naturally existing between them to an exclusively corporeal dimension. This is an impoverishment and a grave loss. As we noted earlier, the "sex education" commonly given today in most countries is a misnomer. It is not sexual education at all, but rather "de-sexing" education. It educates young people not to grow into mature men and women, but to become unisex citizens. Given the special richness of the feminine character, the failure to understand and develop specifically sexual traits or qualities probably limits a woman's mature development more than it does a man's.

One almost unavoidable result of unisex education is the de-personalization of the body. The body becomes something extraneous to the person, something a person can use for enjoyment, as he might use a guitar or a hamburger or a Coke. And then every sort of sexual gratification becomes logical, absorbing— and unimportant. In sexual activity, one is not using or abusing one's own person or another's, but rather gratifying oneself (and perhaps the other) by using something extrinsic to both. History has more than once witnessed the destructive effects of this dualism.

Fashion

Fashion tends to be a powerful factor that can favor or hinder the achievement of a true sexual identity. It usually makes its impact more at the level of appearance than at that of reality, and where it holds too much sway it can place a premium on external or bodily elements that have little to do with genuine sexual identity. A healthy independence from fashion, besides revealing a greater maturity of character, makes it easier for a person to make up his or her own mind about what it means to be a real woman or a real man.

The custom of dueling may have served to steel some fainthearted men to be brave. Yet the bravery of the duelist was almost always more apparent than real, for it was so often driven by *the fear of being considered cowardly* by others, something that reveals an immature and dependent character with standards of personal conduct shaped by what one thinks others may think. Russian roulette marks an extreme of this psychological immaturity. Beneath the utter recklessness it shows lies an adolescent fear of the presumed opinion of one's peers—an opinion that a person of average psychological discernment would dismiss as not worth having.

Many psychologists consider that subservience to fashion is even more powerful among women in making or marring their growth in sexual identity. Certainly if a woman both lacks independence of character and has little insight into the sexual makeup of men, the force of fashion can lead her into choices that scarcely favor her development.

Few women are "leaders" of fashion; most tend to follow it. Individual variations are more likely to echo the dominant tone of current fashion than to depart from it. The desire to be more fashionable is often accompanied by the fear of being too different. And yet it is the woman who is clearly "different" that often appeals most to men, all the more so if the difference expresses a greater femininity. "Women can't be attractive if they do everything that men do. . . . Don't men like women to be different from themselves? They used to."[29]

When bodily exposure establishes itself as a norm of fashion, disapproval in the name of morality sounds outdated to many. Bypassing any moral issue, the student of anthropology may still suggest that girls or women who readily submit to this norm show little awareness of the varying ways in which they can provoke sexual interest on the part of men, and perhaps need to ask themselves if they really want to be the object of the type of interest they are tending to provoke.

Within a couple of decades, the women-in-slacks fashion has established itself almost universally in the Western world. While no one is likely to suggest that this fashion shows any moral lack in a woman, it may still reveal an insensitivity towards the importance of sexual identity, coupled with a lack of psychological discernment of masculine appreciation and compounded by a weak yielding to peer pressure.

Take the case of a mixed party where a woman dressed in a skirt realizes that all the other women present are wearing pants. Will the ensuing self-consciousness resolve itself into embarrassment, vis à vis the women present, at her own lack of "fashionableness?" Or will she be acute enough to realize that she is almost certainly the one of the whole group who appears as most feminine to the men present? Not all women with the psychological discernment to assess the situation so may be independent enough to act in consequence. Then the natural desire to be interesting and attractive to the other sex yields to an unliberated submission to the peer pressure of fashion.[30]

---

29. Willa Cather: *A Lost Lady*.
30. Trousers can be elegantly cut and elegantly worn by a woman; but can they be worn with feminine grace? While the answer may not be clear it is still worth pondering.

Complementarity and Integration

Unless the relational-psychological aspects of sex are seen as intrinsically linked to its bio-physical nature, little sense will be made of human sexuality. Sexual identity must be considered as something given (and therefore to be accepted), before it can also be proposed as a goal to be conquered. Few reactions are more alienating and self-destroying than to contest the objective and given aspects of one's human nature.[31]

Part of the mission of each sex is to "nourish" the other in his or her sexual identity, thus helping each individual person in the development of a fuller humanity. But today there is not enough masculinity around to nourish women, to bring out their femininity, and so to facilitate their human maturity. Nor is there enough femininity to inspire men and help them towards the development of proper masculine humanity. Our contemporary world is suffering from a lack, not an excess, of true sexuality; ours is in danger of becoming a sexually starved, and therefore a humanly underdeveloped, generation.

As we have already noted, a society is more human in nature, the more it is made up of well-developed representatives of the masculine and of the feminine modalities; and of their interrelationship. Hence, society itself, that is, the totality of the individuals who compose it, will appear more—or less— human to the extent to which an integration of feminine and masculine values is present and operational in it; or, contrariwise, absent. This is why the contemporary loss of sexual identity is a matter of deep concern.

"Today it is recognized that woman's ideal is to *bring feminine characteristics to their fullness in herself and in society*, thus increasing harmony with man and with the masculine features that seem to have conformed modern culture in an over-dominant way. It is a matter of *respecting the difference* between both types of characteristics, and *seeking the complementarity*, and not any opposition or incompatibility, between them."[32]

"Both sexes are entrusted with the same tasks: the family and the management of the world. According to this view, there are no tasks exclusively reserved to men or to women. In other words, the private and the public spheres correspond to both. Historically, however, it is a fact that woman has been restricted to the private sphere and man has exclusively appropriated the construction of the world, dedicating scarcely any time to the family. This supposes an imbalance which needs to be overcome. In short, one could summarize the situation by saying that culture needs to find a mother and the

---

31. *The Diagnostic and Statistical Manual of Mental Disorders* of the American Psychiatric Association lists "Gender Identity Disorder" among other psychic disorders. Given as a diagnostic criterion is, "persistent discomfort about one's assigned sex or a sense of inappropriateness in the gender role of that sex" (*DSM-IV* (1994), p. 533).
32. R. Yepes: op. cit., p. 271.

family a father."[33] There is much insight in this. It is indeed necessary that both men and women should be active in the private sphere[34] as well as the public. But insofar as it is true (and it is always a generalization) that woman's natural approach is more "person-concerned" and man's more "activity-concerned," women's greater participation in public life should serve in particular to counter and remedy the depersonalized character of so much of contemporary life. To achieve this, many women may well need to rediscover (and, if necessary, have the courage to follow) their natural tendency to professions that are person-oriented.

Unless one grasps the unique value of femininity and masculinity, it becomes impossible to understand the need for true sexual *formation*, which can help each one attain a personal human identity modeled diversely according to whether one is a man or a woman. To see opposition rather than complementarity between the sexes leads to a disruptive feminism or "masculinism" obsessed with a "struggle for power" which tends to reduce all aspects of men-women relationships to opposition. Modern Western society, at least, is witnessing an increasing division and a lack of reciprocal trust and respect between men and women, which constitute an alarming cultural phenomenon. That such a situation should develop between the two halves of humanity is a matter of utmost gravity.

An analysis of sexuality today might well conclude that there remain as many male and female bodies as before, and the reality of their mutual physical attraction; but fewer masculine and fewer feminine *persons*, capable of exercising a truly human and humanizing mutual spiritual sexual attraction and inspiration.

---

33. B. Castilla, op. cit., pp. 88-89.
34. In relation to the family in particular, it is not a lessening of woman's maternal vocation that is needed, but a revival of the paternal vocation of man.

10

MARRIAGE

Fulfillment Through Sexual Gift
and Union

We have considered the interactive role of sex in the development of the human person. Sexuality, in its natural design, has an inherent power to draw the person out of self and above self: rising out of self-centeredness through the inspiration of new values hitherto perhaps only vaguely experienced in a person's own self, and never in the totally singular way that they are now found in another.

That the sexual attraction can also present itself in an egocentric and grasping way, at times even violently, is undeniable; a fact which gives the impression that some original plan for man seems to have gone wrong, especially with regard to sexuality, since this now appears as a mysteriously problematic area of life where truly human appreciation and admiration often run the danger of being submerged in mere physical desire. So true is this that if sexual formation does not succeed in awakening and inculcating a more properly human awareness of sexuality—as an admirable complement to interpersonal existence—merely physical bodily attraction will tend to radically mold the attitude of each sex towards the other, with the result that an individual of the other sex is seen more and more as a body to be desired and enjoyed, and progressively less as a person to be admired and respected.

In married life itself, the conjugal act, which should be the most distinctive expression of married love and union, can in practice—unless there is extreme care and delicacy on the part of the spouses—become an act of one-sided ego-istic possession rather than a love-act of mutual donation. Then it separates rather than unites. However, these conflictive aspects of sexuality are marginal to our considerations here.

The sexes mutually attract and should inspire each other. For Julián Marías the hope of human happiness is largely polarized in the other sex: "Perhaps the greatest focal point of happiness lies in the relationship with the other sex."[1] Most people still consider that the fulfillment of this hope is to be found in marriage. Is this romantic expectation, which seems to have always accompa-nied humankind, a mere illusion? Would the human condition be better if we could get rid of this hope or see it die out?

The common and general attraction between the sexes tends to be-come particularized in one man and one woman being specially drawn to each other. They sense a unique complementarity which may gradually lead on to a desire for a personal union—not of a transient nature but on a permanent basis. This radical interpersonal heterosexual union has (with isolated exceptions) characterized human society and been the lot or aspira-tion of the immense majority of mankind from the start. It is this union which we call marriage.

Despite the degeneration or degradation (such as polygamy or marital tyranny and abuse) that marriage has been subject to from the earliest times, it is striking that the aspiration of finding a special companion of the opposite sex—a spouse—with whom to share life, with its ups and downs, has been a constant in human history, regarded by almost everyone as a major goal for personal fulfillment and a necessary condition for happiness.

In fact, it is hard to say which is more remarkable: that world literature has celebrated human love with many more romances based on its hopes and aspirations than comedies or tragedies based on its deceptions; or that each successive generation, despite accumulated experience, has failed to lapse into cynicism about marriage,[2] continuing to encourage their youngers to look for a good match, and celebrating one marriage after another as an event to be marked by particular family and social joy. We do not tend to congratulate the person who is making a speculation on the Stock Exchange; yet we rejoice with the one who is getting married.

It would be doubtful progress for civilization if the joy of a wedding lost its peculiar quality, and were regarded or listened to with skepticism.

---

1. op. cit. p. 318.
2. Which has not been altogether without expression, from Monostikoi's "Marriage is an evil that most men welcome," to Arthur Schopenhauer's "To marry is to halve your rights and double your duties."

Sexual Giving and Conjugal Giving

Human love between a man and a woman, if deep and genuine, develops into a desire for union in both body and soul. Ideally these two aspects of human sexual love—love of body and love of soul—should be in harmony; in practice they often are not. If the bodily aspect is allowed to assert itself too much, the spiritual growth of love may be arrested or even destroyed. The natural physical instinct of love is to possess the body; its natural spiritual instinct is to respect the person. Love, if it is true, quickly senses any danger latent in a touch, a caress, a kiss, and it refrains; or cuts the physical act short once it realizes that what perhaps began as a tender expression of self-giving affection is quickly turning into a thoughtless desire for egoistic self-satisfaction.

If an incipient sexual attraction is to lead on to and mature into a marriage with a real promise of happiness to it, the couple need to ensure that the sexual instinct (always present, and in itself inclined to mere bodily union) is *not allowed to get ahead of the conjugal decision* by which a man and a woman make a complete surrender of themselves, in body and in person, to one another, so forming a union capable of fulfilling all the human meaning of sexuality. To give one's body without giving one's self is to turn one's human sexuality into a lie; it is to deceive another, and/or to be deceived by him or her, regarding the very truth that human love demands. To give oneself temporarily, in and with one's body, is not really to give but just to lend. Nothing is actually *given*, unless it is given totally, forever. To "lend" oneself, in the sexual use of one's body, is to degrade the dignity of self, of body, and of sexuality.

So, in passing from friendship to love to engagement, along the way that leads to marriage, it is important to bear in mind that certain corporal signs have different meanings in themselves, and that even the same sign can be made to express different attitudes or emotions. A handshake can be cold or warm; an artificially warm handshake tends to introduce an element of insincerity into a relationship. A kiss between lovers is seldom less than warm; all the more reason for those who are not yet married, but love and want to respect each other, not to permit an expression of affection that in itself signifies a greater dedication than their present relationship warrants. If each is fully sincere with himself or herself and equally so with the other, it will be easier to recognize what is adequate—or not—to the situation in which they find themselves; what is a true expression of their love—as it presently exists not just in feeling but in actual personal commitment based on mutual respect—and what would be a false expression, because it seeks to take all it can get without being definitively prepared and pledged to give all it can give.

When two unmarried persons allow the physical attraction between them to find its outlet in sexual intercourse—in other words, in what of its nature is a conjugal act—then they are either "playing at being married" (a play-acting which has a disastrous effect on the real thing if it comes), or else they are simply reducing the sexual act itself—which is humanly meant to be a sign of total, enduring and unconditional self-surrender—to a mere (though perhaps more intense) expression of *what is as yet but a temporary and uncommitted affection*. In either case they have already ensured that their physical union with the person whom they may eventually marry can never be experienced as what it is designed to be: a unique act shared only with the spouse for whom one has kept oneself, and with whom now at last one experiences a union never before known.

The spousal love of an engaged person is meant to have a virginal consummation. Only those who make the effort to come to marriage as virgins can experience the truly singular joy of marital donation. This is the positive meaning and value of virginity: to keep oneself so as to give, to have something unique to give, in a gift that is given only to a spouse.

To give one's self, one must first possess that self. Self-possession is not shown by promptness of feelings or strength of desire, but by self-control. A feeling towards another person is seldom to be trusted—and the other person should seldom trust its expressions—unless it has been checked and confirmed by both mind and will.

The passage from friendship to attraction, from attraction to engagement, from engagement to wedding, is the gradual transition—which only in its last stage becomes definitive—from "you and I" to "us." The "we" of a married couple is something unique—a "we" that can almost be conjugated in the singular.

The conjugal instinct tends towards an interpersonal donation and acceptance of a quite singular nature: a privileged and committed choice of a "partner" in a common life enterprise where each spouse "belongs" in a unique way to the other. The donation is mutual, and implies mutual *acceptance*. Mutual gift *and* acceptance are of the essence of the interpersonal marital covenant.

Conjugal love calls for total gift and total acceptance. This two-way challenge of totality is posed by the very nature of such love. To know oneself loved is among the greatest needs of the human person. Yet no one can reasonably expect to have this need satisfied unless he or she is ready to love. The quality of love one is prepared to give in marriage is the most one can hope to receive.

T. S. Eliot echoes the aspirations and the possible deceptions: "Oh, I thought that I was giving him so much, and he to me! And the giving and the taking seemed so right: not in terms of calculation of what was good for the persons we had been, but for the new person, *us*. And then I found we were only strangers. And that there had been neither giving nor taking, but that we had merely made use of each other, each for his purpose. That's horrible. Can we only love something created by our own imagination? Are we all in fact unloving and unlovable? Then one *is* alone, and if one is alone, then lover and beloved are equally unreal; and the dreamer is no more real than his dreams."[3]

---

3. *The Cocktail Party*, Act 2.

Giving—or Just Lending—One's Self?

A gift, we have noted, is not a loan. Whoever only lends, never gives. He or she "gives" for a time, but holds on to that "temporary gift." It is mine; I can always claim it back.

Loans are a significant element in social life. The trust and the ease with which we can lend or borrow a book or a tennis racket are a good test of the quality of life in a community. But loans and gifts need to be distinguished. If they are not, misunderstandings or quarrels easily arise, as when someone thinks he is receiving as a gift what was intended as a mere loan or, conversely, someone claims that he only intended to lend what he had in fact originally given. Commercial loans and rentals, where we pay for the use of money or services or property, are also important for the more effective working of society. Their terms and the extent of the claims they give rise to are usually well spelled out in legal documents.

Marriage stands outside all of these social or commercial arrangements or categories. It is not a loan or a mortgage or a renting; nor is it a commercial purchase with a "satisfaction or your money back" guarantee. It is a gift, a mutual gift made between two persons, each one giving self as a spouse and accepting the spousal gift of the other.

Marriage is not "I lend myself to you," but "I give myself." Marriage is not "I accept you on trial . . ."; or "for thirty days . . ."; or "until you break down, or no longer give me satisfaction." It is "I *accept* you."

Anything less than such a gift is not marriage. I lend myself, or I accept you "for a time" or "on this or that condition," is not marriage. People who understand marriage in such a way, or who "marry" on such terms, do not really marry at all. They may say they "tried marriage" and it failed. What failed was not marriage, for that is what they never tried.

In a genuine marriage the couple can say, 'We belong to each other,' because there has been a true marital gift. In a trial marriage, the couple can say, at most, 'We are on loan to each other, and neither of us can tell if or when the other may take back what he or she has lent.'

Some people, perhaps realizing the bogusness of "trial marriage," prefer just to cohabit, for as long as they get on or it suits one of them. It is a poor sexual choice, involving a limited self-donation. It shows little appreciation of one's partner, or little ability to give oneself, or both together; in short, little love.

By married consent a union is established between man and woman that is interpersonal and conjugal. Despite their mutual "belonging," the personal identity—including the freedom and responsibility—of each partner is naturally inalienable. The interpersonal union of two persons does not result in one *person*, but in one unique married *relationship*.

Unilateral self-donation, without the corresponding gift of the other, would be a form of voluntary servitude. Apparent self-donation, not accompanied by a generous other-acceptance, could be a cloak for sentimental selfishness or, worse still, for a calculating instrumentalization of the other person.

As a decision to face the whole of life together, to form an interpersonal "alliance for life" that will end only with death, and to devote themselves together to perpetuating life and love in a family, marriage is certainly not an undertaking for individualists. The individualist's priority is to seek self, protect self, hold on to self. . . . Unless one wages war on that inclination, one will never be able to *give* self. The most one will manage is a self-serving, calculated and temporary loan of self; which is not enough for marriage.

For individualists, a real marital decision is always hard. If they do truly marry (already a big step in the process of becoming less individualist), they will still find it hard to make their marriage a success; hard, but not impossible. On the contrary, if the love that inspired their marital decision was genuine, the decision itself already marks a first major break with the self-centered and self-protective attitude of individualism. Married life remains a continuing challenge to open out from self and self-seeking to something far more worthwhile. If what inspires the challenge is love, the contest can be won.

All of us tend of course to be individualists; and we need to be personalists, discovering, understanding, responding to values in others. Nowhere is this personalist quest more vital than in marriage.

Self-donation is a step toward overcoming the selfishness that always tends to block and frustrate interpersonal relations; but it is a step that needs completion. In the case of marriage, self-donation is not real or effective if it does not involve the conjugal acceptance of the other. "Love can endure only as a unity in which a mature 'we' finds clear expression, and will not endure as a combination of two egoisms, at the base of the structure of which two 'I's are clearly visible. The structure of love is that of an interpersonal communion."[4]

Conjugal love is the highest form of human love, higher even than parental or filial love. Yet we should note something that might seem peculiar but is logical: being higher, it is harder to live. It is not often that parents abandon their children; children more often leave their parents. A breach of conjugal fidelity, even as an isolated episode, has always been regarded as a grave act of betrayal. A society which begins to consider such a betrayal as something to be expected and almost normal—as seems to be happening in some parts of the Western world today—shows a grave loss of its human values.

---

4. Wojtyla, K.: *Love and Responsibility*, p. 88.

The Three Essential Properties of Marriage

Three principal characteristics distinguish marriage from other relationships between persons and indicate its uniqueness as an interpersonal communion. These are: (1) the exclusiveness of the relationship (the man accepts the woman as his only wife, the woman accepts the man as her only husband); (2) the permanence—until death—of the union in which they commit themselves; and (3) the readiness to share with one another exclusively, their complementary procreative power.

Together these *values* place each of the spouses in a singular and privileged situation towards the other. The eminently personalist character of these values, and of the relationship they constitute and characterize, ought to be obvious (even if some people appear not to see it). No less evident is the correspondence of these values to the most fundamental aspirations of human love: "I am yours; you are mine; we belong to each other"; "Forever"; "in a union whose fruit will be a child who, being *ours*, will at the same time be the *incarnation* of our love." It is extremely important to grasp that these three main characteristics or values[5] of marriage—its unity, its openness to children, the unbreakable nature of the spouses' relationship—are of an essentially human and personalist nature.

It is also important to seek the *intrinsic* justification (which is much the same as saying the natural good) of these constitutional values of marriage; otherwise one could yield to the modern complex that considers them artificial impositions with which an outdated tradition wants to restrict personal freedom. The fact is that they represent fundamental modes by which spousal love between a man and a woman finds free and concrete expression. They are links which people in love desire to create. For them they are a source of joy. No sound anthropology can accept that people regard the prospect of remaining definitively bound to the one they love, as too risky for personal happiness. The risk, for whoever is really in love, is not to find oneself too bound to the loved one, but rather to see love dissolve or to lose it through a lack of commitment.

"But, if the other person leaves me in the end, I too want to be 'free.' . . ." Genuine love does not reason that way. Yes; it is true that one cannot absolutely answer for the love or fidelity of the *other person*; but some uncertainty in that sense always remains in human relations. The love that is deep and genuine does everything in *its* power—it binds itself to the maximum to the beloved one—and it trusts (it can do no more) that the unconditional sincerity of its own love will provoke and guarantee an equally committed love

---

5. In more traditional terms, the three augustinian "bona" or goods. cf. two canonical articles of mine: "Personalism and the *bona* of Marriage" (*Studia canonica* 27 (1993), 401–412); "Personalism and the traditional goods of marriage" (*Apollinaris*, 70 (1997) 305–314).

in the other person. For that very reason, a love which bases itself on calculation is not a genuine love, and will be met with an equally superficial love, limited in its scope and not likely to last. "The fear of making a permanent commitment can change the mutual love of husband and wife into two loves of self—two loves existing side by side until they end in separation."[6]

In love, just as in life itself when all is said and done, one risks everything. Whoever wants to eliminate risk at any cost, ends up disqualified for a life or a love with a truly human purpose or dimension.[7]

If you give yourself, you grow; and in that sense become more vulnerable to attack. If you don't give yourself, you remain smaller and perhaps easier to protect. But it is your egoism that you will be protecting, and you will find it attacked from every quarter.

The major in Hemingway's story "In Another Country," worships his wife. When she dies, he exclaims, "A man must not marry. If he is to lose everything, he should not place himself in a position to lose that." The cry is understandable as an anguished reaction in a moment of near-despair. But it is not true to the psychology of love or of values. What is really worth loving is really worth committing oneself to—even if we know we must lose it in the end. (Humanly speaking, after all, everything will eventually be lost.)

Suffering, perhaps a lot of it, is indeed likely to result from any intense interpersonal commitment which breaks down. But only weak personalities are held back by the fear of possible future emotional injury from committing themselves to a present love which deeply attracts them. Such a lack of commitment, when commitment is worthwhile, will leave their character marked with the sign and awareness of failure.

The unbreakable nature of the marriage bond constitutes a guarantee that a person is not going to be used and then tossed aside. Each spouse has a right to that guarantee coming from the other, and the duty to give it; and if one does not feel capable of this, then one has the duty not to lead the other person into deception.

Marriage, seen in this overall personalistic and human light, is essentially a mutual and generous self-gift directed to the good of the spouses and to offspring. The modern tendency to see marriage not as a commitment but as a way of self-satisfaction, as an adjunct to passing pleasure or as a mutual arrangement for temporary companionship, drains any sexual relationship of its immense potential for happiness and fulfillment. One trivializes marriage by regarding it as a "useful" facet to life which must always be open to

---

6. John Paul II, Homily in Washington, D.C. Oct. 7, 1979.

7. Prenuptial agreements determining how the property should be divided in case of divorce are not uncommon today. This is to commence with an undermined marriage, built on an initial lack of trust.

change—on a par with a house or a car or a hobby. To take the approach of "this relationship will last as long as its advantages outweigh its disadvantages for *me*," is to treat your partner as a prop for selfishness, as an object and not as a person, and less still as a spouse—whom one wants to make happy.

United, but Distinct

The challenge of marriage is to create a unity between two distinct persons, with the peculiarity that it is created around, and not at the cost of, the differences between them. If the attempt to create this unity fails, the ensuing separation will leave each of the two more immersed than before in individual loneliness. It is not by dint of changing the other that each will reach and integrate into marital unity, but rather by changing himself or herself and adapting to the other. Whoever really loves, wants to do whatever the beloved one wants. Marriage is not a process of reformation of your partner, but of adaptation of yourself. This way each spouse reforms himself or herself, and thus becomes a more open and loving person.

A couple must learn to love each other *with their defects*. Since we are all self-centered, there is more realism than cynicism in the idea that the marriage covenant is 'a mutual commitment between two egoists to help each other to form a bond stronger than their individual selfishnesses.' Nor should one appraise cynically the confidence that people in love have in the power of their love to overcome selfishness.

In the same way, conjugal love must build upon the real factors characterizing such an interpersonal situation. A main factor is certainly present in the *different* ways of being of each spouse. "I, as I am": "You, as you are": these are two existential facts to be integrated into the relationship. This integration is possible only if conjugal love is real—that is, committed and voluntary, rather than simply emotional—and if each spouse strives to make the voluntary aspect prevail, when necessary, over the emotional.

Conjugal love may or may not be something that one spouse *feels* for the other. It is not essential that such love be emotional; it is essential that it be voluntary. That is what makes it committed love. Genuine love is love of the will; it loves with facts, not just with words. "What I am" *is a fact* (not "what you think I am"); "love me as I am—with my defects; and I pledge to try to love you too in the same way." Conjugal love is always ready to learn.

It is not easy to accept a person as he or she really is. There will sometimes be rebellions and strong temptations to abandon the other spouse. But if one has taken one's commitment in earnest, it is a question of beginning again. "I will love you with your defects," is the norm for married people. To live up to this norm requires generosity and humility, expressed above all in readiness to begin and to begin again, and time and again.

In certain cases the defects of the other spouse may provoke pity for one-self, rather than impatience or rebellion towards him or her. This self-pity, which can especially beset some married women, is worse, for it induces a paralysing passivity that impedes the efforts necessary to save or reestablish a normal marital relationship.

David Copperfield's Aunt Betsey was a bossy but wise woman. She refused to intervene to correct or form the very childish girl her nephew had married: "You have chosen freely for yourself, and you have chosen a very pretty and a very affectionate creature. It will be your duty, and it will be your pleasure too, to estimate her (as you chose her) by the qualities she has, and not by the qualities she may not have. The latter you must develop in her, if you can. And if you cannot, you must just accustom yourself to do without them. . . . This is marriage."[8]

Two people can only remain united in marital love for as long as their continued efforts aim at building a true conjugal union endowed with the strength and unifying power that marriage in its natural design should have. Those who ignore this design are likely to find that whatever they build fails to draw each out of the dominant self-centeredness which is always the real obstacle to happiness; and that in the end it proves too fragile to last.

For a marriage to work. it is not enough that the couple learn to love each other. They have to love something else together. The more noble that some-thing else is, the more strength it will give to unite them and keep them in love and growing in love.

Humanity is at its highest when it gives itself. And self-giving is at its highest when it is creative. Through conjugal sexuality, man and woman find a creative form of self-giving.

The natural plan of marriage is that it should issue in children—the nor-mal fruit of the physical union of husband and wife and the sign of their mutual openness to the potential of their shared sexuality. There is no truly fulfilling marital relationship unless it is open to offspring. A marriage so closed "on itself" that it does not want children is bound to fail, for if the spouses are not open to children—to the fruit of their sexual union—they are not fully open to the richness of their love, nor are they unreservedly open to each other.

The fulfillment of unity between the spouses "represents both a task and a challenge. The task involves the spouses in living out their original covenant. *The children* born to them—and here is the challenge—*should* consolidate that covenant, enriching and deepening the conjugal commu-nion of the father and mother. When this does not occur, we need to ask if the selfishness which lurks even in the love of man and woman as a result of

---

8. Charles Dickens: *David Copperfield*, Ch. 44.

the human inclination to evil is not stronger than this love. Married couples need to be well aware of this."[9]

The physical union of the spouses, if fruitful, never gives rise to an identical fruit. Each child is a different fruit, a new incarnated expression, of the same conjugal love. Spouses re-express themselves in each child. In a large family, love has had many expressions.

Children do not pull parents apart; they unite them. So often the children are *the* factor that keeps parents united. It is lack of children—or, more concretely, the *refusal* of children—that can pull spouses apart. "We don't want another child," is the same as saying, "we don't want another bond of union. We have two already." Two may be too few to keep you united.

The Conjugal Act

Marriage originates in the spouses' consent, their decision to share life in its blending of joys and sorrows. Their union is consummated by sexual intercourse, which in marriage is called *the* conjugal act precisely because of the unique way in which it ratifies that original marital decision. Spouses understand the true significance of their conjugal intercourse when they see it not mainly as a pleasure-giving act but more fundamentally still as a life-sharing act.

Marital sexual union is of an essentially different nature from sexual intercourse between animals. In animals, intercourse is a response to instinct and is simply aimed at procreation; and this is why so many animals are naturally promiscuous. Human sexual intercourse has a deeper intrinsic meaning than just procreation. It is a privileged conjugal function, which for this very reason too loses its meaning when it is promiscuous.

To be humanly natural, the conjugal act must make sense, not containing in itself some inner contradiction. If it does not express what it seems to express, it lacks sincerity and is a form of deception. What then does the conjugal act express or correspond to? The desire to share in a pleasure-experience with the spouse one loves? As we have just suggested, the significance and importance of the conjugal act goes beyond this. Over and above the sharing of pleasure, it should express, in all truth and fullness, the special relationship of life and love that exists between the spouses, effecting a union of their persons which singularly signifies that love. It is only within marriage that sexual intercourse between a man and a woman can express and effect this. Outside marriage, it takes on an element of falsehood, it becomes a lie, because what it says, or seems to say, is not what is intended by those sharing in it.

9. John Paul II: *Letter to Families*, 1994, n. 7.

Hence, the unique naturalness of sexual intercourse within marriage derives not from its being a means for procreation, nor from the particular sense satisfaction that it procures; but from the fact that it is, in its integrity, the most qualified (though certainly not the only) expression of marital love.

By the conjugal act spouses most singularly show their mutual giving and acceptance of each other. It expresses the exclusive nature of their relation inasmuch as it is the one act they will under no circumstances share with any third person. It is conjugal precisely because it unites two persons in its *spousal* meaning.

Nothing can unite them more, provided they live the fullness of donation and acceptance implied—*signified*—in the act. It is all important to make an adequate analysis of what gives marital intercourse its singularity.[10] Conjugal intercourse is a unitive act, which is at the same time a generative act. These two aspects can be distinguished. The question then arises: can they be separated? And, even more to the point, can conjugal intercourse retain its nature as an act of union, if its reproductive orientation is canceled?

A proper examination of this question needs to take due account of the fact that while conjugal intercourse is evidently a procreative act in itself (an act naturally ordered to procreation), what qualifies it to be a special act of love-union is not so evident. That sexual intercourse is of itself an act ordered to procreation is obvious, since it consists in a meeting of the genital organs leading naturally to the fusion of the masculine and feminine procreative elements. That sexual intercourse is in itself an act of love is not however obvious, especially since it can clearly not be an act of love at all, e.g. as in the case of rape or prostitution.

What element can one distinguish in sexual intercourse between husband and wife which justifies its being regarded as such a distinctive expression of marital love and of the desire for marital union, that it is rightly called the "conjugal act?" Not the pleasure which normally accompanies the act; for then an act without pleasure (as can happen perhaps more especially in the case of the woman) would be lacking an element essential to making it an act of union.

No; it is not the pleasure which may or may not accompany it,[11] *it is what actually takes place* in the act that gives it its unique power to express married love and union. And what takes place is precisely the mutual sharing in reciprocal procreative power.

The singularity of marital sexual intercourse is that in it each spouse in effect says to the other, "with you and with you alone I am prepared to share this unique life-oriented power that a man and a woman possess and can actuate together."

---

10. Cf. C. Burke: *Covenanted Happiness* . . . , pp. 89–100.
11. Pleasure is not the meaning but, at most, a complement of the act.

Every conscious human act signifies something. Actions are the most expressive form of language. They may not speak louder than words, but they should speak no less sincerely. There is something wrong when a person intentionally drains an action of its natural significance, as in the case of the insincere handshake. Then one is engaging in deception of others, and perhaps also in self-deception.

This mutual deception is present in marital contraceptive intercourse. Even if accompanied by love, it involves too much inner contradiction to be an expression of conjugal union. For it always signifies the rejection—the refusal to accept—part of the other person. It drains sexuality of its most richly human and conjugal character—the sharing together of a life-giving experience—and reduces it to the level of a simple sharing of pleasure. Contraceptive intercourse is rather an anti-sexual than a sexual act; it is marked by the fear of sexuality in its full unitive meaning.

The contraceptive spouse rejects his or her partner's conjugal sexuality precisely in its most complementary and truly unitive aspect—its power to create and perpetuate through mutual love. The uniqueness of the marital act being reduced to pleasure, its spousal significance is gone. This spousal significance is in fact contradicted. The husband, in rejecting the wife's fertility, rejects her as spouse. By the act of intercourse, she is made no more unique to him than any other woman. Nor is he made more unique to her than any other man. Conjugal uniqueness is no longer present. Instead of husband and wife, the spouses are merely a man and a woman. Contraceptive sex makes husband and wife strangers to each other.

In contraception the spouses say to each other: "I do not trust this bodily expression of love. I do not trust my body; I do not trust your body." Contraceptive love is calculating by nature. And the love of a calculator, or two calculators together, can never be wholly trusted.

Taking is not giving, although in a mutual gift one takes as well as gives. Taking without giving is not love. Sexual intercourse is only a love-act if it shows and involves self-giving. One does not give oneself to things, one simply takes and uses them; hence, if one does not give oneself in marital intercourse, if one only takes, then one is *using* the other person and treating him or her as a *thing*.

Through contraception, the other spouse is reduced from the status of wife or husband to that of sexual playmate. A contraceptive marriage, where there is no real physical intercourse or union at all, is likely to die of sexual undernourishment, for the couple do not meet in true sexual intimacy or nourish each other sexually as true spouses.

A different (though no less destructive) contradiction marks the relationship of a couple who engage in premarital or extramarital sex. In this case the lie or contradiction—between what their act means in itself (total self-donation and other-acceptance) and their actual uncommitted or conditional relation-ship—is not necessarily the refusal of openness to the possible fruit of their union (that openness might be present), but the rejection of their mutual self-gift in its totality. An unlimited and mutual giving is not yet willed (one or both not being prepared for total giving), or is simply not possible (one or both being bound by an existing marital relationship).

Commercial sex, casual sex, promiscuous sex, temporary or trial sex, have in the end little to distinguish them. They all reduce the sexual gift of self to a insignificant thing, an incident to be bought or sold, a minor favor to be bestowed on acquaintances or temporary friends, or a satisfaction to be sought (eagerly, no doubt) and, once received, scarcely appreciated until perhaps its need is felt again.

An act by which an intense sensation is shared by two people can confer a passing uniqueness on their relationship. But if the act itself is marked by an inherent contradiction, as is also the case of extramarital sex, then rather than being united and fulfilled, the two are afterwards left emptier and farther apart because the sensation does not pertain, as it should by its nature, to an act signifying a deeper union—a union which they either do not want or cannot truly create. They are not yet bound, or they are held apart by other bonds from which they are not free.

Since sexual intercourse (the conjugal act) is the most singular expression of the married relationship, adultery has always been considered the maximum violation of the mutual matrimonial pact and, as we have noted, one of the worst betrayals of human trust.

Complementary Differences

Marriage is a *consortium*[12] or partnership between two people who are equal in dignity and rights, but not therefore identical in function and specific roles. On the contrary, marriage is of its essence a *complementary* relationship; and complementariness implies difference. Recalling what we noted in the last chapter—that man and woman are equal, but different—we can say that marriage represents a totally unique meeting between their complementary differences. The successful development of the marriage community depends on the harmony achieved between two persons who stand in the relation not of friends or associates, but of spouses—where sexual diversity is fundamental to the constitution of their relationship.

When the man fulfils his role as husband and father, and the woman hers as wife and mother, then married and family life can show that dynamic and

---

12. "Consortium" is often used in canonical literature to describe the married covenant or union. Its etymology [*con-sors* = "shared destiny"] makes it particularly fitting.

healthy complementarity that contributes to the growth and maturing of spouses and children. Heterosexuality being essential to marriage in its natural character, the most successful marriages tend to be those where the husband is most masculine and the wife most feminine.

People are often attracted to one another precisely because of differences of personality; and many successful marriages are in fact based on the vigorous effort of the parties to harmonize their divergent characters—a process usually marked by conflicts and reconciliations. Such marriages could easily have failed had the parties made less energetic efforts at achieving understanding; their free will was after all constantly in play. Reaching an agreement is always possible; but not without strong and persistent exercise of personal freedom on the part of each.

Jane Austen has one of her characters suggest that differences of makeup between the spouses tend to favor their happiness: "It is rather a favorable circumstance. I am perfectly persuaded that the tempers had better be unlike. . . . Some opposition here is friendly to matrimonial happiness."[13] While that is not always so, human experience does show that many highly successful marriages are between two people of quite contrasting characters.

Marriage being a communion of love, to posit democratic procedures for the management of conjugal life could be a serious mistake. Marriage does not offer a quorum for the operation of democracy. Three is the least number needed to be able to decide by majority vote. When there are just two, the only way of proceeding is consensus or disagreement. To learn to agree, or to reach a "con-sensus," is part of the conjugal process of learning to live and love together. Two wills each determined to have its way can never keep mere friendship going, let alone marriage. The characteristic affirmation of love— "I want whatever he or she wants"—is much more easily said than lived in practice. But people who give up trying to say it no longer have the approach that distinguishes friendship or marriage and have, at least at that moment, ceased to love.

---

13. *Mansfield Park*, Vol. III, Ch. 4.

11

THE FAMILY
Personal Growth in the Context
of Sexually Structured Love

The human person is born of love; is born for love; is born to learn to love. This, as the summary of what should be the human condition, holds the key to our true growth as human beings. If we need education, it is in love above all that we need to be educated. The natural context, the first school, of this love is the family.

Love, genuine love, cannot be given without a person's wanting to give it. Love, however, can be received without wanting it.[1] The newborn child does not have the will to love; it can not *give* a true love (it will—or should—learn to do so later). But it can *feel* love—or its absence. "The infant is more of a passive recipient of love than an active lover, and it cannot bear hostility."[2]

In his initial experiences of life, the child needs to feel himself the object of a true love which is constant and sure. This is the natural task of the family: parents, sisters, brothers. When this task is fulfilled within the child's first years, it is not difficult for him to begin to understand that the love which he has enjoyed was the result of an effort, and that he ought also make the effort to love.

---

1. It can happen too that, though a person is the object of a genuine love, he or she does not want to receive it, or wants *not* to receive it.
2. Karl Stern: *The Pillar of Fire, New York*, 1951, Ch. 30.

However, if one lacks in infancy this experience of feeling loved—freely and without calculation—the natural desire to be the object of love remains frustrated. This frustration creates and intensifies the sense of loneliness, favoring the development of self-pity that can easily become pathological, especially in adolescence,[3] and even turn in time into a radically antisocial attitude.

It is almost as if we have to be loved by others first before we can set out to love them. If a child has no experience of disinterested love, why should he or she move out of self-protection or try to rise above it? "If I am the only one who loves myself. . . ." It is different if the starting point is: "I know myself loved; now what attitude do *I* adopt towards others?"

In a normal family environment and in normal circumstances (in those that *should* be normal), a child develops under the influence of gratuitous love. Usually his emotional reaction is strongly positive, and this reaction facilitates the long process by which one becomes aware of and learns to fight one's natural self-centeredness, as this begins to make itself felt. What is necessary is not that the child be always satisfied with the love that he or she receives, but that this love be true and genuine.

True love knows when to be demanding. Its demands can provoke a crisis in a child who does not want to embark on the way of coming out of self and responding to values. Parents who are not demanding (justly and patiently) with their children do not give them genuine love; and the children will almost certainly remain selfish. It is easier for a child who has been the object of a generous and unconditional love to react positively (perhaps after some initial hesitation) to the corrections that genuine love does not omit, coming to understand that these corrections also come from love. This way the framework is created for the fundamental experience through which he learns that love is pleasant to receive but difficult to give; that having himself been beneficiary of the generous efforts of his parents (and of his older brothers or sisters), he also must now strive to love: in other words, to think of others, to listen, to be patient, to serve, to forgive . . .

The inevitable first clash of self with its surroundings is produced in the family, which provides the one setting where self-restraint can become more than a matter of acting under fear or coercion, being eventually lived as a willed response to what perhaps initially seemed frustrating, but in the end is sensed to come from love.

These lessons of love-donation-service create an environment which favors education in freedom. They teach in a practical way that precisely because we are free, we are—we ought to be—responsible. We have seen how freedom and responsibility must go together. It is because I am free that I am necessarily

---

3. Some experts hold that adolescent self-pity can be a main root of homosexual tendencies; cf. Gerard J. M. van den Aardweg, *On the Origins and Treatment of Homosexuality*, p. 196.

responsible: towards myself and towards others. Since my freedom enables me to choose, it is I who am responsible for my choices and for their consequences. Wanting to have freedom of choice without assuming the corresponding responsibility is characteristic of a person who is immature or selfish or unintelligent; or perhaps all three at the same time.

Each one is free; with a freedom however that needs to be developed and consolidated, and that can even be lost. The free actions of each one also influence the life of others, making us responsible for at least part of their life, just as they are for ours.

A person is never so unique, or in a better position to appreciate his or her uniqueness, as in the family. "The family is the place in which each human being appears in his or her own uniqueness and unrepeatability. It is—it should be—the kind of special system of forces in which each person is important and needed because that person exists and because of *who* that person is"[4]—i.e. a unique son or daughter of one's parents, a unique brother or sister of one's siblings.

Along with the sense of personal uniqueness, the family offers a specially favorable framework for growth in interpersonality. The education in interpersonal relations proper to the family can be seen under two particularly important perspectives: social and sexual.

Interpersonal Relations in the Family: Education for Social Life

The family is a strongly anti-individualist factor. Sharing is its tonic; solidarity its style. Therefore any social rebirth—that seeks to base its cohesion on something more powerful and positive than individualism—has to begin in the family.

Undoubtedly one cannot correctly understand this formative role of the family without rising above the mindset which regards the general goal of education as that of forming *independent* persons, that is, persons who are self-sufficient, separate and "not-connected." This mindset has tended to be dominant in modern educational psychology, but many experts are now beginning to cast doubt on its validity. "If society favors the separate mode over the connected one, it is a problem we all must address. In this context our profession may have a special responsibility—to reexamine the concept of separation-individuation as the major goal of adolescence [the goal of building of a non-dependent personality]. We need not consider the complete differentiation of the self from the family to be the ideal goal. Individuals who retain

---

4. K. Wojtyla: "The Family as a Community of Persons": *Person & Community*, op. cit. p. 316.

strong ties and an orientation to relationships may be more, rather than less, mature than those who separate more completely from the family."[5]

a) In the first place, the family is a school of *understanding of authority*.

      The family is a school where authority can be seen as the difficult exercise of duty, rather than the arbitrary wielding of power, and where the concern to exercise that duty in a just fashion can prove itself. It is the (by no means easy) task of parents to exercise authority so. One should add that parents who take the time to reflect need not even find it such a difficult task. In a recent televised discussion between parents on what to permit or to deny teenage children, one father recalled an approach he found effective with his fourteen-year-old daughter. Challenged with an over-urgent request, "Daddy, is it all right if I go out with Tom and his friends tonight?," the father replied: "If you want an answer right away, then the answer is No. Now, if you are prepared to sit down for ten minutes, tell me about the plan, and discuss it, then it is just possible the answer may be Yes." He was teaching his daughter that decisions, including permissions, require thought.

      If a child does not learn in the family that authority can be respected as a power coming from and appealing to love, he or she is not likely to see it later on as anything other than a force to be evaded or resisted. A society where authority is so conceived—as physical or coercive power, no more—rests on a shaky foundation.

b) The family is also a school of *fraternity*; of participation, generosity, co-responsibility, disinterested and gratuitous service, within a community.

      Wise parents will find ways of involving their children, or at least the older ones, in decision-making about family affairs. This prepares them for a more participative approach to social living later on.

      The full importance of the sibling relationship emerges only if we consider its social as well as its personal dimension. What is at stake here is strikingly brought out if we think about the predictable consequences of a situation in which a brother-sister relationship is not possible—as happens more and more today in one-child families, where there is *no sibling to relate to*. In the past such situations tended to be an exception; today they are becoming the rule in many parts of the West.

---

5. McDermott, Robillard, Char, et al.: "Reexamining the Concept of Adolescence" (*American Journal of Psychiatry*, vol. 140 (1983), p. 1321). This study notes how Carol Gilligan "compared the 'connected person', who emphasizes physical and emotional care for others and a marked concern for the survival of relationships, with the 'separate person' who considers relationships in terms of reciprocity between separate individuals and who operates by a system of rules that has been worked out without consideration of the other person's feelings. Gilligan studied girls and found that they view themselves predominantly as 'connected.' . . ." (ib.).

A child with several siblings, even if he or she has more than the normal dose of human self-centeredness, will find it hard to resist the solvent force of family life on individualism. The same child without any sibling will lack the natural environment to purify his or her individualistic tendencies. Even if the parents make every effort to be firm and just, the handicaps of the one-child situation usually can only be very partially ameliorated. If the child has careless and indulgent parents, the adult he develops into will labor under the deep disadvantage of a spoiled environmental history.

Perhaps we have not yet weighed (though we are beginning to experience) the social effects on the only child of this lack of natural domestic induction into the experience of fraternity. The danger is increasing that the very term "fraternity" will be left with a purely ideological content, existentially incomprehensible to most of the people who, as children and adolescents, never knew what it means to have a brother or sister.[6] From where will they draw the inspiration or example that can teach them what is involved in treating others fraternally, within the general framework of society?

The family is a school of human-social life in which there is constant opportunity to grow in understanding, tolerance, service, forgiveness. It is a school where one learns that there are reasons for sharing and helping others to share. "The experiences of inequality and interconnection inherent in the relation of parent and child, give rise to the ethics of justice and care, the ideals of human relationship—the vision that self and other will be treated as of equal worth, that despite differences in power, things will be fair; the vision that everyone will be responded to and included, that no one will be left alone or hurt."[7]

Napoleon's mother, Letizia Ramolino Bonaparte, also called "Madame Mère," had eight children. On one occasion (after her second son was already Emperor of France) she was asked which of her children was her favorite. Her answer (given with motherly sense, we can presume, because political tact was of little concern to her) was immediate: "Whichever is in greatest need." Few people besides mothers are capable of this scale of preferences. And yet does a society not show radical dehumanization if it contains people in great need (perhaps also through their own fault) who have nowhere to turn where they can feel themselves accepted and loved?

Most communities have limits of tolerance. As a result, the person who violates them may be declared or become a social outcast, forfeiting membership

---

6. Cf. A. Sicari: "The family: A place of fraternity": *Communio 20* (1993), p. 303.
7. C. Gilligan, *In a Different Voice*, op. cit., pp. 62–63.

in society and losing their social privileges or rights. The family, constituted with deeper human roots, should be able to take more strain. The human condition of being a spouse, a parent, a child, a brother or sister, is put to its ultimate proof when someone has lost every claim except the one of belonging to a family; and that ultimate claim prevails over every injustice or selfishness. The Prodigal Son of the Gospel is the great illustration of how humanity at its most selfish can still be welcomed where family spirit is strong. Dostoyevsky philosophizes the point in Marmeladov, a drunkard and wastrel who neglects his family and is ill-treated by his wife, yet keeps coming back to them: "I mean, every man must have at least one place where people take pity on him."[8] Robert Frost echoes the idea: "Home is the place where, when you have to go there, they have to take you in. . . . Something you somehow haven't to deserve."[9]

The family appears as the natural home not only of children but also of the aged. Just as the very young need special care, so do the very old. The increasing weakness attendant on old age is a call on the care-giving capacities of grown-up sons and daughters. Christopher Lasch writes: "The modern problem of old age . . . originates less in physical decline than in society's intolerance of old people, its refusal to make use of their accumulated wisdom, and its attempt to relegate them to the margins of social existence."[10] Lasch puts it impersonally. It is not just "society" but particular families (at least in the West) that are increasingly unwilling to care for their aging parents or grandparents, and exclude them from their natural home. Contemporary psychological studies of the family testify to the individualistic or selfist philosophy of "self-related well-being" that would justify this exclusion, in virtue of the right to be free from excessive "stress"; and even view with dismay current demographic trends which indicate "that *the risk of becoming a care-giver* at some time over the life course is likely to increase."[11]

Families with "Personality"

The family is the first and most natural school of values (and response to values) in which young people should grow and develop. It is of course not the only school. Over recent centuries, parents have tended to forget that they are the first educators, delegating or abandoning their responsibilities more and more to outside educational establishments (at primary, secondary or university level); often without much awareness of the standards operative there.

---

8. *Crime and Punishment*, Part 1, II.
9. "The Death of the Hired Man."
10. *The Culture of Narcissism . . .* , p. 207.
11. Cf. Nadie F. Marks: "Does it Hurt to Care?" *Journal of Marriage and the Family*, vol. 60 (1998), p. 951 [emphasis added].

This whole situation has been significantly modified over the last few decades. The outlook of young people nowadays is molded more by the atmosphere of the recreational or sports centers they frequent than by what they hear in the classroom. But the real "school" which dominates the making or unmaking of social and personal values is constituted by the media; it is a school, moreover, that is potently present within the home itself. The progression from films to television to videos and now to the internet, means that social values can no longer be considered an *outside* factor with regard to family life. Through the media, the social culture makes its way daily into practically all Western homes, profoundly influencing the values (if any) that are being inculcated there.

It is not our concern here to offer any judgment on the predominant values that are picked up in an atmosphere dominated by TV and the Net. Some parents who are not satisfied with them may try to regulate their entry to the home. It will not be an easy task, and could provoke a negative reaction in young people if they feel they are being controlled or subjected to censorship, in comparison with their friends. Other parents may attempt an alternative that is not any easier but, if they can manage it, is far more effective. It has to do with the creation of what can best be termed a strong "family personality."

One way of defining a strong personality in an individual is to say that the person influences (for good or for bad) more than he is influenced. A family with a "weak personality" is going to be influenced, and perhaps dominated, by the values or anti-values surrounding it. Parents are not doing their job unless they are trying to endow their family with a strong and distinctive personality. That means creating a forceful, interesting, and attractive family atmosphere or family life, expressed in active care, friendship, loyalty, and solidarity, and *also* in *activities* that both develop talents in the children and, above all, interest them. What sort of activities? It would probably be a mistake to over-specify them. Activities will have to be looked for, tried out, improved, discarded and replaced by others, and carried out either simply by the family members themselves or, more reasonably and ideally, in conjunction with other like-minded families. Amateur theatrics, musical groups, sports mini-competitions, chess championships, debates . . . are a few of the activities that come to mind. Inventiveness will discover many others, and family personality will be all the richer for having its inventiveness tested.

Parents can know they have come up with a winner—for the time being—when their house begins to attract other children, who come because "at X's house you always have a good time." This sort of endeavor is helped by having a large family. It is equally helped by having a large number of like-minded friends. But what is most decisive in the end is the initiative and dedication of the parents themselves.

Interpersonal Family Relations and Sexual Education

a) *brothers-sisters.*

- The fact that the brother-sister relationship is the only inter-sexual association virtually never upset by unregulated instinct, turns the family into in an irreplaceable school of sexual education. It should be in the family first of all that girls and boys, helped by their parents, learn to discern, understand and appraise how the masculine way and the feminine way of being human are different, and how much respect they merit.

The point can be verified when a boy who has never had sisters sets out on his first attempt to relate more particularly with a girl. He is likely to experience a series of awkward inadequacies which, without special good will on both sides, will be difficult to compensate for.

As we said earlier, it is not by *imitating* the opposite sex but by *learning* from it that a person grows in the sexual identity which is so important for maturity in life. This learning process is more easily carried out in the family setting, between siblings, than anywhere else.

As sisters and brothers come to understand, learn from, and depend on each other (to the accompaniment no doubt of quarrels and reconciliations), they are preparing themselves for marriage and for the family that each will probably establish in the future.

b) *parents-children.* And more concretely:

- *father-daughter*; at the start perhaps a less close relationship than that between mother and daughter. With time, as a daughter grows, her father will tend to look to her and not only to his wife for tenderness. Fundamentally this is a tribute to his fatherly masculinity and to her daughterly femininity.

- *mother-son.* It is normal for a son to have a special reverence for his mother; and, as he grows, also to assume a protecting attitude towards her. Is this an insult to her weakness or a tribute to her femininity? It is in any case a sign of masculine development in the son.[12]

---

12. These brief points could be expanded in many directions. Consider, for instance, the following perceptive passage: "What a boy gets from experiencing the dependable love of a father is a deep personal experience of masculinity that is pro-social, pro-woman, pro-child, and not at odds with love. Without this personal experience of maleness, a boy (who like all human beings is deeply driven to seek some meaning for masculinity) is vulnerable to a variety of peer and market-driven alternative definitions of masculinity, often grounded in real gender differences in aggression, physical strength, and sexual proclivities. . . . Similarly, a girl raised without a father does not come to adolescence with the same deep experience of what male love feels like when it is truly protective, not driven primarily by a desire for sexual gratification" (Maggie Gallagher: "(How) Does Marriage Protect Child Well-Being?" in *The Meaning of Marriage*, Spence, 2006, pp. 210–211).

Paternity/maternity is where husband and wife share most and are most united. Motherhood, which is so threatened today, can recover its dignity only if the dignity—and responsibility—of fatherhood is also restored. Only man can be a father, only woman can be a mother. There is a lack of realization today of the privileged uniqueness of each of these complementary anthropological facts.

A family lacking in either father or mother is an anomaly. It happens accidentally at times, for instance because of the death of one of the parents. *Wanting* to build a one-parent family is folly, and a grave injustice besides. A form of modern irresponsibility is that of the unmarried woman who wants to have a child—as a means to "fulfill" or "enrich" herself. Perhaps she does not realize it, but what she wants to acquire is a handicapped child, deprived from the beginning of the presence of a father.

In some way such a woman recalls the granddaughter of Susanna Tamaro's *Va' dove ti porta il cuore*, who goes to buy a dog and, by preference, purchases a handicapped one. But in that instance the girl was moved by her heart; and Buck, the dog, already existed in his handicapped state. In the case we are considering, it is the woman who imposes the handicap—on a child (and not on a dog). If she is acting from the heart, it is a selfish and superficial heart that emerges. "But I will be both father and mother to him; he will find enough in my love." Will he? Perhaps what is present here is not just considerable irresponsibility, but a considerable amount of conceit as well.

Children need not one parent, but two; not just a mother's love, but a father's as well; not one who will do the work of two, but two who will together do the work of two. Children need that, and are entitled to it. A major motivation to keep a marriage together, when it is threatened with discord between husband and wife, is their realization that the love they together can give to their children is unique, and that the children have a fundamental human right to their parents' effort to maintain and pass on that love.

ооо

At the start of this chapter we said that the human person is born of love, and is meant to learn to love, in a family setting. And yet, there is a growing number of persons today who have reason to feel that they were not born of love; and who perhaps have never experienced anything that could be called a family. Nevertheless, they too have a family and a family life, if only they and we could see it: a matter that depends on where our anthropological perspectives end. This consideration leads us to the next chapters where we speculate on what there may be, in and for man, "beyond" anthropology.

PART 3

TRANSCENDENCE

✷ ✷

12

BEYOND ANTHROPOLOGY?

According to the anthropological view we have proposed, the pattern and condition of personal growth could be summed up as follows: openness to values, discernment of values, response to values, assimilation of values.

In this "anthropology of values," man cannot realize or fulfill himself from within. To grow inside, he must open outwards. The quality of the values he finds, as well as the nature of his response to their worth—this is what determines his fulfillment. Thus a panorama of unlimited personal growth extends before each person. Only if one has exhausted all the values to be found in life, or if one has lost one's own capacity to appreciate them and to respond to and assimilate them, does one cease to grow.

We must then maintain an open outlook, without letting ourselves be trapped and dwarfed in a closed view of life. Yet an anthropology of "openness," if seriously proposed, finds difficulty in determining its own limits. It runs into a number of fundamental questions to which it may not be able to offer any sure answer within its own terms of reference.

If man cannot achieve fulfillment without being open and looking beyond himself, how open must he be? How far does the openness of man's view extend? What in other words are man's ultimate horizons? If a satisfactory answer cannot be given to these questions, in such a way that they can be considered closed, then anthropology itself must leave them open. If man's own development depends on his being open to higher values, the progress of anthropological science also calls for a particular openness. A closed view of man is always limiting. Anthropology's last word about some of the basic questions raised by man may honestly have to be, "we do not know." Each one may then feel called to investigate whether the answers that anthropology cannot provide may possibly be found in some other area of investigation.

Is Death the End?

Man's physical life follows a curving path—upwards towards a moment of maximum development, and then gradually downwards in the decline of later years. The development of man's psychic or spiritual life is not necessarily the same. Many people seem to conserve and increase the vigor of their spiritual faculties right into older age. In theory, since the values and riches of life are inexhaustible, there seems no reason why a person should ever cease to grow spiritually.

However, a very blunt fact seems to put an end to all growth and development: the fact of death. No one escapes death. Death is the one absolutely certain anthropological experience that lies before each of us. Is it the final experience? Is death the last thing that happens to the person? In other words, is death really the end of each individual's life?[1]

Certainly, just as birth is not a sufficient explanation of the beginning or origin of each one's life, so death is not a sufficient guarantee of its end. Man's inquiry reaches naturally farther in both directions. What answers can he come up with?

If death is the final destination for each person, then we are all heading for nothing. All development then leads to final extinction. The values one has gradually found and by which one has been nourished—nature, beauty, art, music, scientific discovery, loyalty, friendship, love—remain for others; but as for me, I disappear definitively from the scene. And if the world itself, and not just each individual person, is to come to an end, then everything ends in nothing. Values are little more than passing illusions. Or, more properly, it is we who in our passing are little more than illusions, and Macbeth's words no longer seem exaggerated; life is no more than "a walking shadow, a tale told by an idiot, full of sound and fury, signifying nothing."[2] Nor could one dispute Sartre's conclusion to *Being and Nothingness*, that "man is a useless passion."[3]

---

1. "The first absolutely certain truth of our life, beyond the fact that we exist, is the inevitability of our death. Given this unsettling fact, the search for a full answer [to the meaning of life] is inescapable. Each of us has both the desire and the duty to know the truth of our own destiny. We want to know if death will be the definitive end of our life or if there is something beyond—if it is possible to hope for an after-life or not": John Paul II, *Fides et Ratio*, no. 26.

2. Shakespeare, *Macbeth*, Act V, Sc. V.

3. *Being and Nothingness*, p. 784.

No serious study of man can ignore the fact that he dies. Psychologists insist on need to face this fact, and even urge its tranquil acceptance—learning to "be at home" with death—as an integral part of self-acceptance and a means of avoiding alienation. "We must be at home with fear of death and with the enigma of death if we are not to become alienated from our nature and destiny and lose basic contact with who we are and what we are about. Acceptance of personal mortality is one of the foremost entryways to self-knowledge. Human maturity brings along with it a recognition of limit."[4]

This is not convincing. The person who refuses ever to advert to his mortality is certainly not mature. But the "recognition of the limit" shown by acceptance of the inevitability of death, does not make one more "at home" with the *enigma* represented by death. Whoever cannot find an explanation to this enigma always senses himself alienated from his nature and from "what he is about." All of us, at least in our youth, sense that we "are about" something really great, that our nature and destiny aspire to the infinite (to what knows no limit). If maturity and true self-knowledge ultimately mean realizing how groundless all these aspirations are, the effort to be genuinely "at home" with death—regarded as the absolute limit and real end—surely involves a self-acceptance that, in its radical frustration of what is most natural to a person, becomes indistinguishable from the deepest self-alienation.

Only a superficial anthropology, therefore, can avoid the topic of death. The fact that each one will die is as certain in anthropology as the fact of a common humanity. Yet the peculiar difficulty of this anthropological fact—that no one escapes death—is also evident. For all of us who think or write about death, it remains a "something that happens to other people," but a *future* fact for me. I can observe the deaths of others, and am at times obliged to do so. I can verify the end of one life after another—life in the basic mode as I myself currently experience it. But whether this gives way to a different mode or a different level of life, I cannot say. And the people who perhaps could say—those who have already died—do not speak to me. Or, if they seem to do so, am I to count on such testimony which so many current scientific views would disqualify?

Insofar as the study of man is not just of theoretical interest but of practical concern for the individual, death is the most important question of all to clarify: a question that anthropology can and should ask, yet apparently cannot answer.

The person who *is*, may choose to be unconcerned about his origins or about when he *never was*. He can hardly be equally indifferent about whether or not he *will be*. To learn from the past, which cannot be changed, so as to

---

4. Herman Feifel: "Psychology and Death. Meaningful Rediscovery": *American Psychologist*, vol. 45 (1990), p. 541.

shape the future, which still lies in our hands, is an often enunciated rule of life. How far does my future extend? Just to death? Or beyond? Just during time as I know it? Or continuing in an unknown measure of duration that some call eternity?

Death is too tremendous a prospect for anyone to be calmly "at home" with it, or to draw much therapeutic reassurance from being told there is nothing beyond it. When Harry Potter is astonished that someone can casually accept death, Professor Dumbledore dismisses his amazement with a simple "after all, to the well-organised mind, death is the next great adventure."[5] Dumbledore is, of course, not really explaining death—just leaving it as an unexplored venture. But in his philosophy it remains a personal adventure to be undertaken, and a great one, not the end of one's story. In this view, to look on death with indifference is a sign of a poorly organized mind.

Each human person finds his life fixed between two points, birth and death. We can more or less know how the world was without us; we do not know how we may be without the world. The certainty of death favors the human sense of "the beyond," opens up the "great unknown," and leaves before us, unanswered, the vital questions of whether there is *anything* in that "beyond"; and if there is, *what* it is; and, even more importantly for each, whether I will have some share or be present in that beyond, and what kind of share or presence that may consist in.

There may indeed be nothing beyond this visible limited life we are living. Nevertheless the very curiosity of our human mind cannot help wondering if there is not something *more* to life than what meets our present eye, at the same time as the hankering after values tends to make us hope that there *will* be more, and also that it will be *better* than what we have so far experienced.

The "idealism of youth" may be just a cliché of the past; or a perennial characteristic of adolescence—which is simply being more quickly lost today through contact with a real world apparently bereft of genuine ideals. It may be optimism to hold that most young persons, at some moment in their early years, still cherish high ideals; it may be more realistic to hold that nowadays few do. Whatever the proportion, it does seem that not many adults who recall having had great ideals as adolescents would now say that the ideals are still there in all their greatness. Is this inevitable? Must people always "lose their fairylands?"[6] Is it possible that such idealistic dreams correspond to nothing? Are they a mere illusion? When a young person dreams that he or she is meant for something great, is that an insight into the deeper nature of his or her existence, or just a high point of auto-suggestion or self-deception—as it must be if death truly draws the final curtain?

5. J. K. Rowling, *Harry Potter and the Philosopher's Stone*, p. 215.
6. Cf. H. Belloc: *Cautionary Verses*, Preface.

If death is absolutely the last act for each of us, then indeed each person ends in solitude; and all the love and fellowship of life are little more than passing fantasies of happiness. Another passage of Hemingway's comes to mind, more poignant still in the light of his own death. "There is no lonelier man in death, except the suicide, than that man who has lived many years with a good wife and then outlived her. If two people love each other there can be no happy end to it."[7] If two people love each other and nothing else, then it is hard to see what happy end either of them can have. But such a constricted love is at best the union of two egoisms each of which feels that all he or she needs is satisfied in the other. A love of that kind is bound to end in disillusionment; certainly at death, and indeed perhaps long before. As we saw in chapter two, genuine love for another tends to draw a person out of self-centeredness. It opens the horizons of one's life to a new awareness of goodness and values. We could follow out Viktor Frankl's idea that "love does not make one blind but seeing" by saying that such love turns a person into a "seer," one with a prophetic vision that sees values even beyond death. A false prophecy? Who can tell? What does each one say to oneself inside? What does he or she hope for?

Self-actualization or Self-transcendence?

Can a clue to the problems posed by death be found in that remarkable fact about man that we have noted—his tendency and apparent need to go beyond and *transcend* himself? Transcendence in our context means man's desire[8] to surpass himself and the limitations of his own nature. "The real aim of human existence cannot be found in what is called self-actualization. Human existence is essentially self-transcendence rather than self-actualization . . . ; self-actualization cannot be attained if it is made an end in itself, but only as a side effect of self-transcendence."[9]

This is the paradoxical position of man. If he is to become himself, he must become more than himself; and even in achieving what might seem to be his maximum, he wants to become still more. Does this anthropological analysis, which appears to be well grounded, mean that man is constitutionally designed for ultimate frustration in the sense that no human life can ever fulfill all its potential?

---

7. *Death in the Afternoon*, ch. 11.

8. Which either corresponds to a capacity, or just reflects an illusion. Imagination, dreams, hopes, ambitions. . . . There is so much inside each one of us that stretches beyond the surrounding reality and perhaps beyond the realm of what seems possible. Reality is limited; human ambition is not. In the last analysis, one of two conclusions must be drawn from this restless inner world of ours: either human dreams are just illusions and vain hopes, or else man points to something more than man.

9. V. Frankl, *Man's Search for Meaning*, pp. 112–113.

Either one leaves this question without any real investigation, or else one opens anthropological inquiry itself to the possibility not only that man *wants* to transcend himself, but that *something actually exists which transcends man*— some reality or way of being, some mode of life, that is more than human but to which man's life is also naturally directed. If that is so, then something or someone "more than man" offers the key to what man is, possibly also to why he is, and perhaps to what he can in fact become.

But, it may be objected, does anthropology not overstep itself if it extends its inquiry to issues that go "beyond" man—life after death, trans-human or transnatural life? Surely what transcends man does not fall within anthropology? The objection loses its apparent force in the face precisely of the anthropological fact that *the desire for self-transcendence is native to man*. If man has a natural tendency to transcend himself in search of ever greater values and realities, if he has a natural repulsion towards the idea that death marks the final end and total destruction of his own existence, if he has a natural desire to possess and enjoy unlimited knowledge and goodness, then either we write off these deep-rooted human tendencies and attitudes as nonsense and absurdity, or else we allow that it is logical and reasonable to hypothesize a *mode of existence*—beyond our present experience—in which these values can be attained and enjoyed, as well as living beings (and perhaps one ultimate Being) who are in possession of such values or from whom the values themselves proceed. Thus, even if it cannot proceed farther, anthropology has every grounds not just to admit but to firmly assert that to propose hypotheses concerning an after-life, a mode of perfect existence, a *Being* in unlimited possession of all values, is humanly reasonable from every viewpoint, since some such hypotheses occur naturally to man within his own experience and reflections.

Anthropology may not be able to give adequate answers to all the questions that arise from man's longing for self-transcendence. But it must allow the legitimacy, within its own field dedicated to the consideration of man, of the questions themselves.

God as an Anthropological Hypothesis

Obviously, the capacity or tendency to form a notion of an "afterlife" or of a Divine Being does not prove that either really exists. Nevertheless, any truly rational and consistent anthropology cannot but accept the logic with which these notions themselves are formulated.

Here we are brought face to face with the advantage—or, depending on one's inclination, the disadvantage—of an anthropology of values: it leaves man potentially open to "everything." Once he reflects on his capacity and need for truth and goodness, for wisdom and beauty, he realizes that there is no end to it, for his potential and hunger cannot be satisfied with anything less than the infinite.

Man finds precisely *in himself* the capacity—the vital need—to enter into contact with what surpasses the visible or physical dimensions of his existence. The very scope of his intellect and his will transcends what is finite; he finds himself naturally led toward the infinite. In words of the Second Vatican Council, "as a creature man experiences his limitations in a thousand ways. At the same time he feels limitless in his aspirations and destined for a higher form of life."[10]

Human knowledge and creative ability—in science, philosophy, technology, art—grow constantly and are far greater than the capacity of any single individual to make his own. The greatest geniuses contribute so much—and yet so little, in proportion—to the whole in its never-ceasing growth. The greater the genius, the broader will be the perspectives opening before him or her: of new knowledge, new discovery, more progress. The perspective of knowledge is limitless; as is that of practical research and experiment; of exploration through earth and space; of creative development in form, literature, art, music . . .

The very scientific spirit animating the pursuit of knowledge, if it is true to its own nature, rebels against the idea of one day coming to the end of its task because it will have discovered everything. No genuine scientist would ever accept the assertion, "Now there is nothing more for us to know." The field of science naturally appears as lacking in boundary or limits. Man, in other words, in his mind's search for truth, finds himself necessarily projected toward the infinite.

The same happens with the will in its search for good. The lover thinks the loved one perfect, only to find, if they marry, that he or she is not. Then comes the alternatives: the (hard) option of learning to love the imperfect, or the (unwise) option of trying to make the imperfect perfect.[11] Wisely worked out in some cases, unwisely in others, what underlies that constantly repeated human story is the desire for perfection.

God, at least as an hypothesis, is also a human question, one therefore to be examined on the anthropological level and not exclusively in the realm of theology. No serious consideration of man can prescind from his sense of God; his desire to enter into a relationship with the infinite. Even on a natural level, it is difficult to escape the impression that man is a reflection of something higher; given his awareness of this, his personal destiny is frustrated if he does not seek to discover, know, and appreciate transcendent reality.

---

10. *Gaudium et spes*, no. 10.

11. There is of course a third alternative: the "pragmatic" option of ceasing to love, or of looking for an "easier" love. It is an option that involves an even more radical contraction of one's horizons.

No doubt not all anthropologists will accept the validity of such reasoning, and the conclusions it leads to. Perhaps, then, one could legitimately distinguish between a "great" anthropology, open to all that man can aspire to, and a "small" anthropology that reduces man's aspirations to his material or physical needs, allows a narrowly predetermined area for his "spiritual" experiences, and firmly declines to speculate on whatever might go beyond that.

Which of the two establishes anthropology on a more scientific basis? Since we are dealing not with an exact science but with one which necessarily builds from certain presuppositions, there is no sure and verifiable answer to this. Which is a more open and complete analysis of man? Let the reader decide.

Halfway Born?

Where do our reflections on man lead us? What does it mean to be "open" to values? What is the ultimate nature and source of the values which can really fulfill man? If in this work's first eleven chapters (where the objective was to establish the main parameters of a sound anthropology) the transcendent dimension of man was purposely avoided, it now seems that no anthropology can be sound if it completely ignores man's desire for transcendental perspectives—regardless of where they may tend to lead. Anthropology is not called to pronounce on what lies at the end (or "at the other side") of the perspectives, but neither can it fail to take account of these perspectives.

Anthropologists with a closed world view can never explain the glaring disproportion between the unlimited aspirations man has within himself and the narrow panorama of life that their anthropology offers. Their reduced view of man seems to be based on *a priori* suppositions which in the end reveal a preference—that is, a free choice of the will, rather than a necessary and rational conclusion of the mind—for a sort of "Homunculus anthropology." In Goethe's *Faust*, "Homunculus," a nineteenth century "in vitro" concoction, is given a certain degree of humanity by a knowledge-crazed scientist; but he is not given enough. He is conscious of his incompleteness: "To come to being is my keen desire." He is "a shining dwarf," and feels himself "only born halfway."[12] So much of modern anthropology leaves man as a dwarf, not even halfway born, with no hope of attaining the state of being which is his deep desire.

Such hopelessness can drive a thinking person mad. Nietzsche, an undoubted genius who left a deep mark on much of modern thinking, erected a philosophy of nihilism. Rejecting all "received" or objective values, he left man to put what he wishes in their place, and thus to fulfill himself—as a true

---

12. *Faust*, Part II, Act II.

Superman—on his own terms. It seems significant and not merely ironic that this philosopher of self-creative superhumanity—rooted in nothing—lapsed into an insanity covering the last eleven years of his life, to his death in 1900.

That man is capable of looking above himself and needs to do so, is a truth which helps discredit the cliché (the repetitious saying and the unexamined feeling) that being a believer makes man smaller, while being an atheist makes him bigger. It is the exact opposite. The recognition of a personal God means overcoming all the bounds of reality, of time and space. It is, as Paul Claudel wrote, to set out on "the one way that really satisfies our need for space, and leads us to something other than fallen bridges and marshes, towards horizons ceaselessly renewed."[13]

Wanting to Meet the Artist

It is not empty space or distant horizons, however broad, that man seeks. His desire for transcendence will not stop there. His hunger for values, his search for truth and beauty and goodness without limit, is bound to end in frustration if it is not also a quest for dialogue and communion. Man is not fulfilled by impersonal values, however great; he wants to find and commune with the person from whom these values proceed. In the face of values, the open spirit always "wants to know the artist." It is a sign of closedness—of having a narrow outlook and a poor and unambitious spirit—to prefer to contemplate "anonymous" works, lest admiration might have to turn into tribute to a person. As we saw in chapter seven, the petty jealousy of self-centered pride can block the way to ever-greater fulfillment.

Values are never perfect if they do not offer the possibility of dialogue. We cannot carry on a conversation with an abstraction, no matter how perfect it is conceived to be. An impersonal god, incapable of dialogue, offers man no promise of fulfillment.[14] When perfection or near-perfection is encountered, the reasonable human reaction is to seek its intelligent and personal origin; also in order to be able to dialogue. Contemplating Niagara—since we cannot talk with a waterfall—the natural response is "Praise be to you, O God."

What is the real and ultimate value of values? Are they no more than concepts? Are they just subjective impressions? Or are they objectively great? Is beauty, for instance, greater than me? Or is my capacity to appreciate beauty greater than beauty? Is beauty a passing attribute? Is it a mere product of my mind? Or is there a Beauty that really *is*; which, moreover, I can not only admire and even love, but also commune with? Can I converse with Beauty,

---

13. Paul Claudel and André Gide, *Correspondence*, 1949, p. 196.

14. Human love tends to idealize and even to "deify" the loved one, easily believing that the values the beloved offers or represents are perfect; and wanting absolutely to commune and converse with him or her.

with Goodness, with Truth, as I converse with a person? Can I converse with a Someone who *is* Beauty, Goodness, Wisdom, Truth, Happiness, and Eternal Life, all in one? Can I commune with such a Someone: share my life with him, and participate in his life? If the answer is Yes, then I am faced not with the problem of God, but with the limitless possibilities that God opens to me.

The "problem of God" is in the end the problem of the man who does not manage or does not want to accept the existence of the Infinite. So, remaining out of touch with the fullness of reality, he is left without any ultimate key to his own nature, and his life is always felt in practice to be enclosed within four walls, or to be a corridor leading up (or down) to an end that is either a full stop or else a plunge into total darkness.

As we have noted, the central question posed by anthropology—"What is man?"—is not just one of scientific interest to specialists in the field. It becomes a question of utmost personal interest to all of us. For each one, "What is man?" equals "Who am I?" No question is more important to the individual. If a person does not know who he is, he is lost. A lost person, unsure of his identity, looks for some reliable source of information or for someone he can absolutely trust, to solve the mystery of his own life and existence. Only the one who stands before God can truly solve the problem of personal identity.[15]

Whoever lacks the sense of transcendence cannot think about or deal with man in his most dramatic predicament: placed between everything and nothing, and tending to one or the other. Such a person could never manage to understand, let alone to create, truly great art or literature—whose proper subject is always man. The great themes of freedom and responsibility, good and evil, virtue or sin, fortune or destiny, cannot be set in any context of real importance, nor do they lend themselves to any truly dramatic treatment, in the absence of belief in the transcendent dimension of man. When the background of such belief is lacking, man and topics about man always remain small, marked by ultimate and pathetic futility.

It is not irrelevant here to note the distinction between the agnostic and the atheist. The agnostic attitude is not totally unreasonable: for it may be a consequence of an inability to overcome the 'objection' to the existence of God offered by all the violence, suffering, and injustice that marks our world. But even then one would expect the agnostic to *hope* that there is a God, despite everything. The attitude of the atheist—preferring to eliminate God—is unworthy of man. It can be compared to the attitude of a person who is on principle hostile to the possible discovery of a hitherto unknown play of Shakespeare or symphony of Beethoven. Could there not be something in all of that rather like Salieri's jealousy towards the work of Mozart?[16]

15. Cf. John Paul II: *The Theology of the Body*, Pauline Books, p. 36.
16. As portrayed in Peter Shaffer's play *Amadeus* (1979).

If this line of reasoning is sound, no one who reflects on life and takes it seriously can remain satisfied with dogmatic atheism. But, it may be objected, is this necessarily so? Am I not entitled to say: "God and eternity are pure hypotheses for me; they fall outside any experience of mine, and so I can rightly ignore them?." You are; but only at the cost of *preferring* a life without any real explanation, which is basically an unscientific and irrational approach.[17]

However, without pressing that point here, let us continue to reflect on what does fall within human experience. We have spoken of death—a future experience for all of us. There is another reality that enters into our everyday experience and constitutes a problem no less critical for our understanding of man: the presence of evil in the world.

The Problem of Evil

A question that at some time faces all of us is what attitude to adopt toward the world, and especially what judgment to make of it. Is the world good, or is it bad? One may answer that it is both; but the inquiring mind will still ask, what is the explanation of this mixed-up, good-bad world? What can be its peculiar origin? Does it have just one source, producing both good and bad? Or are there two separate sources? May it not be more logical to suppose that the good comes from a good source, and the bad from a bad one? If so, how do they relate? Are they in conflict (as they so often seem to be inside each one of us)? If so, which of them is stronger?, which is going to prevail?

People believe in God because when all is said and done it is impossible, for anyone who really thinks, not to do so.[18] People believe in God because they want an adequate explanation of things, and unless one posits a personal, all-powerful God, the world has no reasonable explanation at all. It remains irrational and absurd, and no one wants to live in the context of total absurdity. People believe in God as the ultimate origin of things. But, swayed by the evidence of evil in the world,[19] this basic and natural faith is often accompanied (today perhaps more than ever) by the temptation not to believe in the *goodness* of God. And so people can end up believing in hidden forces and spirits: in good ones and (perhaps more easily) in bad ones. Belief in God gives way to belief in gods: invisible, powerful, and often malignant powers. The current vogue of spiritism suggests that such a process is in active operation today.

---

17. Cf. Appendix I: *Science, Reason, and God.*

18. Cf. ibid.

19. Commenting on "the terrible experience of evil which has marked our age," John Paul II made this observation: "Such a dramatic experience has ensured the collapse of rationalist optimism, which viewed history as the triumphant progress of reason, the source of all happiness and freedom; and now, at the end of this century, one of our greatest threats is the temptation to despair": *Fides et Ratio*, no. 91.

Only Christianity "saves" God—saves our knowledge of God—from this temptation, revealing to us a God who has turned suffering and evil into opportunities to show an all-powerful love. We may not be able to explain (and we certainly should not try to "explain away") the presence of evil. We may be at a loss to understand the reason for suffering. But God's goodness has been placed beyond all doubt. That is why the Incarnation alone provides a sufficient and optimistic answer to the presence of suffering and evil. God has not taken evil away but *has chosen to suffer it himself*, with sufferings that show the extent of his love and become a source of hope and a means of salvation for us.[20] God himself has come among us, to live this checkered human life of ours. In becoming Man in Jesus Christ, God reveals how much he values and loves the world, and gives us an example—*the* example—of how evil, however great, can be absorbed and overcome in a love that is infinite. In doing so, he has shown that he is loving and powerful enough to use evil for good, and great evil for great good.

In the whole of history no greater act of evil has occurred than the Crucifixion of Jesus Christ—God become Man, put to death by men. Yet Jesus himself turned the very Crucifixion—his voluntary submission to death on the Cross for our sake—into the greatest act of love in the annals of mankind.

In this way, evil is not ignored or explained away, but it is set side by side with an infinitely stronger and greater Goodness. The optimism which this gives rise to—that "good is stronger than evil"[21]—is at the heart of the Christian faith.

Salvation

The presence of evil in the world is an immense mystery that must distress every thoughtful person. We should be neither obsessed with nor depressed by it, for it is something we can neither fully grasp nor solve. We should try not to make any personal contribution to this evil, not even by negative attitude or criticism, whenever (as is usually the case) this can have no positive effect; and if possible we should try to reduce it. We can also choose to ignore that evil, although (except in the depressive person) this is seldom more than the isolationist attitude of one's not wanting one's peace of mind disturbed.

No doubt we would like everything and everyone—including ourselves— to be good. But many things are not good. Many people seem not to be good. And I myself, if I take a deep look inside, may hesitate to say that I am good— in any event not as I would like to be.

---

20. cf. John Paul II's encyclical, *Salvifici Doloris* (1984), passim.
21. "bonum fortius est quam malum": Thomas Aquinas, *Summa Theologica*, I–I, q. 100, art. 2; I–II, q. 29, art. 3, etc.

Evil, then, is not just the external problem constituted by what I see around me. It is also the intimate and personal problem of what I find within me. Each one of us, if he knows his own heart, is acutely aware that he is "divided against himself"; that he appears (at least to himself) as a sort of split personality in his actions, often not wanting to do, but doing, what his conscience disapproves of, and often again wanting, but failing, to do what his conscience approves.[22]

We are free; yet we are often pulled (irresistibly, it seems) in ways we would rather not go. Our fulfillment lies in opening out, and our tendency is to close in. We are made to admire, and we lapse into envy. We would like to be self-forgetful and generous, and are frequently calculating and stingy.

We could adapt and apply here one of Pascal's thoughts: "man's greatness and his miseries are so visible that any true anthropology must necessarily teach us that there is some great principle in him of greatness, and at the same time some great principle of misery."[23] Any realistic anthropological analysis discovers in man all the indications of some grave imbalance or disruption rooted in the very depths of his being and constantly influencing his thoughts, desires and choices. Natural anthropology can offer no adequate explanation of this, and still less suggest a remedy. But it must take cognizance of the fact; otherwise it remains a surface science, content to study man's external conduct and social interaction but failing to consider the inner workings of his spirit. The study of man leads on from one fundamental question to another: *What* am I?—*Who* am I?—*Why* am I?[24] Then, passing from philosophical detachment to existential anguish: Why am I *so*? And, finally, Why do I find it apparently beyond my powers to be as I wish to be?

Anthropology would not be genuine, it would be falling woefully short of its goals, if it did not dwell on questions regarding the wounded inner condition of man and his longing for healing. However, having posed the questions, it must leave them unanswered. It would overreach itself if it were to point to any one way of healing or redemption. It is only from a revealed source that knowledge of any real redemption for man can come.

G. K. Chesterton, holding that there is no other optimistic theology but that of Catholic Christianity, recalls the remark of a friend of his: "Anyhow, it must be obvious to anybody that the doctrine of the Fall is the only cheerful view of human life."[25] It is truly the only view that offers an explanation for

22. cfr. *Rom* 7: 15–24.
23. *Pensées*, p. 83. Pascal of course does not say "anthropology," but "religion."
24. "A cursory glance at ancient history shows clearly how in different parts of the world, with their different cultures, there arise at the same time the fundamental questions which pervade human life: Who am I? Where have I come from and where am I going? Why is there evil? What is there after this life? These are the questions which ... have their common source in the quest for meaning which has always compelled the human heart. In fact, the answer given to these questions decides the direction which people seek to give to their lives": *Fides et Ratio*, no. 1.
25. *Autobiography*, Chapter 7.

our internal conflicts and contradictions, placing them at the same time within the context of a divine plan of salvation.

The very man who faces the need to overcome self-centeredness—to rise above self and open out from self, so as to be human—finds in practice that he can never fully succeed in the endeavor. This, in christian terms, corresponds to our inability to save ourselves. We are in a fallen state, and cannot rise on our own. Hence comes the necessity of salvation and the need for grace: for a constant help from above to fight against our defects and to realize our ultimate goal.[26]

The concern of anthropology is natural man; the role and activity of grace fall outside it. However, the study of man on the natural plane remains a fundamental presupposition for tackling the subject of salvation operated by grace, since grace builds on nature and does not succeed in building well if nature is not adequately understood—in its main elements, possibilities, finalities and defects.

How High Can We Rise?

If man is open to infinite values and will always remain dissatisfied if he does not attain them, it seems that there can be no real fulfillment for him unless in the end he either "becomes" God, or else somehow "possesses" God. The first alternative, conceived as an immanent process, is unreal and unthinkable. It is not possible to "become" infinite. The infinite really exists, or else it cannot come to exist.

The second alternative is conceivable. Man's aspirations go as far as to reach God, in whom all values are infinitely present. Since God is the ultimate "Value" and the source of all values, man's total fulfillment depends on his being open to God, responding to God, "assimilating" God—so that God becomes man's, becomes *mine*. These are limitless ambitions and aspirations; their actual achievement clearly depends on God himself permitting it and opening the way to it.[27]

Christian belief is that this incredible fulfillment is in fact possible for man, precisely because God has wished it and made it possible. If this is so, this second alternative in a certain sense absorbs the first. The early writers of

---

26. The *Encyclopaedia Britannica* presents grace as "the divine influence operating in man for his regeneration and sanctification." The Council of Trent describes (actual) grace as a "gift of God and an inspiration of the Holy Spirit . . . giving the impulse that helps the penitent make his way toward justice" (*Denzinger*, 898).

27. The idea that man can "be God" has been an ambition—a vague longing or a proud deception—in all civilizations. But the idea that God could become man is so totally original that it could not come from human reason, neither humble nor proud—though the humble man can accept it, once it is revealed.

the Church did not hesitate to say that "God became man so that men might become gods."[28] In possessing God, in sharing his life, man "becomes" God in a participatory but real way. So Christianity offers in fact the fullness—divine fullness—of personal fulfillment to everyone.

You can "have" God, but only if you let him do the sharing, and according to his plan. If you try to take him over or to supplant him, in the end you reduce yourself to frustration, sinking to a subhuman level.

Understanding man has become important as never before, both for the personal faith of those who follow Christ and for their work of bringing the Gospel to the world. Disbelief in man has become almost as great a danger today (even for Christians) as disbelief in God. Jesus shows his belief in man; he saves man and offers a new image of man that reflects God and leads to God. Unless Christians believe in man—not just in the Man, Jesus Christ, but also in every single person around them as someone capable of acquiring the new likeness that Christ wishes to give them—they are not likely to have or retain a strong belief in God, and they will be less able to find him in their own souls or to reflect him to others.

Man was originally made in the image of God, and therefore in a limited but natural way *reflected* God. Even "fallen" man offers some image of God. But if he falls farther, the likeness becomes more and more obscured. It is a process which is evidently taking place today. As man grows more alienated from himself, more distorted in the human image he reflects, he looks around and finds no image of a God capable of attracting him and offering him hope. So, the theological difficulties of unbelievers, springing from their negative idea of God, are compounded by anthropological difficulties, inasmuch as they have acquired such a flawed idea of man. If their very understanding of man is deformed, they are not likely to be drawn to God through Jesus Christ.

As for Christians themselves, if they are to reflect a more convincing image of God, they must possess and project a more adequate image of man. Deep in the hearts of unbelievers there always remains the perhaps unacknowledged desire to find God. If they are not attracted by the image of man Christians reflect in their human lives, they will not begin to be drawn by the Christian God.

An early Christian apologist addressed to the pagans the reproach that perhaps it was their defective humanity (that they could and should try to correct) which prevented them from understanding and being drawn by the God of Christians: "If you say to me, 'Show me your God,' I will reply: 'Show me your man, and I will show you my God.'"[29] Modern pagans might well be entitled to address a slightly different reproach to today's Christians: "Show

---

28. St. Augustine, *Sermo* 128.

29. "Si dicas: Ostende mihi Deum tuum, dicam tibi: Ostende mihi hominem tuum, et ego tibi ostendam Deum meum": St. Theophilus of Antioch: *Ad Autolycum*, lib. 1, 2, 7 (PG 6, 1026).

me your humanity, show me in your lives something of the humanity of the Christ you profess to believe in, and then I may be more drawn by the God you say loves and saves us all."

Albert Camus was revolted by the persistent heritage of nineteenth-century Victorian self-justification and other-condemnation. In a world (for him) without God or absolute values, he felt that everyone must admit his or her guilt before a minimum of human understanding and solidarity could become possible. In *La Chute*, he writes: "When we are all guilty, that will be democracy."[30] It is indeed possible that an admission of guilt by each one (at least to himself) might result in greater mutual understanding and provoke a more active humanitarian pity. But it would probably be a bitter pity, like that of Dr. Rieux in another work of Camus, *La Peste*, who saw men as victims of a merciless world, of their own misery, and of the selfishness of others. If such a "democracy" could bring men together, it would be in the solidarity of a meaningless and loveless society. Christianity is the democracy of all being guilty; but also of all being loved, forgiven, cleansed, and fitted for a new life.

---

30. This view is, of course, just the opposite of contemporary humanistic psychology's insistence that we all be declared, or declare ourselves, guiltless. A sense of guilt is considered to be destructive of self-esteem, and no morality is acceptable which asks one to level a finger at oneself or to "repent" of one's actions. "Therapy" has replaced the admission of guilt and the need for forgiveness, while therapeutic counseling is professedly aimed at the rehabilitation of self-love: "I was able to renew my self-esteem. I learned again to like myself." The paeans of Philip Rieff's *The Triumph of the Therapeutic* (first published in the mid-1960s) have a hollow sound forty years later.

13

TRANSCENDING
From What, To What?

The anthropological outline presented in the main part of our study was based on certain first principles. Man is not yet man: in other words, each individual is not yet all he that can come to be. Man therefore is a being "in the making." His fulfillment—that is, the full development of the personal life he is capable of—lies ahead of him, as a goal to be worked for and achieved; or missed. Man is free. His fulfillment depends on his efforts and his free choices,[1] and so this fulfillment is not something that each one attains automatically. The person who makes wrong choices, accepting options that undermine, reduce, or paralyze his human potential, will never reach fulfillment, but may on the contrary end up in human failure and frustration. Man is not self-sufficient.[2] He must grow towards self-fulfillment; but that can only come about through a process of opening out—towards values; values to be discovered, appreciated, responded to, assimilated.[3]

---

1. In a certain sense, a "free society" could be described as "one that allows me *to make the effort* to realize myself."

2. Nevertheless much of modern psychology is leading people into the rudimentary error of believing in an immanent human sufficiency, in a fulfillment that can be achieved solely from within. Christianity says: No, "our sufficiency is from God" (2 Cor 3:4).

3. This anthropological analysis of human fulfillment—that man's realization depends on his somehow turning "away from" himself or being led "out of" himself in response to values, especially as present in others—will strike many as paradoxical and perhaps downright alienating. Yet it is certainly

The purpose of our subsequent analyses was not so much to offer the reader blueprints, or ready-made strategies, as to open horizons and to provoke questions. No one knows exactly where he is going or what lies ahead of him. Each person's existence is a series of question marks: about the choices to be made at the next crossroads, about the general direction of his life, and about the final goal it is leading to. Only you can say whether the answers you have at hand give sufficient sense to your life—or still leave it, in its major aspects, as a mass of hypotheses and, ultimately, as an unresolved enigma.

In the preceding chapter we touched on some of the reasons why man, faced with his limitations, wants to overcome and reach beyond them. "Man transcends man": this means in effect that man wants to surpass himself and his own limits. He wants to test and reduce the hypotheses and solve the enigma. He wants explanations that really explain.[4] "People seek an absolute which can give to all their searching a meaning and an answer—something ultimate, which serves as the ground of all things. In other words, they seek a final explanation, a supreme value, which refers to nothing beyond itself and which puts an end to all questioning. Hypotheses may fascinate, but they do not satisfy. Whether we admit it or not, there comes for everyone the moment when personal existence must be anchored to a truth recognized as final, a truth which confers a certitude no longer open to doubt."[5]

The horizons of anthropology inevitably transcend the limits of man. Once we raise our eyes from the earth, we are looking out "onto" infinity.

In this last chapter we want to return to certain major questions dealt with earlier in general terms, but kept nevertheless within an earthbound perspective, and see what answers to them might occur to a mind open to transcendence. Again it is up to the reader to decide whether these further insights, now offered from a broader viewpoint, can help resolve his own personal questions; or whether he prefers to remain with the answers, along with the doubts, he already has.

Before doing so, however, it is good to dwell for a moment on something that the reader has no doubt noticed, as implicit more than explicit, in the anthropological exposition we have been unfolding: the idea of "human nature," as something objective and given.

---

not new, being even more drastically present in the evangelical norm that we must "lose" our life so as to find or save it (Mt 10:39). This same norm permeates the modern philosophy of christian personalism which therefore, although new in name, is directly rooted in the message of Christ. Quoting the key formula of the Second Vatican Council—"man can fully discover his true self only in a sincere giving of himself" (*Gaudium et Spes*, no. 24)—John Paul II writes, "the Holy Spirit, strengthening in each of us 'the inner man,' enables man ever more fully to find himself through a sincere gift of self. These words of the Pastoral Constitution of the Council can be said to sum up *the whole of Christian anthropology*": *Dominum et Vivificantem*, no. 59.

4. See Appendix One.

5. *Fides et Ratio*, no. 27.

The Issue of Human Nature

We said that man is free, even if he is not a law unto himself. He has his own life in his hands—as raw material which he can turn into a truly human and fulfilled existence, or into one that has gone off its rails and is running amok. The sensation of having so mismanaged one's life that it is now altogether out of control is frequently met in fiction and in fact. Dorian Gray, in Oscar Wilde's novel, gives himself over to a life of vice, although no one can notice it from his serene features. He himself, however, is conscious of the "various moods and the changing fancies of a nature over which he seemed, at times, to have almost entirely lost control."[6] What does it mean to "lose control of one's nature?" Why should we have to control that nature? Is it in order to *become* what we can naturally become, and so be fully human? Is it for fear of that *unnatural* something that we could also become, thus practically ceasing to be human? Both possibilities, we believe, lie before each one of us.

We hold that there is such an objective reality as "human nature," and that it is given to each of us as a gift and as a program, as a resource and as a goal that can be realized. But we also believe that this gift of human nature can be mismanaged to the point of total human frustration.

Anthropology is surely not intended to be (and has little interest if it is) restricted to the esoteric study of primitive societies. And one could question its utility and interest if it were a sort of science of "abstract man," removed from all actual reality. What is needed today is an anthropology which seeks to be a science of man as he actually exists—or, perhaps more exactly, as he can exist and needs to become if he is to be truly human. The principles it proposes should have the effect of showing man how to be man in practice, and how to avoid the alternatives: ending up with a poorly fulfilled humanity, or as a totally dehumanized reality.

It is true that up to this point we have spoken little of "human nature." It is also true that "human nature" (along with the related concept of "natural law") is generally considered a "politically incorrect" notion, and carefully avoided by many philosophical or anthropological schools of thought today. Yet the whole of anthropology is an attempt to interpret the phenomenon of man: what he is or seems to be, and (since he is a living, free and changing being) what modes of change make him *more* human, more a man, and what modes limit his growth in humanity or perhaps frustrate it. What else, then, is the science of anthropology than the study of what is implied in "being human"—that is, in possessing a human nature? If there is no such thing as "human nature," if human beings have nothing in common—no truths or values, no rights or duties, no rules or possibilities or limits, that apply to them all—then can there be any anthropological science or study of "man" at

---

6. *The Picture of Dorian Gray*, Ch. 11.

all? How then could people be called on to live together in a human way? Would real social life or a truly human society even be conceivable?

We spoke earlier of "human rights"—the defense of which is properly regarded as the bulwark of a democratic and just society. Unless the reality of a common human nature is acknowledged, do any valid grounds exist for appealing to "human rights," precisely as rights that belong to each of us by the simple fact of our being human? From this, and not from any government, state or positive law, our human rights draw their inherent legitimacy, which is such that any law violating them, whatever its source, is intrinsically unjust and has no power to bind consciences.

Human beings can be an object of an anthropological study only if, with all their individual differences, they have something fundamental in common: basic faculties of intellect and will, human rights and duties, conscience, shared needs, a specific human sexual identity and a natural tendency towards the peculiarly human phenomenon of marriage. That "something fundamental in common" is what we call human nature. If it does not exist, is there any sense in calling some actions "unnatural" or "antinatural?" Or can anything be natural to man? Do we actually mean anything when we speak of "humanity?" Does it make sense to qualify certain acts as "human" and others as "inhuman?" What do we mean by "human rights?" On what grounds can a person or a regime be accused of "crimes against humanity?"

Steel has its nature and, according to the quality achieved in its production, will withstand certain pressures and loads, and collapse under others. Engineers and architects need to know the nature and quality of the steel they are thinking of using in their projects. Can we—should we—say that, somewhat similarly, man has a nature according to which much, but not anything or everything, can be fashioned; that he can achieve definite goals and find fulfillment in responding to certain demands, while the attempt to live as if one were made for no goal (or, more importantly, as if one were bound by no limitations) can lead to frustration and perhaps total collapse? Can we say that knowledge of man's nature—of its potential, its powers, and its limits—is essential for each one in order to tackle the task of building his own life? And that whoever tries to build his humanity without knowing what is genuinely human and what is not, runs a grave risk of undermining that humanity through his choices and actions, and of gradually dehumanizing himself?

Nature and Freedom

These questions are inseparable from any consideration of the human freedom we studied in Chapter Two; of its power and limitations. Are all men free? Or better, ought all to be free, in the sense that those who are not free are deprived of something proper to man? Our answer here is a strong affirmative.

Is freedom a human right—something due to human nature? The reply is an equally strong affirmative. Does freedom go so far (as Sartre held that it does) as to be itself the first and only "value," which entitles us to shape or create our very nature as each one wishes?[7] Here we would answer with an equally strong negative, and add that those who "exalt" freedom to this extent do not understand freedom, do not understand man, and in the ultimate analysis are offering a formula for anthropological suicide.

"That man is free who is conscious of being the author of the law he obeys."[8] A "radical" assertion of some fifty years ago which does not withstand much critical analysis.[9] In any case it is not probable that many secular psychologists or philosophers today would subscribe to it as it stands; they would not finding it radical enough, balking especially at two words which many have come to regard as incompatible with human freedom and dignity: "law" and "obeys." Yet they might have little difficulty if the sentence were modified to read, "that man is free who is conscious of being the author of the values he holds." The peculiar modern sensitivity to language which this reveals can be passed over. It is more to our point to note that the two phrases express the same basic view: man's freedom depends on his being able to define the terms on which he is or will be free. Does such a "philosophy" make sense? Can any man actually do that? Is being free or being freed simply a matter of defining freedom in one's own terms? Or is what we have here the phenomenon of man's wanting to "free" his life from any objective rules of development or from limits to his possibilities?

"I have no given 'nature'; I am my own life-project; I make myself. My project, both in its formulation and in its realization, is conditioned by nothing else than what I choose."[10] There is no such thing as a 'nature' within which I must work, or a 'truth' that rules me from above. I am free to make my own nature, my own truth, and my own values. For many people today, the "self" has become the ultimate criterion of everything, and "is defined by its ability to choose its own values."[11]

---

7. "Certain currents of modern thought have gone so far as to exalt freedom to such an extent that it becomes an absolute, which would then be the source of values": *Veritatis Splendor*, no. 32.

8. Robert F. Knight: "Determinism, "freedom," and psychotherapy," *Psychiatry*, vol. 9 (1946) p. 256.

9. It could be reasonably paraphrased: "that man is free who is author of the rules of the game he plays." But will anyone else play that game with him? The formula reflects the psychology of childhood, and makes for a total isolation. Yes, it is typical of the child to want the rules of a game to be subject to his authority, and to try to change them whenever they do not suit him. The child who regularly insists on changing the rules of the game ends up playing alone.

10. For Sartre, as we noted, freedom is the only "given" man has; he works on from there as he likes. But to accept any one given element is already to posit a "nature." How does one then justify the exclusion of other elements from that given nature - e.g. the power to think, to discern, to judge . . . ?

11. Bellah et al.: *Habits of the Heart . . .* , p. 75.

This is the outlook described by Pope John Paul II in his 1993 encyclical *Veritatis Splendor*: the outlook of those who hold not only that freedom and nature have no essential interdependence, but that the very concept of "nature" is a threat and an enemy to freedom. For them, "nature needs to be profoundly transformed, and indeed overcome by freedom, inasmuch as it represents a limitation and denial of freedom. . . . This ultimately means making freedom self-defining and a phenomenon creative of itself and its values. Indeed, when all is said and done, man would not even have a nature; he would be his own personal life-project. Man would be nothing more than his own freedom."[12] Nature needs to be "*overcome* by freedom!" What the Pope describes is man at war with himself; man pitting his freedom against his nature—against any idea of an objectively given or limited nature.

In any case, whether one's nature constitutes a limitation to be overcome or a possibility to be realized, one needs to *know* it. If a captain is unfamiliar with his ship and ignores its capacities and limits, or if he chooses to navigate with no heed for the forces of wind, currents, and water, he is not likely to reach port.

When considered in its most important and bluntest context, our freedom means the freedom to be human, but also the freedom not to be human. It means the power to make ourselves more human, to humanize ourselves; but also the power to make ourselves less human, to dehumanize ourselves. Since I am human, I am free.[13] But since I am free, I can dehumanize myself and lose my humanity, and freely lose my freedom with it. This of course is meaningless to those for whom the very idea of "being human" is itself meaningless.

We have the power to define our character—but not our nature. My choices indeed make me: not necessarily according to what I want to be, but according to the natural consequences of the choices themselves. Bad choices make for bad consequences. I can freely cast myself into the shape of a thoroughly unpleasant and unhappy "me."

The view that each person is by right "self-defining" not only involves the denial of a common human nature, but undermines the very basis of any truly human society marked by freedom and animated by mutual respect. It puts each individual potentially at war with all the others, each of whom is presumably also seeking to fulfill himself by an exercise of a freedom that draws up its own rules and knows, or wants to know, no limits. If society is not held together by a voluntary consensus on common values and laws, it will disintegrate, or else will end under the rigid control of the most powerful. "This view of freedom leads to a serious distortion of life in society. If the promotion of

---

12. *Veritatis Splendor*, no. 46.
13. Precisely because freedom springs from our being human, it is conditioned by the limits of our humanity. We may be "free" to attempt things "beyond" our human nature, but we are not of ourselves free to achieve them; and if what we choose is destructive, we can destroy ourselves.

the self is understood in terms of absolute autonomy, people inevitably reach the point of rejecting one another . . . , society becomes a mass of individuals placed side by side, but without any mutual bonds. . . . At this point everything is negotiable, everything is open to bargaining: even the first of the fundamental rights, the right to life. . . . The "right" ceases to be such, because it is no longer firmly founded on the inviolable dignity of the person, but is made subject to the will of the stronger party. In this way democracy, contradicting its own principles, effectively moves towards a form of totalitarianism. . . . When this happens, the process leading to the breakdown of a genuinely human co-existence and the disintegration of the State itself has already begun."[14]

To his own imagination, the "self-defining man" appears as a virtual giant. In reality he tends to shrink into a dwarf, losing freedom, horizons, and happiness in the process. Only in opening himself to transcendence can he freely aspire to all he is made for. "Whatever diminishes man (whatever shortens the horizon of man's aspiration to goodness (harms the cause of freedom. In order to recover our hope and our trust at the end of this century of sorrows, we must regain sight of that transcendent horizon of possibility to which the soul of man aspires."[15]

Values

Let us turn from freedom and nature to values, which we considered especially in our third chapter. "Values," in our presentation, are the key to man's growth and fulfillment. Freedom is a value; but without the existence and discovery of other values, freedom itself loses all value, because it is reduced to the power of choosing between worthless things.

In that sense we saw that the importance of freedom depends on the availability of worthwhile things to choose. The more things there are to choose, and especially the greater their value, the more our human freedom appears as a great possession. Narrow the field of choice or reduce the worth of what can be chosen, and a person's effective freedom is diminished. Most people would hold that the freedom of a desert island or a concentration camp offers little that could fulfill man.

We leave the reader with the problem—because it is up to him to solve it—of how to acquire adequate standards by which to judge values, distinguishing higher from lower, and ultimately being able to distinguish genuine, true values from those that are false. It is not indifferent for the type of life one is likely to have, whether one places money higher than love in one's scale of

---

14. John Paul II, *Evangelium Vitae*, no. 20.
15. John Paul II, Address to the General Assembly of the United Nations, October 5, 1995.

values. Only a very superficial appreciation of freedom stops at the *power* to choose, and attaches little importance to *what* one chooses. Not everything which attracts is a value that enriches life. If one cannot distinguish authentic values from those that are false, it is practically speaking impossible to achieve fulfillment and to avoid frustration. Underlying the crisis of freedom besetting man today is a crisis of values. Unless man recovers his values, he will never recover or have effective use of his freedom.

Contemporary education imparts few criteria by which to differentiate between true and false values,[16] or even between those that are higher or lower. "It is essential that the values chosen and pursued in one's life be true, because only true values can lead people to realize themselves fully, allowing them to be true to their nature. The truth of these values is to be found not by turning in on oneself but by opening oneself to apprehend that truth *even at levels which transcend the person*. This is an essential condition for us to become ourselves and to grow as mature, adult persons."[17]

"Levels which *transcend* the person. . . ." There, in the last analysis, is the biggest issue facing each one of us. Whoever recognizes his personal incompleteness and insufficiency, and opens—responds—to values and to others, has engaged in battle against the temptation to put self at the center of his universe. If one perseveres, one's horizons grow. One's response becomes a quest for absolute values. One becomes more and more open to the idea of transcendence.

Do I want to transcend myself? If not, I will stay stuck and locked within myself, no matter where I get to. Life certainly yields little to the person who has no ambition. But is it then enough to ask myself, How high do I want to reach? How great do I want to be? How far do I want to go? People, after all, can climb very much higher and go very much farther than where they are now and still not transcend themselves, because they always take themselves with them. To transcend self is to take a jump beyond self, to go so far as in some way to leave self behind, to look so high as to have lost sight of self.

Is this a contradiction in terms? Does "losing oneself" not represent the ultimate alienation? Yet we have recalled the Gospel paradox of the need to lose one's self so as to find one's self. Not every loss of self-attributes is negative. Loss of self-consciousness or of self-pity can be an immense liberation. A person can "forget self" in response to a great value, losing self in reverence and admiration. And that is truly to transcend self.

Thomas More, outstanding lawyer, famous humanist and Chancellor of England, was someone who gave every indication of believing in life and believing in himself. A man of enormous resourcefulness, confident in his

---

16. Thomas Aquinas sees our lack of discernment about values as a consequence of original sin: "The result of this disorder in man is that he does not appreciate things at their true value": *Summa contra Gentiles*, III, Ch. 141, n. 7.

17. *Fides et Ratio*, no. 25.

views, yet as free from arrogance as he was from subservience to others; a man fond of life, fond of others, admired by all: and yet nothing in him shows the least trace of vanity, self-absorption, or concern with self-image. Many regard him as the greatest Englishman of all time. Nevertheless, this man, who believed in himself, believed in more than himself. His human greatness and appeal are inseparable from his possession of a personal hierarchy of values and his fidelity to it. The preface to Robert Bolt's *A Man for all Seasons* expresses this splendidly.

"Thomas More," says Bolt, "as I wrote about him, became for me a man with an adamantine sense of his own self. He knew where he began and left off, what area of himself he could yield to the encroachments of his enemies, and what to the encroachments of those he loved. It was a substantial area in both cases for he had a proper sense of fear and was a busy lover. Since he was a clever man and a great lawyer he was able to retire from those areas in wonderfully good order, but at length he was asked to retreat from that final area where he located his self. And there this supple, humorous, unassuming and sophisticated person set like metal, was overtaken by an absolutely primitive rigour, and could no more be budged than a cliff. . . . What first attracted me was a person who could not be accused of any incapacity for life, who indeed seized life in great variety and almost greedy quantities, who nevertheless found something in himself without which life was valueless and when that was denied him was able to grasp his death."

So it is not a question of not believing in oneself, but of believing in something "more than oneself." If you are not able to believe in anything more than yourself, you may end up not believing in anything worthwhile at all. Then, logically, comes the temptation to suicide—the final (though not inevitable) recognition of the inadequacy of the self one once wished to believe in as an absolute.

The United States of America in the nineteenth and early twentieth centuries was the land of limitless opportunities and boundless frontiers. Admirable qualities of enterprise, fortitude, and optimism marked the pioneering Americans who pushed their country's borders ever forward. Yet there were already students of the American phenomenon who wondered—what would happen when the frontiers end?

In a sense they have ended today; or have been turned into dead ends. Self or self-esteem, money or prestige, has become the irresistibly beckoning frontier. No small part in this has been played by humanistic psychology which proposes the contented inner self as its goal and ideal, and which has come to dominate American education and outlook over recent decades. Self, the center of each one's diminutive world—"his little world of man"[18]—

---

18. Shakespeare: *King Lear*, Act 3, Sc. 1.

becomes the creative source of everything, even religion. And everything, even religion, becomes a prop to the "creative" (but objectively shrunken) self.[19]

The concept of self-denial was mentioned in chapter nine. Some regard it as perhaps the most negative and frustrating idea in Christianity. They fail to grasp how it is to be understood, which is precisely in the sense of *selfishness*-denial: the refusal to build one's life on self-centeredness, to shrink and become small, to close around oneself. Those who want to grow must open out from self. We have the lungs, but we don't have the air; the breath that gives life has to be drawn in from outside.

Then, is the ultimate ideal, for each of us, just that of "celebrating myself?"[20] Is self-contentment synonymous with happiness? Can contentment with self last beyond temporary situations or passing moods? Can I attain a condition where I will celebrate without limitations of time or persons? Is it possible to enter into a celebration where the jubilee is of all in all and with all? The Bible says it is possible, and calls that jubilee the joy of the Lord.[21]

America—indeed the whole western world—stands in need of new frontiers which challenge the individual to escape from the prison of self-centeredness and the illusion of self-contentment, and to open out, in commitment, to higher goals.[22] It is urgent to discover new—or old—horizons of genuine fulfillment.

Which Can Go Farther, Imagination or Reality?

There is one human faculty that seems unconstrained by natural limits: the imagination. Inside his mind, a very imaginative person can "create" without limits. However, the "reality" he or she creates remains "virtual," not real. One can, of course, pass from the virtual to the real—if what is imagined is within the bounds both of possibility and of the person's powers of artistic or practical execution. Then it may be endowed with a consistency and reality of its own. This is more to "incarnate"—give body or form to—a value, than to create it. So, only in this very qualified way can we be said to "create" values. An imaginative person can invent and tell a story and even find the creation of this value easy. A hungry man can imagine a square meal, but cannot create it—though he may be able to go out and buy or earn it, even if perhaps not easily.

---

19. Cf. *Habits of the Heart*, p. 229.

20. See Walt Whitman's poem, "Song of Myself," whose first line is, "I celebrate myself."

21. See *Matthew*, 25:21.

22. Yet for forty years humanistic psychology has been confidently preaching the gospel of non-committed self-sufficiency and praising "the triumphant therapeutic [which] has arisen out of a rejection of all therapies of commitment" (Philip Rieff: *The Triumph of the Therapeutic*, p. 254). No real healing comes to the solitary self that has been led to believe nothing is worth committing oneself to. As therapy this is not a triumph but a devastating failure.

Man cannot live off imagination alone. Imagination can provoke wonder, but the life of the person who is able to wonder only at imaginary things may collapse at any moment. One's life grows as the ability to admire and wonder at reality grows; it shrinks when this ability deteriorates. The Second Vatican Council says: "the human spirit must be cultivated in such a way as to lead to a growth in its ability to wonder, to understand, to contemplate, to make personal judgments, and to develop a religious, moral, and social sense."[23] It is significant that the first capacity highlighted here is the ability to wonder—at what is real, not just at fiction. Without that, man will never understand reality in any depth, his judgments will be flawed and superficial, his religion (if he has any) will be mere formalism, and his moral and social sense will never be inspired by respect for others or a sincere interest in them.

"Our sense of wonder, in the philosophical meaning of the word, is not aroused by enormous, sensational things—though that is what a dulled sensibility requires to provoke it to a sort of *ersatz* experience of wonder. A man who needs the unusual to make him "wonder" shows that he has lost the capacity to find the true answer to the wonder of being. . . . To perceive all that is unusual and exceptional, all that is wonderful, in the midst of the ordinary things of everyday life, is the beginning of philosophy. And that, as both Aristotle and Aquinas observe, is how philosophy and poetry are related. And Goethe, in his seventieth year, ended one of his short poems, *Parabase*, with the words: *Zum Erstaunen bin ich da*, which might be rendered by saying "to marvel is my *raison d'etre*." Ten years later Eckermann records him saying that "the very summit of man's attainment is the capacity to marvel. . . ." The capacity to wonder is among man's greatest gifts."[24]

The ability to admire stirs us to emulate what can be emulated, and to be astonished at and grateful for what is so far beyond us that we realize we can never reach or imitate it, even though we also understand that to be able to admire it is in itself an enrichment.

Education at all levels today does little to disturb the individual's concern with the image of self, rather than with its true worth. This squares with the prevailing tendency of modern life to form persons capable of taking in little more than the surface of things, content with appearances rather than realities. In more and more young people the longing for wonder is stirred (for shorter and shorter periods) by virtual reality, but not by the reality that makes up their customary lives. They readily follow Hollywood into fantasy worlds— worlds moreover often characterized by violence and imbued with fear—and return with a diminished appreciation of the everyday reality and the ordinary people around them; less able to treat them familiarly and humanly, to trust

---

23. *Gaudium et Spes*, no. 59.
24. Joseph Pieper: *The Philosophical Act*, pp. 100–102.

them, or simply to be at home with them. Not much will change until educators learn once more to communicate to their students enthusiasm for real values, and to elicit in them the capacity to be impressed by everyday things and to admire others.

It is said that the last thing, the last value, to die is hope. The person who has lost hope is left with no positive human reason for living. Then fear alone may make him continue to live. A rational and deep optimism is open only to the person who hopes, with firm faith, that death is not the end of this life—with its promises and deceptions and ultimate limitations—but the beginning of a new life that surpasses our wildest imaginations and dreams. The power of such faith and hope transformed the lives of the early Christians and, through them, the world. How forcefully it permeated the message of those who first preached in the name of Jesus Christ! It echoes time and again through the letters of the apostles. "We rejoice in our hope of sharing the glory of God" (Rom 5:2); "creation waits with eager longing for the revealing of the sons of God; for the creation was subjected to futility, not of its own will but by the will of him who subjected it in hope; because the creation itself will be set free from its bondage to decay and obtain the glorious freedom of the children of God" (Rom 8:19-21); "in this hope we were saved" (Rom 8:24); "since we have such a hope, we are filled with confidence" (2 Cor 3:12); "through him you have confidence in God, who raised him from the dead and gave him glory, so that your faith and hope are in God" (1 Pet 1:21); "see what love the Father has given us, that we should be called children of God; and so we are. The reason why the world does not know us is that it did not know him. Beloved, we are God's children now; it does not yet appear what we shall be, but we know that when he appears we shall be like him, for we shall see him as he is. And every one who thus hopes in him purifies himself as he is pure" (1 Jn 3:1–3). This is to hope for everything; it is impossible to hope for more.

Many people today are haunted by a sense that their life is running out of values. Looking back may help them; but to be able to look forward is the only real solution. Values from the past may be treasured, but are not enough. Without a firm conviction that the future can bring better things, one's taste for life turns sour, one's very desire to live may go. Good memories, looking back; good hopes, looking forward.[25] Even when the former are not there, the latter can still offer life-saving support.

If we are to believe St. Paul's half-veiled confession, it seems he was allowed to have a momentary glimpse of heaven while still here on earth: "I know a man in Christ who fourteen years ago was caught up to the third heaven—whether in the body or out of the body I do not know, God knows.

---

25. Contrast the emptiness Robert Frost depicts in "The Death of the Hired Man," "And nothing to look backward to with pride,/And nothing to look forward to with hope"; though the looking backward is of more genuine profit when inspired by *gratitude* rather than pride.

And I know that this man was caught up into Paradise—whether in the body or out of the body I do not know, God knows—and he heard thing that cannot be told, which man may not utter" (2 Cor 12: 2–4). Perhaps he had only been dreaming, although he seems quite convinced that his experience was more real and more vital than anything he had known before in his life. "No eye has seen, nor ear heard, nor the heart of man conceived, what God has prepared for those who love him" (1 Cor 2:9). He leaves us to make what we wish of what he saw—or imagined. Are we capable of that much imagination, if it was imagination? Are we ready for so much reality, if it was reality? What greater difference than that between the person who believes in God and the person who does not? Which of the two has wider horizons? Which lives a bigger life? In which life is there more space in which to breathe?

Conscience: Whose Voice?

In chapter six we looked at the extraordinary phenomenon of conscience, that singular voice speaking from within and passing judgment on one's actions. There we suggested that, more than the voice of the intellect, conscience appears as an echo of *a prior voice* of truth. Anyone who takes conscience seriously must be seized by a sense of awe: "These are not just my thoughts. There is something higher and deeper behind this: something in me, and yet above me." Is there not another pointer to transcendence here? To follow one's conscience not only guides one's actions along a path of duty, it raises one's heart and one's whole perspective higher. This is why Cardinal Newman considered conscience to be one of the most compelling proofs, and certainly the proof that is most interior and personal to each of us, of the existence of God. He was, of course, speaking of those who take conscience seriously.

Examining the awareness of duty and the force of conscience, Newman concluded: "all this is an intimation, a clear evidence, that there is something nearer to religion than intellect; and that, if there is a way of finding religious truth, it lies, not in the exercise of the intellect, but close on the side of duty, of conscience, in the observance of the moral law."[26] Newman's observation goes to the heart of the matter. Without a readiness to face up to duty, without a will geared to the moral struggle involved in following the demands of a sincere conscience, no one is likely to *think* himself into accepting the existence of God.

Anyone seeking seriously to understand his own life will pause at length over the problems and pointers offered by the phenomenon of conscience. How to explain this voice of judgment on my actions, a voice that I have not called up or appealed to, and that judges me according to standards I have

---

26. Cf. Wilfrid Ward, *Life of Cardinal Newman*, vol. II, p. 330.

not chosen? How to explain that even if I make up my mind to ignore these standards (say, with reference to chastity), and tell others that they are meaningless to me since I no longer believe in sin, I can much more easily convince others than persuade myself that this is so?

How, then, explain the mysteriously independent status of conscience? It speaks with authority, requires obedience, and will not be silenced. If I do not like what it says, I can try to be deaf to its questionings, commands or prohibitions. By insistently centering my mind on arguments that seem to justify what I prefer to do, I may gradually reduce my conscience to the apparent status of a minor scruple speaking from the background or periphery of my existence, and even to the category of an alien voice, a simple reflection of extraneous influences to which my life has been subjected. Yet, reduced and all, it still speaks—and not from the outside, but from the very depths of my being. It is a part of myself that never ceases, however muffledly, to call for a hearing. To the very end of my days, my inner sincerity, and perhaps my whole destiny, depends on my readiness to respect, and not to want to ignore or instrumentalize, this most intimate expression of my worth and dignity.

Like most people, I can probably present myself as self-contented and quietly self-sufficient *on the outside*, while not being at peace inside—there where no one can penetrate unless I open myself, where I am completely alone in my own privacy. Or am I in fact never completely alone? Why is it that I often cannot silence this voice of conscience, charged at times with tones of reproof? Is it so independent because it is in fact the voice of another? Is there Someone on whom I can never really close the door of my privacy?

This is the point where some people panic and run away. They are afraid to follow out any line of reasoning that could lead from conscience to God. And, not having got beyond the idea of God as a rival to their ego or as a spoilsport to their whims, they are afraid of having to meet God. Ironically, in turning away from a false idea of God, they are running away from a real part of themselves: that most intimate aspect of their faculty of self-knowledge where God has made himself specially present and where special access to him is possible.

To others it seems the height of immaturity and foolishness to be afraid of figuring oneself out. They want at any cost to get to the depth of this mystery of conscience. If it is not just my voice that speaks, it must be the voice of someone else, someone who knows me more truly than I know myself, and who also knows better than I the true value or effect of my actions on my life.

Once conscience is seen as an echo of truth, it is more easily sensed to be a reflection of love. It can then be listened to, and asked questions of, as the loving voice of someone who knows us from within and, with full respect for our freedom, tries delicately, wisely, and affectionately to show us the right and the wrong roads that keep appearing at every juncture of life. Then it no longer appears as a voice to be afraid of. What is rather to be feared is our capacity to turn away from it.

Callista, the heroine of one of Newman's novels about the early Christians, still pagan but more and more drawn to Christianity, explains her awareness of *Someone* (not "something," as her fellow pagans consider their god), who speaks inside her. She asks a pagan philosopher if he believes in one God. "Certainly," he answers, "I believe in one eternal, self-existing something." But she replies that she feels God in her heart. "He says to me 'Do this; don't do that.' You may tell me that this dictate is a mere law of my nature, as to joy or to grieve. I cannot understand this. No, it is the echo of a person speaking to me. . . . My nature feels towards it as towards a person. When I obey it, I feel a satisfaction; when I disobey, a soreness—just like that which I find in pleasing or offending some revered friend. So you see, I believe in what is more than a mere 'something.' . . . An echo implies a voice; a voice a speaker. That speaker I love and fear."[27]

The voice of conscience is firm—but quiet rather than loud. Therefore I must be prepared to fine-tune my reception of it, in order to gradually get its message in greater clarity. Newman says that conscience, "is so constituted that, if obeyed, it becomes clearer in its injunctions, and wider in their range, and corrects and completes the accidental feebleness of its initial teachings."[28] The opposite is also true, however. If a person, with all the strength of a selfish will, deliberately turns a deaf ear to the initial and almost imperceptible, but highly personal, voice of conscience, he can come to confuse all the signals arising from within, and end up being guided not by the voice of conscience, but by that of selfishness—with all its capacity for self-deception.

A thinking person can decide (regardless of whether this is wise or foolish) to ignore the question of death, leaving it for a more or less remote future when it overtakes him. Conscience cannot be dealt with in this way. It is too irremediably and urgently present to be ignored by anyone who takes himself seriously. It gives advice unasked for, approves some of our actions, condemns others, and just will not go away. It speaks, and demands to be heard. It claims authority, and we feel the force of that authority without being able to deny or explain it.

To describe conscience as a voice of judgment is not to suggest that it always judges negatively. It would therefore be an error to think of it as no more than a disturbing inner voice of self-recrimination, apt to render a person's life intolerable. No. To command and to prohibit are the important functions of conscience. If one goes against its commands or prohibitions, then comes the reproach, precisely in the form of a *self*-reproach: "*I* have done wrong; I have

---

27. John Henry Newman: *Callista*, Ch. 27.
28. *Grammar of Assent*, Ch. 10.

done what I should not have done, or I have failed to do what I ought to have done."[29] If on the contrary one follows the imperatives of conscience, it will signify its approval, usually by ceasing to speak, perhaps at most with a simple, "Well done; now get on with the rest of your life." It is wise, however, not to dwell too much on the approving conscience. To do so can foster that self-satisfaction which in turn easily leads to self-deception. We can be certain about the occasions when we acted against conscience. But that we have acted in full accordance with conscience, and that conscience itself has guided us properly, can only be a matter for hope. St. Paul is not aware of sin, but still is not totally sure of himself: "I do not even judge myself. I am not aware of anything against myself, but I am not thereby acquitted. It is the Lord who judges me" (1 Cor 4:3–4).

Anyone with experience in psychological or spiritual counseling has known people with unhealthy and exaggerated feelings of guilt, out of all proportion to any possible wrongdoing. Nevertheless, while one can be haunted about possibly wrong actions, one can be indifferent about really wrong ones. The latter is probably the worse pathology. And yet there is something still worse.

A person can purposely seek to be free from *any* suggestion (coming from outside or inside) that he has done wrong. There is a healthy sense of having done wrong; and there is an unhealthy persuasion—which at times amounts to a pathological determination to be convinced, with a conviction that others must not shake—that one has never done wrong. It is the contemporary obsession with self-esteem, that predominant Victorian and modern "value" we mentioned earlier: craving for personal approbation, posturing for a perfect self-image, striving to create virtual virtue.

The mindset of our age is to put self first, to be Number One in our own interests and estimation. Self-protection may seem reasonable; yet if it means closing in on self, it is an effective block to self-fulfillment. Self-esteem has a legitimate scope, but becomes dangerous when cultivated as a priority. Self-protection, just like self-esteem, is a favorable mood for self-deception.

Self-esteem, in any case, must remain an ambiguous concept for a Christian. The Christian estimation of self—his or her sense of identity—always has two sides to it: "I am a son or daughter of God" (an overwhelming truth which is a constant source of consolation and peace); and "I am a sinner in need of forgiveness and redemption" (an inescapable conviction of having done wrong and of being in peril, to one's last moment). The two appraisals are true; only Christianity makes it possible to combine the two in a life of war and peace.

---

29. Note how it speaks: the admonishment does not come as from an outside source or an extraneous judge, saying, "*You* have done wrong." It is I myself, from the depths of my self-awareness, who reproach myself, saying, "I have done wrong." We have stressed the independent status of conscience; it is not a yes man of my mind or my will. Nevertheless, it is *mine*; it is part of me.

The "selfism" of humanistic psychotherapy has no place for sin, guilt, repentance, or forgiveness; it offers peace on easier terms. In building self from self, it sees personal experiences not only as singular to each one but also as the *right* experiences for him, so as to construct a unique self. "Weaknesses" become strengths, "defects" become rightful traits of character; it all depends on how one chooses to see them. How far this is from the Christian approach to personal weaknesses! If the Christian need not lose peace over his defects it is because God continues to love him—despite them. But these defects still threaten his growth. He needs to fight them, trusting in God's grace so as to overcome, and returning to the fight whenever he has failed. Selfism proposes a totally different norm. A defect is a hindrance to growth when it is "ego-*dystonic*," i.e. a disturbance to one's personal sense of well-being. One can fight to get rid of it; but that may not be necessary, for it can be neutralized or, rather, integrated into a positive pattern of "growth" through a new personal decision of accepting it as part of "me" and therefore "right for me." And so, by a simple change of approach, one achieves an "ego-*syntonic*" contentment: self-esteem from within, without limit or reproach, and on one's own terms.[30]

✿ ✿ ✿

In our anthropological analysis, openness/acceptance toward values emerges as the key to personal development. The fullest and happiest life is that of the person who has many genuine values—in possession or in firm hope—along

30. These unusual terms of differentiation—"ego-dystonic" and "ego-syntonic"—were given coinage by the American Psychiatric Association in the twenty-one-year process (1973–1994) through which homosexuality was gradually removed from the classification of a psychic disorder. *The Diagnostic and Statistical Manual of Mental Disorders*, the official diagnostic manual of the APA, was first published in 1952; the second edition, *DSM-II*, in 1968. Both unqualifiedly classify homosexuality as a mental disorder. It appears as the first among "Sexual Deviations," being followed by fetishism, pedophilia, transvestism, etc. (*DSM-II*, p. 44). Regarding all these deviations, the general observation is made: "Even though many find their practices distasteful, they remain unable to substitute normal sexual behavior for them" (ibid.). In 1973 the governing body of the APA voted to eliminate homosexuality from the category of a psychic disorder. *DSM-III* (1980), in adapting to this vote, invoked a concept of *syntonia/dystonia*. "Homosexuality that is ego-syntonic is not classified as a mental disorder" (p. 282), although "ego-dystonic homosexuality" is still categorized as a psychosexual disorder (261; 281–282). This is further explained: "a homo-sexual arousal pattern that is unacceptable to the individual would be ego-dystonic, whereas, if the individual were not distressed by the pattern and experienced it as acceptable, it would be ego-syntonic" (p. 359). This peculiar distinction was maintained, albeit in a rather veiled way, in *DSM-III-R*, the revised 1987 edition (see pp. 561 & 296), and then dropped completely in *DSM-IV* (1994) when any mention of homosexuality disappeared from this well-known and influential manual. A full account of this process, and of the considerable contention it generated among psychiatrists themselves, is given in my article, "Psychiatry: A 'Value-Free' Science?" (*The Linacre Quarterly*, vol. 67 [2000], pp. 59–88), which is itself drawn from a Sentence of the Roman Rota, *coram* Burke, of July 9, 1998 (Latin and English versions published in *Monitor Ecclesiasticus*, vol. 125 (2000–II), pp. 254–331).

with a high capacity to appreciate them. The person, in other words, who manages not to get used to his situation; who keeps his appreciation and his acceptance alive.

Thus the process of fulfillment is one of appreciation and response, of admiration, of readiness to look up and to break narrow and confined horizons, so as to assimilate and be filled. Is there a limit to this process? Is death the end and frustration of all fulfillment? We left the answers to the reader; and, with a final comment, we will still leave them there where they belong—with each one.

Presupposing that death is not the ultimate frustration—*believing* that death marks a beginning more than an end[31]—man's capacity for transcendence now takes on the character of a potential for infinity, for eternity. Man becomes *capax Dei*, capable of living the very life of God.

I can find my fulfillment only through and in another "I." Only by giving myself to another "I," abandoning myself and losing myself in Him, can I find my own real self, become myself, in becoming more than myself.

"Christian revelation excludes reincarnation and speaks of a fulfillment which man is called to achieve in the course of a single earthly existence. Man achieves this fulfillment of his destiny through the sincere gift of self, a gift which is made possible only through his encounter with God. It is in God that man finds full self-realization. This is the truth revealed by Christ. Man fulfills himself in God, who comes to meet him through his eternal Son. Thanks to God's coming on earth, human time, which began at creation, has reached its fullness. 'The fullness of time' is in fact eternity; indeed, it is the One who is eternal, God himself. Thus, to enter into 'the fullness of time' means to reach the end of time and to transcend its limits in order to find time's fulfillment in the eternity of God."[32]

God: On Stage or Off Stage?

This is the point at which we take leave of the reader, but not without a reference back to the "Niagara Falls syndrome" mentioned in an earlier chapter. Any deliberate limiting of wonder is a refusal of fulfillment. To feel reduced by the achievements or greatness of others is to reduce oneself in fact. "I will look up, but not to any height, not as far as it is possible to see," is an impoverishing choice of shortsightedness.

---

31. I say *believing*, because there is no way of *knowing* that there is a life after death, just as there is no way of knowing that there is *no life* after death. Regarding an afterlife, atheistic denial is just as much an act of faith as is Christian hope (see Appendix One). The agnostic who admits he doesn't know, is at least sincere (though hardly happy and self-contented) about his ignorance. He *is* ignorant. The atheist is a believer, no less than the theist. The former chooses negative faith—to believe in ultimate annihilation. The latter chooses positive faith—to believe in ultimate deification.

32. John Paul II, *Tertio Millennio Adveniente*, no. 9.

Aware of the cramping power of jealousy, I must learn to use envy as a stimulus to emulation, and if emulation is beyond me, to admiration; ready to admire to the utmost limit, and hoping that I may encounter what can be admired without any limit—a value and, behind the value, a person, capable of stirring me to the joy of unending wonder.

An anthropology of values may not lead on to the discovery of God, unless due heed is given to what was noted in chapter seven; the fact that it is seldom difficult to admire the work of some artist or athlete who is dead or at least totally unknown to us, whereas admiration or appreciation may prove less spontaneous and more difficult if we happen to know the talented person. In other words, it is easier to translate appreciation of a work into admiration for the artist when the latter has, so to speak, disappeared from the stage, has become a glory of the past but is not a real and present danger, a living and active threat to my personal glory or self-esteem.[33]

Insofar as this is so, it can provide a clue to why some people prefer never to let God onto the stage of their lives. God, if He exists, cannot ever be relegated just to the past. He is present in the life of each one, and to admit his presence means to face up to the need to build everything around a new frame of reference. I do not occupy center stage, even in my own life. God does; and only if I learn to discover and admire his action can I learn to play my own role to the full and successfully—even triumphantly.

It is certainly true that if I let God onto the stage of my life, a lot of things will need readjusting. There is a piece to be played from beginning to end: my life. I am the protagonist; the main part is mine. But as regards the script, it no longer appears as something that I must make up as I go along. There is a plot—a superb one—already set, composed specially for my individual talents, and in which I can more than excel myself. The main lines of the script are already there, together with plenty of scope for me to fill in, or to make impromptu interpretations. The Writer, who is the greatest Master of scripting, is also Producer and Director, and of such outstanding talent that to be the leading player in the piece is—if I am able to grasp this—a much more extraordinary bit of luck than if I were my own writer-producer-director, playing—perhaps—to a world TV audience (or, perhaps, before a lethargic group in a back street theater). My privilege is that I have been chosen by the greatest Director as star in a one-time-only performance, to go down in history and to be played before an audience of all generations, who are not only wholeheartedly with the Director in his choice of leading actor, but also fully confident that I can play a masterful role.

---

33. The greatness of someone like Napoleon was lessened by his self-centeredness, always wanting more glory for himself. Such greatness is small when compared to that of the non-self-centered person who is able to *respond to glory* and who does so, rather than seeking it simply as a means to inflate his own ego. He grows more; paradoxically he becomes greater.

This is the final dilemma and choice. If I am not capable of looking out and looking up, of forgetting myself and responding, I will remain in my own self-sufficiency—for what it is worth. If, because absolute independence is my non-negotiable ideal, I am not capable of any lasting commitment to anything or anyone, I am most likely headed for total isolation and utter loneliness.[34]

T. S. Eliot urges the need to avoid "the final desolation/Of solitude in the phantasmal world/Of imagination, shuffling memories and desires." His Celia comments, "That is the hell I have been in." And the reply comes: "It isn't hell/Till you become incapable of anything else . . ."[35]

A last word about this possible final destination. If I am incapable of admiration and wonder, if I have not combatted petty jealousy towards men, I may fall victim to a diabolic jealousy towards God. For I can indeed choose to be the limit of my own horizons, the maximum object of my own esteem, the ultimate value in my own life. What, then, will I give in exchange for my life? What price can I put on it? What is it worth? And, as my years come to an end, what *was* its worth?

If God does not exist, my life, in the end, is worth nothing.

If God exists, my life, in the end, is worth—*can* be worth—everything.

My life is not yet a completed project. It has its present worth, more or less satisfactory to my eyes and more or less corresponding to its possible worth, but changing ever day. What will be its definitive worth? That is up to me. My life—a life still in the making—is in my hands and those of no one else. In the end—in the definitive beginning—it will be what I have made of it.

---

34. "Absolute independence is a false ideal. It delivers not the autonomy it promises but loneliness and vulnerability instead": *Habits of the Heart*, p. 247.
35. *The Cocktail Party*, Act 2.

Appendix I

SCIENCE, REASON, AND GOD

"Most believers," we are told in a recent study, "will agree that their belief is not a scientific one, and many are attracted to the idea that science and religion give complementary accounts of the universe, describing the same ultimate reality from different sides, as it were. However, this still does not explain how religious statements can give knowledge of one particular aspect of reality, unless they are testable by some sort of experience. This remains one of the most basic philosophical problems about religious claims."[1]

An overly quick reading of this passage might miss the transition it makes from the empirical realm to the philosophical—a transition as unjustified as it is common. Whoever reflects seriously about life (which the philosopher, among others, is supposed to do) quickly realizes that human knowledge cannot be reduced to what is verifiable by empirical testing or direct personal experience. Otherwise, one would have to maintain that historical statements are not scientific, and go on to deny to history itself the status of "knowledge." Legal science progresses by means of rationally thought-out arguments and conclusions, without these being subject to empirical proof. Reliable knowledge of life, and credible answers to the questions life poses, must derive from clear reasoning. But only those who are unaccustomed to thinking clearly, or

---

1. L. Stevenson & D. L. Haberman, *Ten Theories of Human Nature*, 1998, p. 73.

to the whole process of rational debate, will wish to limit knowledge to what can be empirically verified.

Thoughtful believers will probably agree that their belief is not scientific, within the terms of the *empirical* sciences. But that is in no way to say that it is not rational, or that a question such as the existence of God cannot be rationally dealt with. Nor would the thoughtful believer readily accept that *physical* science can examine and explain "the same ultimate reality" as does religion, simply from a different angle. Science just does not reach or try to explain ultimate reality; and I know of no scientist who claims that it does. The approach characteristic of science is, rather, to hold that, in the process of clarifying the nature of things, more can always be investigated and, hopefully, discovered.

Logical positivists prefer to exclude investigation into the question of "ultimate reality," holding that there is simply no answer to it. Yet the truly rational person is not content with this arbitrary limiting of the scope of reason and rational investigation. The search for "ultimate reality" or "ultimate explanations" touches the very heart of all human reflection. We have seen that man does not explain himself, that anthropology leads "beyond" anthropology and points to something beyond its own proper field. Physical science itself would be adopting an "a priori" or dogmatic approach if it were to exclude the possibility that its investigation into the nature or explanation of things could open up horizons which transcend its own domain. Just as anthropology points to transcendence, so physics leads on to metaphysics.

"Meta-physical" (beyond physics) does not mean "meta-rational" (beyond reason). One's mind is capable of reaching much farther than the world one sees and touches with the physical senses. Further, it is not true that metaphysical reasoning, being non-empirical, is "a priori," and therefore ideological, prejudiced, or irrational. There is nothing irrational or "a priori" about refusing to shelve the question of "ultimate reality," or about wanting an adequate explanation of the world. Perhaps the explanation finally given cannot be verified by empirical methods (is it possible even to conceive an empirical test that could be "scientifically" applied to an ultimate reality?), but it can be a strictly rational conclusion, as being the only reasonably adequate answer to the question posed.

Certainly, not all problems or questions have to be posed, nor do all those posed have to be answered. Yet, to anyone who takes life seriously, the problem of the world and of human life—their origin and ultimate purpose—is not an insignificant or optional question. It occurs, pressingly, to every reflective person as the key question in the most important and definitive area of investigation facing mankind, and can only be shelved by those who are unthinking or do not wish to think.

Human reason is there to investigate reality. This is the true scientific endeavor. It is evident that reality itself is not limited to the physical or tangible-visible world. Otherwise one would have to deny the reality of the whole of mathematical science, for mathematics is neither tangible nor visible. Whether a mathematical theorem holds true or not has to be examined rationally, but it allows of no empirical demonstration. The teacher who puts his theorem on the blackboard is not following an empirical method; he is not offering a tangible or visible proof of his thesis but is simply, at most, facilitating the application of pure reason to the question of whether it makes sense or not. The whole scientific method in mathematics is rational, but not empirical.

So it is with any scientific examination of the question "Is there a God?" Here the scientific mind has to look for rational evidence. To ask for empirical evidence is to show that one has not even grasped the nature of the investigation. No physical experiments can give empirical proof of the existence—or nonexistence—of God. God is not to be discovered at the end of a telescope, nor does he emerge from a test-tube experiment or a quantum mechanics equation. This is true whether one offers a positive or a negative answer to the question proposed; in other words, neither the existence of God nor his nonexistence can be empirically proved. Hence, the assertion "There is no God" is as unempirical as the assertion "God exists." From the standpoint of empirical science, the first is just as much an act of faith as the second.

When the empirical approach is clearly inadequate to provide an answer to a necessary question, then the human mind will use other rational means in seeking an answer (unless it *prefers* the ostrich-like reaction of wanting not to think the matter out). One considers possible answers—hypotheses—and one reduces the hypotheses to the most reasonable one, eliminating or rejecting those that are empty, far-fetched, or patently absurd. To refuse to consider any hypothesis, just as to refuse to declare which of the possible hypotheses presented strikes one as more reasonable, is a blind refusal to reason.[2]

The *Encyclopaedia Britannica* article on Metaphysics notes that "metaphysics is far from being a simple empirical discipline," and yet "is strictly intellectual in its development," its insights being "derived from reflection on certain evident facts." Metaphysics, at least christian metaphysics, does not begin with *a priori* assumptions about God or another life. It starts with the evident fact of the world as we know it, with its mysterious disorders certainly, but especially with its evident order and design. The reasoning is simple and can be illustrated by applying it to any familiar object—say, the table or desk on which I am writing. The table is old and it is wooden; beyond that I know

---

2. The *Encyclopaedia Britannica* under "Principles of Physical Science" says that the scientist's concern in the following of a hypothesis, "is to convince himself and his critical colleagues that a hypothesis has passed enough tests to make it worth accepting *until a better one presents itself*" (emphasis added). Metaphysical science (applying the "tests" of rational argument), no less than its physical counterpart, does follow this same intellectual procedure.

nothing about it. I have no idea where it was bought or how much it cost. But of one thing I am certain: someone made it. Or, perhaps more precisely and to the point, someone designed it and then had it made. Of that I am sure. An argumentative friend may feel entitled to object, "But how can you be so sure? After all, you have no proof. You cannot discount some other possibility: say, that a tree gradually evolved in its natural growth into the exact shape of that table, drawers and legs and all." Sorry; but I can and do discount that "possibility." I cannot take my friend's hypothesis seriously. He is being argumentative, but neither scientific nor rational. Where you see an evident design, the rational thing is to posit a designer. Not to do so is a *pose*—something proper to a clown or an actor, but not to a thinker.

The question of the origin of the desk thus resolves itself into two hypotheses: one from design, the other from chance. If one has to choose between the two, there can be little question as to which the thinking person will accept. The first is rational, the second is outlandish and absurd.

Let us take away the desk, which does not matter, and put in its place the world—which is the object of our reflection. Following the same metaphysical (rational and hence scientific, although non-empirical) analysis, I conclude, with all the certainty the human mind can attain, that the world came from a designer.

What about Evolution and the "Big Bang?" Well, what about them? The desk also had its evolution; it gradually took shape—by means of someone working on the wood, according to a design. And the tree (from which the wood came), like the Big Bang,[3] also had to have its origin in a design, a Designer, for it to have been endowed with the potential for further growth and possibilities.

In carrying our rational investigation to its limit, we can, of course, keep proposing the further alternatives that emerge. Does admitting that the world we know must have materialized from some initial design necessarily imply some original and primary personal intelligence? As we pursue our investigation here we are again left ultimately with a choice between two hypotheses. Either the world, with all its evidence of design, comes from the plan of an original intelligent Designer (in which case it did come by design); or else it has come from a non-intelligent source (in which case it is a work of chance, and we have in fact denied our admission of design). Again we have to decide which hypothesis seems more reasonable.

---

3. The Big Bang theory is of course a hypothesis about a major stage in the physical evolution of the universe, not about its ultimate origin. The *Encyclopaedia Britannica* describes it as a "theory of the evolution of the universe [which makes] it possible to calculate *the history of the cosmos after a certain epoch* called the Planck time. Scientists have yet to determine what prevailed *before* Planck time" (emphasis added).

Of course. the definitive question is about the origin of the first Designer. How did he get there? Either we hold the first Designer to be non-created, that is, a self-existing being—"always there"—or else we posit a created Designer. But then who designed *him*? We are still within a process and have not yet reached an explanation of its origin. There is no rational end to the investigation unless one posits an eternal, self-subsistent, all-powerful, intelligent being, who is at the origin of everything; in other words, unless one accepts the "God hypothesis." Any other hypothesis is inadequate, totally inadequate, and therefore to be discarded by the unprejudiced scientific mind.

Reason, no less than faith, finds it harder to believe in nothingness than to believe in God. Absolute annihilation is simply an untenable scientific hypothesis for a physicist; so too is the emergence of something from nothing. What is cannot lapse into nothing; similarly, what is cannot come from nothing.

Evident design posits an intelligent designer. The *contra* argument, that the presence of disorder shows the absence of a designer, is a non sequitur. Disorder and apparent chaos do exist, as do evident order and design. Disorder also requires an explanation (and many hypotheses can be advanced to explain it). But its continued existence, even if mysterious and unexplained, in no way takes from the absolute rationality and the common-sense power of the argument that where there is clear evidence of design, one can be certain in positing an intelligent designer. The room or the house in which I work may be in a chaotic state, not having been cleaned or put in order for months. But if I look at the desk on which I work and the house in which I work, all of that disorder does not prevent me from concluding that someone designed them, and that they were then elaborated (perhaps by other agents, and through a long process) until they took shape according to the original conception.

If we pass from disorder to evil, the same applies. The statement, "The existence of evil proves that there is no God," is a non-argument. The existence of evil tends to originate difficulties in understanding *God's ways of acting*, if he exists. But it is no proof of his nonexistence. That God and evil cannot coexist is neither evident nor verifiable.

But, in order to be logical, must we not then admit that the proposition "The existence of the world proves that there is a God," is equally a non sequitur? If it were presented as an *empirical* proof ("It is established that there is a world; hence it is demonstrated that there is a God"), this would indeed be an inadequate argument. But if we abandon the empirical approach (as we should) in favor of rational argumentation and ask, "Can the existence of the world be explained without positing a God?," then any true scientific method calls for pursuit and solution (if possible) of the issue by means of reasoning: taking reasoning, pure reasoning, to the limits where it can rationally lead us. This is what we have just done, through the comparison and elimination of hypotheses. This is to act reasonably and scientifically. Any other procedure is dogmatism or the choice simply not to think, i.e. the rejection of reason.

Let us note in passing that some people not only believe there is no God, but choose to take their disbelief as their presupposition and starting point in any consideration of the matter. There is something bizarre as well as unscientific about this. If one sets out to investigate the possibility that an infinitely good, wise, powerful, and loving Being exists, the logical human approach is the *hope of positive discovery* (the hope that the possibility can be verified), with the feeling, What a pity if it cannot! That was the spirit of the great explorers whose discoveries enriched the life of mankind. Each of us has an explorer inside who wants to discover the infinite. If he cannot, his horizons remain narrower, his life poorer, and he has to live and die with the disappointment. Of course, death may reveal to him that he was wrong.

Atheism: Freedom and Joy, or Deadend and Nausea?

The atheist can, in a sense, be self-sufficient—at the cost of living in a meaningless world. Self-sufficient non-transcendence has always been the most fundamental and the most hollow temptation for mankind.[4] If the intellect, for all its power, is unable to penetrate the shadows that surround the mystery of life and death and to reach the promise of a *personal* "hereafter," it cannot free man from the sense of ultimate futility.

A well-known study of Renaissance civilization pictures the leading men and women of that historical period freed by their "powerful natures" and independent minds from the "constraining christian myths" of heaven and hell, and from notions such as sin, repentance, and salvation (however much these notions still flourished among the uneducated), letting themselves be captivated by "the new liberal ideas of a future life" which hark back to the Greco-Roman ideal of a "pagan heaven," a sort of "transfigured hereafter for great men, pervaded by the harmony of the spheres."[5]

---

4. Pride (which Chesterton once described as the "falsification of fact by the introduction of self") can prevent the intelligent person from seeing how empty this temptation of the intellect is. Newman regarded proud self-sufficiency as the main obstacle to faith: "If I must submit my reason to mysteries, it is not much matter whether it is a mystery more or a mystery less; the main difficulty is to believe at all; the main difficulty for an inquirer is firmly to hold that there is a living God, in spite of the darkness which surrounds Him, the Creator, Witness, and Judge of men. When once the mind is broken in, as it must be, to the belief of a Power above it, when once it understands that it is not itself the measure of all things in heaven and earth, it will have little difficulty in going forward. I do not say it will, or can, go on to other truths without conviction; I do not say it ought to believe the Catholic Faith without grounds and motives; but I say that, when once it believes in God, the great obstacle to faith has been taken away, a proud, self-sufficient spirit": *Discourses to Mixed Congregations* (Disc. 13).
5. Jacob Burckhardt, *The Civilization of the Renaissance in Italy*, pp. 412–413.

But is the progress of a powerful nature really shown, or an independent mind really achieved, by the reduction of an individuals' personal life to nothing more than a passing anecdote which, once told, leaves behind—for others—the memory of a "greatness" (or what one trusts will be considered such) "in harmony with the spheres?"

Is this a liberal and progressive outlook? Or could it not rather reflect the narrow vision of the proud man, accompanied by an antique and snobbish contempt for what satisfies the populace? A vision that, not so strangely, is already dated.

Post-Renaissance rationalism, culminating in the philosophy of the Enlightenment, taught that life is not mysterious; that nature is and can be shown to be self-explanatory; that existence is non-transcendental. Ernst Cassirer, a prominent scholar of the Enlightenment, thus describes the principles from which it worked: "What always prevented the human mind from achieving a real conquest of nature and from feeling quite at home there was the unfortunate tendency to ask for a realm beyond. If we set aside this question of transcendence, nature ceases at once to be a mystery." In the Enlightenment view, Cassirer says, "nature is not mysterious and unknowable, but the human mind has enveloped it in artificial darkness. If we remove the mask of words, of arbitrary concepts, of phantastic prejudices from the face of nature, it will reveal itself as it really is, as an organic whole, self-supporting and self-explanatory. . . . The riddle of nature vanishes for the mind which dares to stand its ground and cope with it."[6]

The thrust and intent of the Enlightenment, and of the rationalist trends that preceded and followed it, was to eliminate all sense of mystery: there is no mystery, everything has its explanation. Before considering if this attempt succeeded, one could well question whether its basic assumption could ever have proved ultimately enriching for human life.[7]

All knowledge is good.[8] But a search for knowledge which sets out from the assumption that everything can eventually be explained, in other words, that knowledge itself is finite, is a search for that deadend we have mentioned before—where nothing is left to be investigated or explained, no sense of possible discovery remains to science, and man's horizons have reached their definitive limit. From the viewpoint of "values" which we have been following, this is an impoverishment. Man would then "dominate" the whole of reality;

---

6. Ernst Cassirer, *The Philosophy of the Enlightenment*, 1951, p. 65.

7. Cf. Albert Einstein's dictum: "The mysterious is the source of all true art and science."

8. More precisely, all knowledge of good is good. Knowledge of evil (of the absence or negation of good) is good if it facilitates a person's avoiding evil. But if evil is not truly understood as the absence of good, but is rather mistaken for good (which can happen), that is not good. The defect there is either the fallibility of the mind (which mistakes evil for good) or the weakness of the will (which, though rightly informed of what is good, prefers evil).

he could look down on everything; but he would have nothing left to look up to. The rejection of mystery is the rejection of wonder. The mind that can explain everything wonders at nothing. It has removed a fundamental element of happiness and fulfillment from its horizons. It has seized the world and closed it in on itself.

But it was self-deception for rationalism to claim that "nature" or the world explains itself. If it had been more clear-thinking (and perhaps more humble), it would have realized that its attempt was bound to fail. If it had been more human, it would never have wished it to succeed. All it could have done was to reason nature and the world back to an original self-existing cause (in itself an inexhaustible mystery and source of wonder for man); but this it did not want to do. It preferred to be convinced that its attempt to explain away all mystery must succeed.

Not Coping with the Riddle . . .

This persuasion of the Enlightenment that a rational explanation of every-thing had been given, that "the riddle of nature" had been coped with or solved, was congenial enough to the nineteenth century—a period not noted for its depth of philosophical thought. Things were to change during the course of the century that followed.

Somerset Maugham, one of the main British writers of the period between the two World Wars, was a dogged agnostic. He deliberately turned away from the rationalist posture of being able to explain everything. He held, on the contrary, that meaning and explanation are to be rejected; and that the consequence for man will be a new freedom and joy. The following passage from his well-known novel, *Of Human Bondage*, shows him laboring enthusi-astically at this millennial pretense:

"There was no meaning in life, and man by living served no end. . . . Life was insignificant and death without consequence. Philip exulted . . . ; it seemed to him that the last burden of responsibility was taken from him; and for the first time he was utterly free. His insignificance was turned to power, and he felt himself suddenly equal with the cruel fate which had seemed to persecute him; for, if life was meaningless, the world was robbed of its cruelty. . . . Failure was unimportant and success amounted to nothing. He was the most inconsiderable creature in that swarming mass of mankind which for a brief space occupied the surface of the earth; and he was almighty because he had wrenched from chaos the secret of its nothingness. Thoughts came tumbling over one another in Philip's eager fancy, and he took long breaths of joyous satisfaction. . . . In throwing over the desire for happiness he was casting aside the last of his illusions. His life had seemed horrible when it was measured by its happiness, but now he seemed to gather strength as he realized that it might be measured by something else. Happiness mattered as little as pain . . . Philip was happy."[9]

This may be written with a certain style; but does it make sense? Can anyone seriously think that to see life as having no meaning leads to a sensation of power and joy?[10] Why should one exult to discover that failure is unimportant and success amounts to nothing? Why should one be happy to discover that happiness matters as little as pain? If it matters so little, why bother about it—about happiness or pain or meaning or joy? Yet we do bother. Am I to throw over the desire for happiness, precisely so as to feel happy? Maugham's playing with words may have been aimed at fooling himself. I wonder how many of his readers he fooled.

John Galsworthy's epic, *The Forsyte Saga*, shows the nature and development of upper-middle-class "values" during the period from 1870 to 1930. It presents a rich range of characters and of attitudes, from the more convention-bound and unconsciously hypocritical of the Victorian years to the more spontaneous and frankly "carpe diem" of the post-"Great War" generation. The first are formally "religious"; the latter are openly not. But in the philosophy of life of one and the other there is simply no place for the transcendent.

Fleur Forsyte is prototype of the modern young thing of the 1920s. Calculatingly gay and brightly sensitive, she loves "exciting" beauty—beauty full of movement and change. "I can't bear Greek plays; they're so long. I think beauty's always swift."[11] Lasting love or beauty which calls for commitment is beyond her comprehension. No commitment can be definitive; there must always be a way out, a chance of deliverance. It is only logical to reject moral laws once they "stand in the way of happiness and progress. . . . Marriage without a decent chance of relief is only a sort of slave-owning; people oughtn't to own each other. Everybody sees that now."[12] Commercialism has taken over all interpersonal relations, even marriage. The idea of mutual *belonging*, in a committed love of reciprocal self-giving, has been lost. One simply owns or is owned. Therefore the only wise thing is not to depend or be made dependent on anything: just hold on to and live for yourself.

Better to "keep" yourself—even if you keep yourself for nothing. So "young Jolyon," the transitional Forsyte, philosophizes about the post-war

---

9. Somerset Maugham: *Of Human Bondage*, Ch. 106.

10. The American sociologist, Philip Rieff, admits that the rejection of transcendent views is grim. But, he adds, "the grimness is relieved by the gaiety of being free from the historic Western compulsion of seeking large and general meanings for small and highly particular lives" (*The Triumph of the Therapeutic*, p. 59). This ignores the fact that every particular life remains small if no larger meaning can be found for it; and begs the question of what real relief is provided by taking superficial gaiety as a cover for underlying grimness.

11. *The Forsyte Saga*, p. 567.

12. Ibid. p. 607.

generation: "The young are tired of us, our gods and our ideals. Off with their heads, they say—smash their idols. And let's get back to—nothing! . . . Property, beauty, sentiment—all smoke. We mustn't own anything nowadays, not even our feelings. They stand in the way of—Nothing."[13] Galsworthy, who possibly had a residue of the religious faith that Maugham made such profession of denying, at least saw the nothingness to which the lack of values of modern times was leading.

Life, in this view, has no objective end or purpose. Along with transcendence, morality too can be dropped.[14] There are no given norms to guide what I do in or with my life. Morality, if there needs to be such a thing, is something I discover or make up for myself. We see it again in Philip Carey, the central figure in *Of Human Bondage*. He finds the "joyous" freedom of newly found atheism still hampered by the moral baggage inherited from his youth. "He made up his mind therefore to think things out for himself. . . . He determined to be swayed by no prejudices. He swept away the virtues and the vices, the established laws of good and evil, with the idea of finding out the rule of life for himself. He did not know whether rules were necessary at all. That was one of the things he wanted to discover. . . . Philip wanted to find out how he ought to behave, and he thought he could prevent himself from being influenced by the opinions that surrounded him. But meanwhile he had to go on living, and, until he formed a theory of conduct, he made himself a provisional rule: 'Follow your inclinations with due regard to the policeman round the corner. . . .'"[15]

A provisional rule indeed, and flexible enough to permit constant revision. If the prohibitions of 'the law' constitute the maximum limit or risk of morality, then limit can be extended and risk reduced through a progressive 'liberalization' of the law, until it exists simply to sanction whatever anyone wants.

The Hollow People

T. S. Eliot, in line after forceful line of his poetry, shows the lonely emptiness of the spirit which so many of his contemporaries, Maugham and Galsworthy among them, presented as natural and liberating. "Remember us—if at all—not as lost violent souls, but only as the hollow men, the stuffed men."[16]

---

13. Ibid. p. 618.
14. By the late sixties this had become the confident tenet of popular psychology: the true way to self-fulfillment is a life lived within purely earthly dimensions, on one's own terms, and without any bothersome morality. A generation later, it is questionable if most Westerners are convinced that the horizons of their lives have really become broader and richer, or that self-fulfillment flows automatically from a life stripped of a sense of the transcendent and of objective moral demands.
15. Ch. 53.
16. *The Hollow Men*, I.

"Without purpose, and without principle of conduct/In flickering intervals of light and darkness/One thinks to escape . . . but one is still alone/In an over-crowded desert, jostled by ghosts."[17] "It takes so many years to learn that one is dead!"[18] "My self-possession gutters; we are really in the dark."[19] Eliot was understandably impressed by Scott Fitzgerald's *The Great Gatsby*, with its depiction of the Jazz age, "herding its inhabitants"—the bright young things of the 1920s—"along a short-cut from nothing to nothing."[20]

Twentieth-century paganism held out heady promises of both freedom and joy, yet those who followed it found a freedom that stirs no admiration and a joy scarcely worth singing about or celebrating. The backdrop to Robert Frost's poem, "Pan with us," is pagan worship enfeebled by Christianity: still offering gratification, but with no power for human fulfillment and with an underlying sense of worthlessness. Pan, the mythological god of fertility, half-man, half-beast, appears as old and saddened. He could keep up the pretense of playing his pipes, but "Times were changed from what they were: Such pipes kept less of power to stir. . . . They were pipes of pagan mirth, And the world had found new terms of worth. He laid him down on sunburned earth, And raveled a flower and looked away. Play? Play?—What should he play?"[21]

By the middle of the twentieth century, especially after two barbaric World Wars, more reflective minds turned from both hollow rationalism and thoughtless hedonism to an assertive and bitter skepticism lacking in any pre-tense to happiness or self-satisfaction. Jean-Paul Sartre pushed the philosophy of hollowness to its ultimate conclusion. For him, too, life is meaningless. But while Maugham's Philip Carey sees in this a cause of celebration, Sartre is *disgusted* by it. Each thing is alone and disconnected, and in consequence value-less. The only relationship he can establish between things is that they are *in the way of* each other. Things are in the way. *He* is in the way: "I was *in the way* for eternity." Life, without purpose or meaning, is indeed absurd. Absurdity: this is his "key to Existence, the key to my Nauseas, to my own life. . . ." "In fact all that I could grasp beyond that returns to this fundamental absurdity."[22] Those who hold that life lacks any ultimate value or transcendent purpose or meaning have no answer to offer—if they think things out logically—to Sartre's conclusion that such an outlook makes life absurd and nauseating.

Sartre in effect takes Eliot's comments and erects them into his own philos-ophy of nihilism: the worthlessness of life compounded by the exasperating

---

17. *The Family Reunion*, Part I. Sc. 1.
18. Ibid. Part II, Sc. 3.
19. *Portrait of a Lady*.
20. *The Great Gatsby*, ch. 6.
21. The 'flower people' of the 1960s also raveled many things, and looked away—to what? They too ended up finding little in what they chose to play.
22. *Nausea*, New York, 1964, pp. **.

presence of others. Life is indeed no more than an "over-crowded desert"; other people, however unsubstantial their ghostlike existence, are in the way— of my purposelessness. And I, ghost that I am, am in their way.

Sartre's philosophy allows him one ultimate self-satisfaction. He is superior to others because he sees, while they fail to see, the worthlessness and absurdity of the lives with which they pretend to be satisfied. He despises them; they disgust him. Other people are contemptible, stupid and altogether hateful—a feeling he expresses in that phrase: "hell is other people,"[23] the antithesis of all human and democratic feeling and respect.

Indeed, life with others is a sort of hell for those who cannot stand them, find nothing good in them, nothing to appreciate or to rejoice at. But, more than from others, hell comes from oneself: from an empty, isolated, embittered, and unappreciative self. Sartre could have found a deeper analysis of his own position in these lines from Eliot: "What is hell? Hell is oneself,/Hell is alone, the other figures in it/Merely projections. There is nothing to escape from/And nothing to escape to. One is always alone."[24]

In any case it should be granted that Sartre is more rational than the rationalists; for, to anyone who really thinks, there is greater logical consistency in his conclusion that a senseless world must be a source of disgust rather than of joy. The saints—at least in this: their conviction that life must have some transcendent and glorious purpose to be worth living and loving— are more on Sartre's side than on that of the Enlightenment or its rationalist successors; or, again, than that of the jolly (or the lost) generation of the 1920s, the angry generation of the 1960s, or the self-deadening generation of the 1990s: "If life's purpose were not to give glory to God, how contemptible, how hateful it would be."[25]

---

23. *Huis Clos*, Scene 5. Sartre brings to mind Satan's proud contempt towards man, so well brought out in Milton's *Paradise Lost*.
24. *The Cocktail Party*, Act 1.
25. Josemaría Escrivá: *The Way*, no. 783.

Appendix II

INDIVIDUALISM
AND COLLECTIVISM;
PERSONALISM AND COMMUNITY

Over the last centuries the dominant philosophy of self has been individualistic, according to which each is basically "out for" himself, and so "self-interest" becomes the motive power of each one. Since the interests of a single person could seldom prevail alone, people tended to group for certain purposes according to what were felt to be shared interests. So, on the positive side, individualism favored the growth of democratic systems, especially along party lines, by which the power of government is entrusted to majority groups. But individualism has also led to a concept of social life as a struggle among rivals, with progress to be governed by a law of the survival of the fittest.

Individualism originated many abuses and evident injustices especially in the socioeconomic field. This led to the development of collectivism: an economic or political-social philosophy where the life of the individual is seen in subordination to the interests of "the people" or the social whole. If the failures of individualism were so evident that they led to collectivist experiments and regimes, the deficiencies and abuses of collectivism, especially over the last part of the twentieth century, became in turn so clear that the pendulum seemed set to swing back again.

Does this necessarily mean a return to individualism? Does a third alternative not exist? Many think that one does, and that the antisocial elements of individualism—its unlimited selfishness, its lack of solidarity, its exploitation of the less powerful—can find their remedy in this other vision of man and his life, which is called personalism.

In itself, "personalism" simply suggests a philosophy centered on the human person. What, then, is there in this philosophy that distinguishes it from individualism and makes it less an enemy of the common good? Doesn't any tendency to center life on the person, taken as individual, find itself in logical opposition to collective or community interests? To my mind, the answer is No; for between the true interests of the person and those of the community or society there is no logical opposition. There is—there ought to be—a natural harmony. This, however, will be evident only to whoever understands the true nature of personalism, and the radical way in which it is to be distinguished from individualism.

Personalism

Personalism represents a view of man in which his dignity—prior to every social grouping—is underlined. In the dynamism that characterizes the human person, it perceives a call to self-fulfillment through the free espousing of transcendent and lasting values. Personalism takes particular account of freedom: the freedom of the individual and the freedom of others, and therefore it takes no less account of personal responsibility.

Personalism maintains a keen awareness of the dignity and rights of the person, and invites everyone to defend them against any type of violation perpetrated against himself or against others. At the same time it proposes that whoever is conscious of his rights must also be aware of his duties. Personalism therefore does not see any degradation of the person or any loss of status in the duty for instance to obey truth or legitimate authority. Such obedience marks a particular expression of man's dignity; his ability to discern what is worthwhile and to give it a free and active answer.

Personalism insists in a particular way on duties towards others, also seeing the fulfillment of these duties as a means of personal development and self-fulfillment. The person grows as he enriches himself through relations with others: open and generously receptive relationships. The alternative is social isolation and human alienation.

Awareness of the values present in others obviously offers a firm basis and no little help for building the social community. In true personalism there is a natural covenant or alliance between the person—the individual human being—and the community. Personalist participation in the community implies an adaptation not of interest to interest, but rather of person to person, founded upon the consciousness of the dignity and the rights that all have in common. A community not founded on respect for the dignity of the person ends up as a mass without a soul, such as is to be found in a concentration camp, or a totalitarian state, or perhaps a corporate conglomerate.[1]

"The person is a whole; not, however, in a closed sense, since he must be open. The person is not a small god without doors or windows, like Leibniz's monad, or an idol that does not see, nor hear, nor speak. The person tends by nature to social life and communion."[2]

At times it is said that the personalist point of view simply proposes the "centrality of the human subject." Such a phrase does not seem adequate. It could quite aptly express the individualistic view. Moreover, it might suggest an immanentist concept of man, while true personalism always leads to transcendence.[3] Personalism does not and cannot consist in an answer simply to one's self. My own inner resources are not adequate to fulfill me. It is the capacity of self-transcendence which can lead one on to a new and higher level of existence. One comes out of self, rises or is drawn above self, and thus constantly realizes one's self in an enriched and more intense way.

"Personalist" is not to be confused with "subjective"; and less still does it suggest a type of individualist autonomy. The need to distinguish personalism and individualism is all the more important in that the latter might easily be regarded as close to the former, and even be mistaken for it (especially since certain forms of individualism use terminology that seems personalist), and yet individualism is entirely different from, and in fact totally opposed to, true personalism.

Individualism

Some further observations can be made regarding that secular individualism which before (and perhaps after) collectivism has dominated such a large part of modern thought and existence. Seeing the individual as the fundamental and highest good, individualism holds that the interests of the community and of society ought to be subordinated to the individual. Where the individual's interests do not correspond with those of others or of the community,

---

1. How different the spirit, course and outcome of the French Revolution might have been if, instead of "Liberty, Equality, Fraternity," its slogan had been "Liberty, Dignity, Fraternity." It would thus have sidestepped the unresolved and unresolvable problem: the fact that the exercise of freedom, on the part of people naturally possessed of different talents, inevitably leads to real but not necessarily unjust "inequalities." Moreover, instead of vague agendas for making the weak "equal" to the strong, it might have inspired political and social philosophies more seriously designed to protect the fundamental rights of each person against economic individualism or state collectivism.

2. J. Maritain: *Les droits de l'homme et la loi naturelle*, p. 11.

3. "In philosophical anthropology, transcendence—in keeping with its etymology *transcendere*—signifies a surpassing (a going-out-beyond or a rising-above), to the extent that this is verifiable in the comprehensive experience of the human being. . . . Transcendence is the spirituality of the human being revealing itself": K. Wojtyla: *Person and Community: Selected Essays*, op. cit., p. 233.

the individualist will prefer his own interests. Individualism not seldom emphasizes the autonomy of the individual, to the point of transforming this autonomy (often without even being aware of the process) into an absolute value, into a sort of god.

In a certain sense one can say that individualism appears as a type of personalism gone awry. It also underlines rights, but not duties.[4] It demands freedom, but does not accept the responsibility of having to answer for one's own actions. Its judgments tend to be subjective. It promotes arbitrariness in behavior, without being worried about the demands of social life. It is concerned for itself, but not for others—unless the interests of the latter coincide with its own. It tends to make of the individual an autonomous source and judge of right and wrong, leading to a wholly subjective morality that undermines the human community. If it is permissible to me always to follow what seems unobjectionable in my eyes (even if it is absolutely offensive to others), the basis of social solidarity quickly collapses.

Precisely because "what I am," for the individualist, is often very far from "what I want to be," individualism is by no means devoid of ambition. But it can easily be deficient in moral outlook—because one can want (to do or to be) many things one *ought not* to want. The individualist, just like the existentialist, limits any true personal fulfillment if he or she bypasses its moral dimension. The ethical issue begins once one realizes that "I am" does not always satisfy the innermost conviction: "I ought to be." "I am a liar, and I ought to be truthful"; "I am a cheat, and I ought to be honest." That deep interior conviction, "I ought to be," is not a mere "moral imperative," but rather the voice of conscience stirring us to an ambition for truer fulfillment. Moreover, it has a universal aspect to it: I ought to be honest, and so ought others. All of us should be so; and then society would be more human. To be indifferent to these issues is to be indifferent to the primary human quality of personal and social life.

Jean-Paul Sartre would say that we are what we are or what we choose to be, and that no ethical evaluation can be made of these simple facts. Modern popular psychologism, imbued with the same outlook, vigorously rejects the very notion of applying value judgments to personal conduct. But this freeing of the individual from all accountability leaves social life with nothing to hold it together. In effect, to deny the difference between "I am" and "I ought to

---

4. A well-known historian of the 1789 French Revolution, noting that the "Declaration of Rights," one of its founding acts, was a list of rights without a corresponding list of duties, comments that perhaps the National Assembly preferred to pass over this aspect of the civil problem because "rights coupled with duties look suspiciously like wrongs" (J. M. Thompson, *The French Revolution*, p. 88). Liberal movements which sprung from the Revolution did little to allay this suspicion or to overcome the individualism underlying it. Yet it is evident that, rights and duties being correlative, no genuine philosophy of rights can fail to be at the same time a philosophy of duties.

be" means not only to abandon every ideal of personal fulfillment, but also to renounce any and every claim to judge or contest the behavior of others; it is therefore to propose a society where, each one being a law to himself, all interpersonal "rights" are lost. Just as no one has any right in my regard, so I have no right with regard to others . . .

The philosophy of individualistic self-centeredness keeps recurring in new and not-so-new forms. It was the philosophy of the "me generation" which, in the vernacular of the 1960s, wanted to "do its own thing." It was put forward by, among many others, Charles Reich in his 1970 (and long since dated) best-seller, *The Greening of America*. Reich proposed a "new" freedom based on a "recovery of self"; a freedom in which "the individual is free to build his own philosophy and values, his own life-style, and his own culture from a new beginning. . . . The individual self is the only true reality. Thus it returns to the earlier America: [Walt Whitman's] "Myself I sing." The first commandment is: thou shalt not do violence to thyself. . . . The commandment is: be true to oneself . . . . No one judges anyone else. This is a second commandment. . . . Each person has his own individuality, not to be compared to that of anyone else. . . . Being true to oneself is the best and only way to relate to others. . . . To observe duties toward others, after the feelings are gone, is no virtue and may even be a crime. . . . Thus the new generation looks with suspicion on "obligations" and contractual relations between people. . . . To most people, there is something frightening about the notion that no oath, no law, no promise, no indebtedness holds people together when the feeling is gone. But for the new generation that is merely recognition of the truth about human beings."[5]

Yes, there may be something frightening in much of this. One wonders if the final mood of Anna Karenina, and the predictable temper of the "me generation" as the years caught up with it, are all that different: looking back on a life where one has always been misunderstood, and so growing in destructive anger born of the blending of self-righteousness with self-pity. Strip away the veneers of culture and not much separates Anna's mood from that of Jimmy Porter in *Look Back in Anger*, except perhaps that Jimmy, at the end of John Osborne's play, has not yet discovered the bankruptcy of his utter lack of values.

As we saw in chapter eight, trust—and hence closeness to others—tends to evaporate in social life in the absence of common values. If each individual is to build his own unique and personalized "values," he will become in the end incapable of living the true democratic experience of values shared—held and upheld in common—which he, in fellowship with others, can rejoice in and be proud of. The result is total aloneness, the ultimate dead end of individualism.

---

5. *The Greening of America*, pp. 241–245.

Today's "Lonely Crowd" is a crowd made up of "lonely selves."[6] It is doubtful that the lonely self can survive the contemporary loss of any consciousness of universal human values. To have no sense of belonging, of shared goals and responsibilities, of common loyalties and duties, is to turn one's back on the world and on others and to totter over the abyss of one's own emptiness.

"There is no way of my pursuing my good which is necessarily anta-gonistic to you pursuing yours because *the* good is neither mine peculiarly nor yours peculiarly—goods are not private property. Hence Aristotle's definition of friendship, the fundamental form of human relationship, is in terms of shared goods. The egoist is thus, in the ancient and medieval world, always someone who has made a fundamental mistake about where his own good lies and someone who has thus and to that extent excluded himself from human relationships."[7]

E. M. Forster's attraction to modern secular humanism (or to Eastern Nirvana?), where life no longer needs to be seen as a rat race because there is nowhere to go and therefore no one to outdistance or to get the better of, is well brought out in his story, "The Other Side of the Hedge." If only we could discover an "other side" to the hemmed-in road which modern man walks: that dusty, urgent highway where everyone travels fast, thinks just of himself, edges others aside to get ahead. . . . Forster's protagonist pierces through the hedge and finds himself in a new land, among strange people who are not interested in getting anywhere, for they hold that there is nowhere to get to. Somebody invites him to walk along with him. "I found it difficult walking," he says, "for I was always trying to outdistance my companion, and there was no advantage in doing this if the place led nowhere. I had never kept step with anyone since I left my brother"—whom he had abandoned earlier on the civilized side of the hedge because he "wasted his breath on singing and his strength on helping others . . . ," and so got bogged down on the highway.

Yet if there *is* somewhere to get to, and *everyone* can get there, then indi-vidualistic outdistancing of others is even less to the point.

The philosophy of self-definition is the ultimate expression of individu-alism. It is impossible for "self-defined" individuals to meet in a common humanity. Individualism divides and fragments people, just as personalism links them in bonds of unity. "An individual is someone who defines himself or herself away from a crowd, or the more universal mass of humanity in gen-eral. A *person*, on the other hand, actively creates the self through relationship with other persons in social and communal bonds."[8] It is not good that man be alone, or that he think and behave as if he were self-sufficient. He can fulfill

---

6. Cf. David Riesman, *The Lonely Crowd*, 1950.
7. Alasdair MacIntyre, *After Virtue*, 1984, p. 229.
8. P. Allen: "Integral sex complementarity": *Communio*, 17 (1990), p. 537.

himself only through relationships of openness, respect and communication towards others, not of isolation, self-sufficient indifference or exploitation.

Individualism is no friend to the community; it lacks respect towards others (in a particular way towards their freedom), and lacks pride in service. The only bonds it creates with others are those of self-interest (hence the concept it has of society: a series of individuals associated together in virtue of pragmatic interest or simple necessity).[9] Where the individualist does not see his own interest clearly, he will not harmonize with others. The inability to connect one's own fulfillment with that of others is characteristic of the individualist. That again is why it is so difficult for the individualist to have or maintain any deep or genuine self-respect, since self-respect stands little scrutiny unless it is grounded in the sense that one's life is also of benefit to others.

The common good, for the individualist, is a concept to be ignored or at most to be understood in materialistic terms, reduced to standards of living, public services, etc., and valued purely according to economic or ideological parameters, not those which are really human, such as sincerity, loyalty, fidelity, justice and mutual respect. The tendency in an individualistic society is for persons increasingly to regard each other not only as strangers,[10] but as rivals. Everyone is held to be fundamentally selfish and an atmosphere of mutual distrust becomes generalized. To be "only concerned with me"— there is no other safe philosophy for the individualist. John Grisham's clever satire *The Partner* reflects this, and pushes it to its ultimate conclusion: even whoever is intelligent and unscrupulous enough to win out against the whole unscrupulous world will in the end be left hurt and alone if he makes the elementary mistake of trusting any one person.

The individualist ethos tends to reduce life to a rat race of competing egos; and any truly human society disappears. A merciless portrayal of this, in the setting of New York City, is presented in Tom Wolfe's novel, *The Bonfire of the Vanities*. Power, money, pleasure, and especially esteem—however externally given—have become the universal goals. And yet, what begins in self-adulation and continues in need of constant reaffirmation, ends in self-contempt and ultimate self-hatred.

No; individualism and personalism, rather than being variations on closely related philosophical concepts, are in direct contrast and produce

---

9. Within the individualist perspective, "the good of the individual is treated as if it were opposed or in contradiction to other individuals and their good; at best, this good, in essence, may be considered as involving self-preservation and self-defense. . . . For the individual the "others" are a source of limitation, they may even appear to represent the opposite pole in a variety of conflicting interests. If a community is formed, its purpose is to protect the good of the individual from the "others." This is, in broad outline, the essence of individualism": K. Wojtyla: *The Acting Person*. op. cit., p. 274.
10. "Modern society is indeed often . . . nothing but a collection of strangers, each pursuing his or her own interests under minimal constraints": A. MacIntyre, *After Virtue*, pp. 250–252.

opposed consequences for social as well as personal life. From the social point of view, one can be a personalist and for that very reason be fully centered and integrated into the community. One cannot be an individualist and maintain an authentic spirit of solidarity or of society.

More importantly: fulfillment, for the personalist, is to be sought outside or above the person. The dignity of each one lies in the power to respond, to come out, to grow: not around self, but around what is different from self (with a difference that complements self), and higher than self. The principle of personalism is self-giving response, whereas that of individualism is protective self-interest. The paradox is that the personalist, in giving himself, realizes his own real interest and fulfillment, whereas the individualist, by not giving himself, frustrates it.

A look at the present world reveals many things to be scared of. The most real danger, and the most personal to each of us, is loneliness—the prospect of finding ourselves utterly alone, not only physically but in spirit: appreciating no one, appreciated by no one, loving no one and loved by no one. We cannot escape this fate by retreating into ourselves; that would be to walk further into the danger rather than to avoid or overcome it. We have to come out of self: towards others, towards values, towards all that is of true worth. That has been the theme of this book.

BIBLIOGRAPHICAL REFERENCES

Gerard J.M. van den Aardweg: *On the Origins and Treatment of Homosexuality*, Praeger, New York, 1986

Prudence Allen: "Integral sex complementarity," Communio, 17 (1990)

G.W. Allport: *Personality: a Psychological Interpretation*, New York, 1937

American Journal of Psychiatry: vol. 138 (1981) / vol. 140 (1983) / vol. 147 (1990)

American Psychiatric Association: *Diagnostic and Statistical Manual of Mental Disorders DSM-III-R* (Third Edition, Revised): 1987 / *DSM-IV* (Fourth Edition): 1994

Thomas Aquinas (1225–1274): *Summa Theologica*; *Summa contra Gentiles*

Aristotle (384–322 BC): *Rhetoric*

St. Augustine (354–430): *In Ep. ad Parth.*; *Sermo* 128

Jane Austen: *Mansfield Park* (1814)

James Baldwin: *The Fire Next Time*, 1963

Robert N. Bellah et al.: *Habits of the Heart. Individualism and Commitment in American Life*, Univ. of California Press, 1996

Hilaire Belloc: *Complete Verse*, London, 1970 / On "Rasselas"

Robert Bolt: *A Man for all Seasons*, 1960

Charlotte Brontë: *Jane Eyre* (1847)

Emily Brontë: *Wuthering Heights* (1846)

Jean de La Bruyère: *Les Caractères* (1688)

Jacob Burckhardt: *The Civilization of the Renaissance in Italy*, 1878

C. Burke: *Covenanted Happiness: Love and Commitment in Marriage*, Scepter, 1999 / "Psychiatry: A 'Value-Free' Science?": *The Linacre Quarterly*, vol. 67 (2000), pp. 59–88 / Sentence of the Roman Rota, *coram* Burke, of July 9, 1998: *Rotae Romanae Decisiones*, vol. XC, pp. 512–543 (Vatican Press, 2003)

Albert Camus: *La Peste* (1947); *La Chute* (1956)

Thomas Carlyle: *On Heroes and Hero Worship* (1841)

Ernst Cassirer, *The Philosophy of the Enlightenment*, Princeton University Press, 1951

Blanca Castilla: *La Complementariedad Varón-Mujer*, Madrid, 1993 / *Persona y Género*, Barcelona, 1997

Willa Cather: *A Lost Lady*, London, 1961

G.K. Chesterton: *Autobiography* (1936); *Charles Dickens* (1906); *Orthodoxy* (1909)

Paul Claudel: *Le Soulier de Satin* (1928)

Paul Claudel and André Gide: *Correspondence* (1949)

Christopher Dawson: *Progress and Religion* (1929), Ch. 9

Charles Dickens: *David Copperfield* (1850)

Fyodor Dostoyevsky: *Crime and Punishment* (1866)

Ann Douglas: *The Feminization of American Culture*, London, 1996

Albert Einstein: *What I Believe* (1930)

George Eliot: *The Mill on the Floss*, 1860

T.S. Eliot: *Complete Poems and Plays: 1909–1950*, New York, 1950
Britannica CD. Version 1997 (Encyclopaedia Britannica Inc., 1997)
Michael Ende: *La Prigione della Libertà*, Longanesi, 1993
Erik H. Erikson: *Identity: Youth and Crisis*, New York, 1968
Existentialism (Philosophical Library), New York, 1947
Erich Eyck: *Bismarck and the German Empire*, London 1958
Herman Feifel: "Psychology and Death. Meaningful Rediscovery": *American Psychologist*,
    vol. 45 (1990)
Joseph de Finance: *L'Affrontement de l'autre*, Rome, 1973
F. Scott Fitzgerald: *The Great Gatsby*, New York, 1926
E.M. Forster: *Howards End, London*, 1910; *Collected Short Stories*, 1947
Viktor E. Frankl: *Man's Search for Meaning*, London, 1987; *The Doctor and the Soul*,
    New York, 1967
Sigmund Freud: *Civilization and its Discontents*, 1930
Robert Frost: *The Poetry of Robert Frost*, New York, 1969
Maggie Gallagher: "(How) Does Marriage Protect Child Well-Being?," in *The Meaning
    of Marriage: Family, State, Market and Morals* (Eds. Robert P. George and Jean
    Bethke Elshtain), Spence, 2006
John Galsworthy: *The Forsyte Saga*, London, 1949
Carol Gilligan: *In a Different Voice*, Harvard University Press, 1982
Johann Wolfgang von Goethe: *Faust* (Part I, 1808; Part II, 1832)
John Grisham: *The Partner*, London, 1997
M. Heidegger: *Kant e il problema della metafisica*, Genoa, 1962
Ernest Hemingway: *Death in the Afternoon*, 1932; *To Have and Have Not*, 1937
A. E. Hotchner: *Papa Hemingway*, New York, 1968
Henry James: *The Beast in the Jungle* (1903)
John Paul II: S*alvifici Doloris* (1984) / *Dominum et Vivificantem* (1986) / *The Theology
    of the Body*, Pauline Books, Boston, 1997 / *Centesimus Annus* (1991) / *Veritatis
    Splendor* (1993) / *Letter to Families* (1994) / *Tertio Millenio Adveniente* (1994) /
    Address to the UN General Assembly (October 5, 1995) / *Evangelium Vitae* (1995) /
    Fides et Ratio (1998)
Christopher Lasch: *The Culture of Narcissism: American Life in an Age of Diminishing
    Expectations*, New York, 1979
Harper Lee: *To Kill a Mockingbird*, New York, 1960
Alan Jay Lerner: *My Fair Lady* (1956)
C.S. Lewis: *The Abolition of Man*, New York, 1955
Richard Lovelace: *To Lucasta* (1649)
Alasdair MacIntyre, *After Virtue*, University of Notre Dame Press, 1984
Julián Marías: *La Felicità Umana: un impossibile necessario*, Milan, 1990
Jacques Maritain: *Les droits de l'homme et la loi naturelle*, Paris, 1945
Nadie F. Marks: "Does it Hurt to Care?": *Journal of Marriage and the Family*, vol. 60 (1998)
Somerset Maugham: *Of Human Bondage* (1915)
William Lee Miller: *Lincoln's Virtues: an Ethical Biography*, Alfred A. Knopf, New York, 2002
John Milton: *Paradise Lost* (1667)
Molière (Jean-Baptiste Poquelin): *Dom Juan* (1665)
Emmanuel Mounier: *Oeuvres*, Paris, 1947

Jean Mouroux: *Le Sens Chrétien de l'Homme*, Paris, 1953

Bernard N. Nathanson, *The Hand of God*, Regnery, 1996

John Henry Newman: *Discourses to Mixed Congregations* (1849); *Callista* (1856); *Grammar of Assent* (1870)

John Osborne: *Look Back in Anger*, London, 1957

Blaise Pascal: *Pensées* (1670)

Joseph Pieper: *Leisure, the Basis of Culture*, New York, 1963; *The Philosophical Act*, New York, 1963

Leonardo Polo: *Presente y Futuro del Hombre*, Madrid, 1993

Psychiatry: vol. 9 (1946); vol. 52 (1989)

Charles A. Reich: *The Greening of America*, Random House, New York, 1970

Philip Rieff: *The Triumph of the Therapeutic*, University of Chicago Press, 1987

David Riesman: *The Lonely Crowd*, Yale University Press, 1950

François de La Rochefoucauld: *Maximes* (1665)

E. Rojas: *Una Teoria della Felicità*, Milan, 1988

J.K. Rowling, *Harry Potter and the Philosopher's Stone*, London, 1997

George Santayana, *Spinoza's Ethics, Introduction* (1910)

Jean-Paul Sartre: *La Nausée* (1938), *L'être et le néant* (1943), *Huis Clos* [No Exit], (1944)

Peter Shaffer: *Amadeus* (1979; film version 1984)

W. Shakespeare: *King Lear* (1605); *Macbeth* (1606), *King Henry the Sixth* (1590)

A. Sicari: "The family: A place of fraternity": *Communio* 20 (1993)

Karl Stern: *The Pillar of Fire*, New York, 1951

L. Stevenson & D. L. Haberman: *Ten Theories of Human Nature*, Oxford University Press, 1998

Susanna Tamaro: *Va' dove ti porta il cuore*, (Follow Your Heart), Milan 1990

Gustave Thibon: *Retour au Réel*, Paris 1946

J.M. Thompson: *Napoleon Bonaparte*, Oxford, 1958; *The French Revolution*, Oxford 1945

Leo Tolstoy: *War and Peace* (1864–69); *Anna Karenina* (1873–77)

Anthony Trollope: *Barchester Towers* (1857); *The Prime Minister* (1876)

Fred Uhlman: *Reunion*, London, 1994

Pilar Urbano: *El Hombre de Villa Tevere*, Madrid, 1995

Mark Twain: *Huckleberry Finn* (1884)

Vatican Council II: *Gaudium et Spes* (Pastoral Constitution)

Maisie Ward: *Gilbert Keith Chesterton*, London, 1945

Wilfrid Ward: *The Life of John Henry Cardinal Newman*, London, 1912

Walt Whitman: "Song of Myself" in *Leaves of Grass* (1855)

Oscar Wilde: *The Picture of Dorian Gray* (1891)

Wojtyla, K.: *Love and Responsibility*, London, 1981 / *The Acting Person*, Reidel, 1979 / *Person and Community: Selected Essays*, New York, 1993

Tom Wolfe: *The Bonfire of the Vanities*, New York, 1987

Virginia Woolf: *A Room of One's Own*, (1929)

R. Yepes: *Fundamentos de Antropologia: un ideal de la excelencia humana*, Pamplona, 1996

R. Zavalloni: *La libertà personale. Psicologia della condotta umana*, Milan, 1973